To: Yvonne – with lots of Love and all good wishes

Eric Kilwood.
2/8/07. Love.

peace.

European Christianity and the Atlantic Slave Trade:

A Black Hermeneutical Study

Rev. Dr. Robinson A. Milwood, PhD

Bloomington, IN   Milton Keynes, UK
authorHOUSE®

AuthorHouse™
1663 Liberty Drive, Suite 200
Bloomington, IN 47403
www.authorhouse.com
Phone: 1-800-839-8640

AuthorHouse™ UK Ltd.
500 Avebury Boulevard
Central Milton Keynes, MK9 2BE
www.authorhouse.co.uk
Phone: 08001974150

© 2007 Rev. Dr. Robinson A. Milwood, PhD. All rights reserved.

No part of this book may be reproduced, stored in a retrieval system, or transmitted by any means without the written permission of the author.

First published by AuthorHouse   4/12/2007

ISBN: 978-1-4259-9439-6 (sc)

Printed in the United States of America
Bloomington, Indiana

This book is printed on acid-free paper.

Dedication

Accomplishments are tabulations of a journey in life. Life's journey can be unpredictable. Some areas are pleasant and memorable. Some are vicissitudes karmically designed to serve the formations of one's character, development and contributions to society and one's profession.

It is philosophically significant to immortalise positive things. When this is done, the persons who have been the foundation stones of one's life should be inscribed on the memory and the appreciated legacy of the individual's personality.

I am very fortunate to have had a mother and father that if I were divinely given the chance to choose my parents again, I would definitely choose my late mother and father. Therefore with love, respect and thankfulness to God, I dedicate this book to my mother (Sis) and father (Papsi), who taught me by example how to fear and love Almighty God, and to love and to accept all people equally.

Secondly, to the members, and officers of the Methodist Church, Stoke Newington Circuit, who have supported my ministry through many, many difficult storms, struggles and challenging times without fear or doubt, but with confidence and trust, I share this dedication with them and give my thanks in sempiternal abundance to you faithful and caring flock that the church has appointed me to serve. I salute you all with my pastoral care and love without any hesitation and abatement. Shalom.

Robinson A. Milwood
2007

Acknowledgment

The Atlantic Slave Trade has engaged my theological and philosophical, hermeneutic and intellectual appetite since I was studying a post-graduate course, in "Problems in the Philosophy of Religion". My main academic concern was "suffering and evil". Researching theodicy, theology, moral evil, pain and suffering, I found that there was no mention of racism or the Atlantic Slave Trade. The study left me deeply disturbed and intellectually rapacious to delve into the evilness of the Atlantic Slave Trade. Somewhere along the line, perhaps because of my academic past and the influence of the most pressing topics of those times, I first focussed my studies on Liberation Theology and, later for a second doctorate, I researched Biblical Hermeneutic and Liberation Theology.

Professor John Hick in his fascinating book *Evil and the God of Love* says:

> "The world has the right to hear Christian voices, however inadequate, on the theological problems of evil, and the recent Christian literature on the subject, although extensive there are major gaps."

For me, the most pertinent gap in the accounts of the Atlantic Slave Trade is precisely in the history of Christianity and the Christian churches over those 400 years. There can be no logical and sagacious interaction between theodicy, theology and philosophy without the inclusion of the Atlantic Slave Trade. To ignore the Atlantic Slave Trade is obviously a blatant denial of a major and significant period of African history, European history, British and American history. But British, European and American scholars of theology and philosophy have ignored the subject. However, as Professor Hick tellingly points out, "Having thus opened up the resources of past Christian thought, one should be willing to use them in formulating a contemporary response to the challenge of evil to the Christian faith".

I believe the Atlantic Slave Trade, with all the callous brutality of enslavement of Africans for 400 years and with the conscious involvement of the major denominations, i.e. Anglican, Roman Catholic, Baptist, Methodist, Presbyterian and Moravian, is a fundamental challenge to the churches today in this 21st Century. I have consciously chosen to make a black hermeneutical study of the Atlantic Slave Trade because of my historical and ethnological linkage to the Atlantic Slave Trade. Integrated within this study nevertheless are the works of a number of white academic historians from Europe, Britain and America who have not considered in any appreciative way the significant contributions of numerous black slaves in North America and the Caribbean, especially those who have, through their eschatological sufferings, struggles, insurrections and rebellions, made achievable the passage to abolition and emancipation. These were slaves such as Cudjoe, Samuel Sharpe, Bogle, Nat Turner and others whose insurmountable determination brought about their emancipation from slavery, which certainly did not arrive through any generosity or humanitarianism of the mind, heart or soul of European political leaders and especially British and American ones.

The relationship between the Atlantic Slave Trade and European, British and American Christians is significant and historically a solid *Sitz im Leben* of Africa today and among African descendants globally is both a legacy and reflection of the Atlantic Slave Trade. I am academically engaged in the study of the Atlantic Slave Trade through commitment to justice, equality and Shalom, first, as a Methodist minister and second for academic justification.

It is difficult or nearly impossible to write a book on this gigantic subject without the support, help and guidance of people who share or are near to the writer in various ways.

I wish to express my profound thanks to my secretary, Mrs Patricia Manyan, not only for her typing skills. but particularly for her patience with me during the typing up of my manuscript. I am deeply thankful to you, my fortuitous sister.

To Miss Yvonne Curtis BSC, MSC, ex student and friend, my profound gratitude for the generosity of her time and intellect in constant dialogue with me on several aspects of this book and for writing the foreword. I am especially grateful for the time given in discussing certain historical and psychological aspects of my study of the Atlantic Slave Trade.

My thanks to Mr. Richard Gibson for editing and proofreading the book. Thanks also to my student Ms Lee Bramble, BA, for assisting with the proofreading.

To the many scholars who have written on the transatlantic slave trade, both black and white, my acknowledgement in spating abundance. Here I have not written or attempted to write an history of the transatlantic slave trade but rather I have attempted to articulate my interpretation of the relationship between so-called European Christianity and the active involvement of the churches in the barbaric and immoral slave trade to satisfy a culture of economic philosophy.

Finally, this work would not have been possible without the patience, love, support and encouragement of Pam, my close confidant, love, friend, prop and motivator. Special thanks, Pam, for the many stimulating discussions we had on the slave trade and for sharing different insights, but particularly for listening to me reading many of my hermeneutical postulations. Pam, you deserve special acknowledgement for all the responsibilities and aspirations we share.

Robinson A Milwood
2007

Foreword

The Atlantic Slave Trade is by definition the greatest period in the history of Africa, Europe, Britain and America. Despite its phenomenal importance, it is not seen as part of the history of Europe, Britain and America in their academic curriculum.

Dr. Milwood has with scholarship and cultural audacity taken a new approach and departure from the chronological history of the Atlantic Slave Trade. He has carefully analysed critically and scholastically, an interpretation of the Slave Trade. This book is scholastic innovation that has been done with the mind of intellectual extrication.

To have placed the church in all its involvements is not a new discovery because it has always been there. But what makes it unique and important in Dr. Milwood's book is his exposure and identification of the church's active involvement in the Atlantic Slave Trade. Dr. Milwood made a number of radical claims that should be forceful instigation for discussions, reflections, re-thinking and even positive changes. Claims such as the psychological damage and spiritual impact on Africa and on African descendants. He has further claimed that Europe, Britain and America consistently underdeveloped Africa, not only with demographic enslavement of Africans, but essentially technologically. Another far-reaching claim of Dr. Milwood is what he calls "European and British Cultural Semantical Christianity". This is a major nub of Dr. Milwood's claim that should reverberate through the major denominations.

Dr. Milwood also had no hesitation in calling into question the 'existence of God' when taking into account the heinous sufferings and dehumanisation of Africans.

It is pretty clear, and Dr. Milwood has acknowledged that he has made no attempt to write a 'history of the slave trade', but he has made the first step to interpret the slave trade. This he has achieved by his incisive approach, his elucidation of complex areas of the Atlantic Slave Trade, and he has equally achieved in showing the destructive brainwashing of the slaves, deliberately and consciously by European and British cultural and semantical Christians.

Dr. Milwood's book is a timely book and a major contribution to the celebration of the bi-centenary of the Abolition of the Slave Trade Act. *'European Christianity and the Atlantic Slave Trade: A Black Hermeneutical Study'* is appropriate for the bi-centenary and comes at a due time encapsulating Africa and African descendants. A major challenge to the Europeans, British and American historians. There is evidence that the legacy of the slave trade continues until this day. Dr. Milwood has indicated that he remains unsatisfied and has began to look at another important aspect of the Atlantic Slave Trade, namely, 'The Psychological and Spiritual Impact, the Absence of Collective Consciousness, and the Legacy of Dysfunctionalism among African descendants'.

Finally, Dr. Milwood's book is written with a broad audience in mind; for the specialist and non-specialist; but most importantly for the general public. I am very privileged to be involved in this scholastic project.

By Miss Yvonne E. Curtis, BSc. MSc.

Contents

Dedication	v
Acknowledgment	vii
Foreword	xi
Introduction	xvii
Chapter 1 Biblical Evidence	**1**
Internal Slavery/Tribal Slavery (Domestic slaves)	6
Chapter 2 Religion And Slavery	**7**
Definition of slavery	7
Religion	12
European Christianity	12
Chapter 3 Definition of Slavery	**17**
Defining the Slave Trade	17
Dr. Vincent Harding	21
Chapter 4 Religious Complexities	**27**
The complexities of ReligionAre religious emotions attached to morality? Or is religion spiritually attached to morality?	27
Black Witness to the Apostolic Faith	32
Chapter 5 Religious Dimension	**37**
Religious dimension	37
Chapter 6 Perfidiousness And Reality	**47**
Veracity and Audacity	47
The Impact of an Evil Commerce	51
Scholarship and the Slave Trade	60
Finally the Cause and Consequences of the Abolition of the Slave Trade Act 1807	61
Chapter 7 Complexed Dilemmas	**67**
Reasons for Africa's Poorness and Under-development	67
European Racial Categories of Race	70

African Religion versus European Cultural Christianity	73
Dr. Yosef A.A. Ben-Jochannan's Contribution	77
Slaves' Recalcitrancy	82
Slaves' Treatments	85
Slaves' Insurrections	87
Chapter 8 Religious Involvements	**99**
Abolition and Emancipation	99
Black Religion and Missionaries	100
The Church and the Plantation Environment	101
Chapter 9 Situational Involvement	**103**
European Christian Cultural Involvement in Slavery	103
The Dilemma and Paradox	104
Chapter 10 Religious Culture And Slavery	**107**
European Christians and the Slave Trade	107
Chapter 11 Desideration And The Approach	**109**
Abolition - The Appetite	109
Paradox and Ambiguity are Coterminous to the Slave Trade	113
Chapter 12 Culture And Religion	**121**
European Religious Intentions	121
European Christianity	121
Chapter 13 Elucidation Of The Slave Trade	**127**
Defining the Slave Trade	127
The Slave Trade and British Scholars	130
Chapter 14 Ecclesiastical Involvement	**143**
Christianity	143
The Anglican Church	145
European Cultural Christianity	151
Anglicanism	151
Planters and Conversion	153
Chapter 15 Religious Paradosis	**155**
What is Conversion?	155
Hugh Thomas' The History of the Atlantic Slave Trade 1440-1870	163

Chapter 16 Correcting The Crime	165
Abolition of Slavery and Emancipation 1807 (Britain) and 1808 (USA)	165
Chapter 17 Effective Or Ineffective	179
Abolition and Emancipation	179
Chapter 18 Evaluation Of Slavery	185
Evolution of Prohibition/Abolition/Emancipation	185
Chapter 19 Slaves' Struggles	189
Struggle for Emancipation	189
Chapter 20 The Quest For Freedom	193
Emancipation	193
Major Events and Rebellions	197
Chapter 21 Facing The Crime	205
The Atlantic Slave Trade Holocaust	205
Chapter 22 Acceptance And Refusal	211
Slave Traders' Attitude to Slavery	211
Chapter 23 Slave Traders And Slavery	217
The Church, Slavery and Emancipation	217
Plantation Owners' Christian Dilemma and Polemics	219
Chapter 24 Slave Vicissitudes	227
Slave and Slave Traders' Conflict and Struggles	227
Religion, Traditions and Beliefs	239
Chapter 25 Eradication Of Slavery	249
The Abolition of European Slave Trade - 1807 British and 1808 American	249
Black Slaves' Symbioticism	264
Black History in the Atlantic Age	269
Bibliography	273

Introduction

There are many names given to the most heinous crime in history committed by man to his fellow man. Among them is the Transatlantic Slave Trade, the Atlantic Slave Trade, the Middle Passage or the Triangular Trade. These terms are commonly used by historians to relate to the same period of history.

The appearance of the Dutch, Portuguese, French, Germans, Spaniards and British on the sacred soil of Africa marked a crucial period of human history. They came first for gold, then many other African minerals and ivory, but when the Europeans discovered that far more profitable was human cargo, they abandoned gold and minerals for human beings and engaged in the capture and selling of Africans into slavery. The trade that continued for 400 years was consolidated by the construction along the West African coasts of various forts and castles.

I have chosen to examine the relationship and active involvement of European Christianity which I defined in my book as Cultural Christianity and the Atlantic Slave Trade. The British historian Hugh Thomas rightly claimed that all the denominations were profoundly involved in the slave trade. I have sought therefore to expose without reservation or hesitation the involvement of the major denominations.

Thomas's statement is not a vacuous generalisation. Rather his statement reveals a fundamental fact of the European and British missionary programme, policy and philosophy, which was justified by the use of African slaves as the main fuel for the expanding economies of Britain and Europe.

They proclaimed the slaves had no soul, that the slaves were property, and they treated them as such. The slaves were cattle, they were animals, they were brutes, and they were certainly not human. They were ignorant. Their minds were declared to be blank of any awareness of cruelty, slavery or subjugation. They were barbaric; they were primitive animals and incorrigible pagans. Given these characteristics, why were the churches preaching to the slaves? What was the moral, spiritual and theological purpose in preaching to animals, to barbarians, to ignorant people? What was their reason for the hypocritical deception in pretending to enlighten slaves if not for reasons of psychological brainwashing? Preaching is to convert, to challenge or to expostulate. The missionary programme was clearly aimed at brainwashing the slave to accept subservancy and obedience as Dr. Mark Christian notes in his book *Black Identity in the 20th century/Expressions of the US and UK African Diaspora*. Dr. Christian called the situation "The Master Enslavers (Race)". The master enslavers were the slave traders themselves, the Royals, the political states of Europe and Britain, but particularly the missionaries combined with the churches in this diabolical act of pulverising and truncating African minds psychologically and spiritually. Yes, I agree with Hugh Thomas. All the denominations, large, major and small were essentially involved in the Atlantic Slave Trade.

The churches had far too long used a cultural recondite approach to avoid facing up to the sins, evilness, wickedness and exploitation of Africans throughout history. The Anglican Church in 2005 made a modest confession and apology, but an apology for a wrong of such magnitude and degree deserves far more substantial reparation.

The churches also failed to acknowledge that the slave trade is an integral part, indeed a significant part of Christian history. They chose to ignore the slave trade as significant to their theologies, philosophies and doctrines.

The Atlantic Slave Trade and European Christianity was chosen by me also because I felt that its significance is so great that it deserves a black hermeneutical study. Many scholars of history have written on the Atlantic Slave Trade period. And most have been written by right-wing historians who in the main have not done justice to the examination and interpretation of the slave trade within the teaching and actions of the major denominations.

I have attempted in this thesis to create a long overdue area for academic investigation and at the same time, to expose surgically through hermeneutical study the essential function of the denominations in the slave trade, and in particular the deadly psychological weapon used by the churches, namely, the Missionary Movement. I have placed the Missionary Movement at the very centre of the slave trade. The Missionary Movement was the vehicle used by the churches to brainwash the Africans and to subdue them. The denominations actually purchased and acquired their own slaves in great numbers, especially the Anglicans and Catholics. The involvement of the Moravians and the Quakers in the slave trade is also of serious concern. I have also used black hermeneutical study to expose and to challenge fundamental concepts such as, theodicy, theology, morality, ethics, philosophy, religion, European and British Christianity - what I call European Cultural Christianity, purely as a culture rather than as a religion.

I have made clear that the major card players in the Atlantic Slave Trade were the Royals, Governments, scientists, philosophers and the churches.

As for the Abolition Movement, I have explained that the historical importance of William Wilberforce has been greatly exaggerated. The myth around his name and role must be corrected. In order to justify this correction, I have revealed the greater importance of the immortal Thomas Clarkson and the illustrious Grenville Sharpe, rather than William Wilberforce.

Perhaps second to Dr. Richard Hart. I have made the dogmatic postulation that at no time spontaneously and unconditionally had Britain and America the intention to abolish slavery. They had no spontaneous intention whatsoever to abolish slavery. There are significant historical facts that substantiate this argument and buttress my thesis. I have argued that it was the slaves through their consciousness and relationship with the cosmic God expressed by their revolutions in Haiti and insurrections elsewhere against

France, Spain and Britain that brought about the abolition of slavery. These rebellions, insurrections and conspiracies were the major and significant factors behind Abolition.

I have clearly delineated that the enslavers used three strangulating weapons to subdue the slaves. These were:
1. European Cultural and Semantical Christianity
2. Fear
3. Brutal punishment

Concomitant with the enslavers was the approval of all the churches abetted by the serious failure of academic scholastic rectitude. I have therefore shown that the subject of the Atlantic Slave Trade and European Christianity and the importance and relevance of the subject demands scholastic rectitude, which I have assiduously endeavoured to abide by in this book.

I have made the dogmatic postulation that Britain and America had no spontaneous and unconditional ambition or intention to abolish slavery. Slavery had become for Britain, Europe and America an economic necessity. There was no moral compulsion whatsoever. There are indeed sufficient historical facts to substantiate this basic argument. In order to cement my thesis, I have argued that it was the slaves through their ontological consciousness and cosmic relationship with the cosmic mind or intelligence of God through their revolution in Haiti against France, Spain and Britain and their rebellions, revolutions, insurrections and conspiracies were the major significant factors that brought about the Abolition of Slavery and the eventual emancipation of the plantation slaves. I have not categorised the denominations as instigators of lesser evil deeds in the slave trade, but the admission must be made that the Roman Catholics and the Anglicans featured more frequently than, say, the Methodists, Baptists or Moravians. I have acknowledged the contributions of the immortal Dr. Eric Williams and Dr. Walter Rodney's contributions to scholarship on the slave trade. While I have indeed also praised both scholars, I am forced by the gravity of the facts to mark out my departure from Williams and Rodney. I have argued in this thesis that Britain and Europe underdeveloped Africa technologically and demographically by the slave trade.

I acknowledge the impact and influence of Dr. Herbert Klein's approach to the historical elucidation of the slave trade. Dr. Klein had no reservation in exposing the Africans' endemic involvement in the perpetuation of the Atlantic Slave Trade. I have followed a similar line to that of Dr. Klein. This thesis could not by a mile encapsulate the gigantic magnitude of any study of the Atlantic Slave Trade period and European Christianity. There are major areas untouched by the scholarship of this work and thesis. I must leave them to others or to a later second volume. I feel sorry that the circumference of this study did not include what I regard as profoundly pertinent: the massive legacies of the Atlantic Slave Trade and their consequences on Africa and African descendants worldwide. Perhaps I might include this at a later date in a second volume.

With academic temerity, I am forced by the economic, political, demographic and sociological gravity of the Atlantic Slave Trade to say that the situation of black people today in the world community and their place in it are a consequence of the legacy of the slave trade, albeit psychological, ethnological, economical, sociological, technological or intellectual. Most pertinent of all are the dislocations and non-gregariousness of black people, briefly the non-existence of black unity and lack of economic solidarity and respect in the world today. In other words, the lack of collective consciousness and the legacy of dysfunctionalism.

I have left the underdevelopment of Africa to the claims of Dr Emmanuel Martey in his book *African Theology Inculturation and Liberation* to expose the political socio-economic level and the anthropological religious cultural level based essentially on the pauperisation of the African person.

Substantiation at all times is of paramount importance to maintain what I call academic rectitude. I have therefore relied on scholars of global eminence, who have all impacted on my heuristical development for this book. Scholars on both sides of the Atlantic have helped my quest, research and commitment to the challenges of this particular area of the slave trade history.

The denominations, it is hoped, should now be mature enough theologically and historically to face up to the heuristic surgical knife that must cut into the reluctance of the churches to confess their active participation in the slave trade and acknowledge how the missionary movement was used for the economic enrichment of Europe and Britain, without any theological and moral concern and conscience.

The facts, be they congenical or repulsive, must be faced. Aware of this, I have neither sought to obscure or minimise the involvement of Africans in the Atlantic Slave Trade. As I have consistently maintained, that academic scholarship must have academic rectitude. Many historians have lost this academic rectitude because they have consciously ignored the fundamental locus of the Abolition of Slavery and the birth of emancipation, which were the slaves themselves, and not the British Government or the Government of the United States in bringing about Abolition. In his book *British Historians and the West Indies*, Dr. Eric Williams has already delineated with good cannon the lack of academic rectitude among a significant number of scholars.

I hope this book will provoke genuine discussion and debate, and the creation of very clear scholarship with rectitude, a significant rethink of European and British theological and philosophical thought, as well as readiness of the churches to apologise publicly to black people. I hope for the stripping away of the churches' rigid structuralism and hope for a fresh look at Africa and African descendants. This book is also a challenge to black people to cultivate a sense of collective consciousness, collective psyche, positive collective black empowerment and calls for the eradication of negativism and dysfunctionalism. I shall crepitate "Praise the Lord" for my sleepless nights, my reclusiveness and the assiduity I had to apply to myself to complete this book as a contribution to the bicentenary commemoration of the Abolition of the Slave Trade Act.

Robinson A Milwood
London 2007

Chapter 1
Biblical Evidence

Old Testament

Genesis 37:36 (*Gen*)
Children born in the house of slave parents became "house-born" slaves such as mentioned in scripture from patriarchal times onward.

Genesis 15:3 17:13 27 Exodus 27 Judges to 14
Debtors who went bankrupt were often forced to sell their children as slaves or their children would be confiscated as slaves by creditors[1]. The Insolvent debtor himself, as well as his wife and family commonly became the slave of his creditor and gave him his labour for three years to work off the debt and then go free. This seemed to be the background to the Mosaic law[2]. Deuteronomy (*DT*) 15:18. Insolvency was a major historical cause of reduction to slaves' deeds in the biblical East.

---

[1] Second King 4:1, Numbers 5:5.
[2] Exodus 21:2 to 6.

To steal a person and to reduce a kidnapped person to slavery was an offence punishable by death in the laws of Hammurabi and Moses[3]. The brother of Joseph was guilty of just such an offence[4]. The price of slaves naturally varied somewhat according to circumstances, sex, age and condition of slaves. In the late third millennium BC, in Mesopotamia (Akkad and Third UR dynasties) the average price of slaves was 10-15 shekels of silver. About 700 BC, Joseph was sold to the Ishmaelite for 20 shekels of silver[5], precisely the price for the patriarchal period.

In later dates the average price for a male slave rose steadily under the Assyrian, Babylonian and Persian empires to about 50-60 shekels.

The law sought like Hammurabi's code five centuries earlier to avoid the risk of wholesale populations drifting into slavery and serfdom under economic pressure on small farmers by limiting the length of service those insolvent debtors had to give to six years[6]. Those who wished to stay in service and keep their family could do so permanently[7]. At Jubilee the slave would be released in any case[8]. In connection with the restoration of inheritance,[9] the insolvent debtors in temporary enslavement similar to the lines of that in Exodus[10] are probably the subject to those in Exodus[11]. In Jeremiah's day the King and wealthy flagrantly abused the law of seven-year release by releasing their slaves only to seize them again and were duly condemned for this very sharp practice[12]. A Hebrew who sold himself into slavery to escape from poverty was to serve his master until Jubilee year when he would go free,[13] but if his master was

---

[3] Exodus 21:16, DT 24:7.
[4] Gen. 7-28.
[5] Gen. 37:28.
[6] Exodus 21:2-6, DT 15:12-18.
[7] Exodus 21:6, DT 15:16.
[8] Leviticus (*LV*) 25:14.
[9] LV 25:28.
[10] Exodus 21:2.
[11] Exodus 21:26-27.
[12] Jeremiah 34. 8:17
[13] LV 25 37-43.

a foreigner he had the option of purchasing his freedom or being redeemed by a relative at anytime before Jubilee[14]. These slaves were the subjects of further specific law and custom that a chief's wives and maidservants might bear children for their master for a childless wife is attested both in the patriarchal narrative Gen 16. Under the law, if a Hebrew girl was sold as a slave[15], her matriarchal status was carefully safeguarded, She might marry her master and be redeemed. If rejected, she might become a properly maintained concubine, but would go free if the master failed to implement whichever of the three possibilities he had agreed to. In Mesopotamia such contracts were usually harsher, having no safeguard whatsoever.

Unlike Hebrew slaves foreign slaves could be enslaved permanently and handed on with other family property[16]. However they were included in the commonwealth of Israel on patriarchal precedent circumcision[17] and shared in festivals. Exodus 12:44 Passover DT 16:11 and Sabbath rest[18]...

A woman captured in war could be taken as full wife by a Hebrew and would thereby cease to have slave status, thus if she was subsequently divorced she went free and did not become a slave[19].

The treatment accorded slaves depended directly on the personality of their masters. It could be a relationship of trust[20] and affection[21] but discipline might be harsh, even fatal[22] although to kill a slave outright carried a penalty[23] of doubtless death ultimately[24]. It is just possible that Hebrew slaves like some Babylonians sometimes carried an outward token of their servitude. In some circumstances,

---

[14] LV 25 47-55.
[15] Exodus 21 7-11.
[16] LV 25 45-46.
[17] Gen 17:10 14-27.
[18] Exodus 20 10:27.
[19] DT 21 10-14.
[20] Gen 24:39 16.
[21] DT 15 and 16.
[22] Exodus 21.
[23] Exodus 21:20.
[24] LV 24 17-22.

slaves could claim justice[25] or go to law, but like the Egyptian spared by David could be abandoned by callous masters when ill.

Throughout ancient history the available documents are a witness to large numbers of people who tried to escape from slavery by running away. However, slaves that fled from one country to another came under a different category. The countries sometimes had mutual extradition clauses in their treaties.[26]

In the Hebrew laws an enslaved debtor was to be released after six years[27] or as compensation for injury[28]. In Hebrew, the word *Mishpot*, which in Latin was transmitted into French and English, denotes a person is free and is in "manumission," and no longer a slave.[29]

Slavery was practiced in Israel on a restricted scale. David caused the conquered Hammerites to do forced labour,[30] and Solomon conscripted the surviving descendants of the peoples of Canaan into his *Mas Obed* legislation or permanent state of labour.[31]. After the war with the Midianites, Moses annihilated his opponents and the warriors of the pharaoh. One in five hundred and one in fifty respectively of their spoils in persons and goods for service were rewarded the high priests and Levites at the tabernacle. David and his officers had dedicated foreigners for similar service with the Levites who served the temple, some of them descendants returning from captivity with Ezra. To these were added, Solomon's servants[32]. Finally a more human spirit breathes through the Old Testament laws and cautions on slavery as illustrated by the repeated injunctions in God's name not to rule over a brother Israelite harshly[33]. Moreover, it should be remembered that by and large the economy of the ancient East was never one, substantially or mainly based on slave labour as in Classical and later Greek and above all in Imperial Rome.

---

[25] Job 31:13.
[26] King 2: 39-40.
[27] Exodus 21:2, DT 15 12-18.
[28] Exodus 21, 26 and 27.
[29] Exodus 21:2 26-27, DT 15 12-13, Gen 34 9-11.
[30] Second Samuel 12:31.
[31] 1 King 5:13.
[32] Ezra 2:58, Ezekiel 44:69.
[33] LV 25, 43, 46, 53, 55 and DT 15:14.

New Testament

In the New Testament Jewish slavery, to judge by the Talmud, remained governed as always by the tight national unity of the people. There was a sharp distinction between Jewish and Gentile slaves. The former were subject to Sabbath/Manumission and the onus fell onto the Jewish communities everywhere to ransom their nationals held in slavery to Gentiles.

By contrast Greek slavery was justified in classical theory by the assumption of a natural order of slaves. Only the citizen class was strictly speaking human, ordinary slaves were merely cattle. The fact remained that throughout classical antiquity the institution of slavery was simply taken for granted, even by those who worked for its amelioration. There was the mass agricultural slavery in Italy and Sicily during the second centuries, between the Punic Wars and Augustus.

Finally, the main stays of slavery were:
(1) birth;
(2) the widespread practice of exposing unwanted children;
(3) the sale of one's children into slavery;
(4) voluntary slaves as a solution to problems such as debts;
(5) penal slavery;
(6) kidnapping and piracy; and
(7) the traffic across the Roman frontiers.

The condition of slavery was everywhere steadily spreading in New Testament times.

Cruelty was condemned by the growing sentiment of common humanity. For instance, the death of a slave in Egypt was subject to a coroner's inquest. In Rome slaves automatically became citizens on manumission. Paradoxically, in the New Testament, the attitude to slavery was significantly different. The 12 disciples of Jesus apparently had no part in the system of slavery[34]. Jesus repeatedly

---

[34] Matthew 21:34, 22-23.

spoke of the relation of the disciples themselves as that of servants to their Lord[35]. Outside Palestine however, where the churches were often established on a household basis the membership including both "Masters and Servants". Slavery was one of the human divisions that became meaningless in the new community in Christ[36]. This apparently led to a desire for emancipation. 1 Corinthians 7:23. Slaves should therefore aim to please God by this service[37]. The fact that household slavery, which is the only kind referred in the New Testament, was generally governed by feelings of goodwill and affection.[38]

Internal Slavery/Tribal Slavery (Domestic slaves)

Two dynamic sentences quoted from Bob Brown's *Pan African Roots* will begin to set the climate for this thesis. "The history of Africa as presented by European Scholars has been encumbered with malicious myths. It was even denied that Africans were historical peoples. It is said there where other continents had shaped history and determined its course, Africa has stood still, held down by internal indecision that Africa [Basil Davidson, *The African Slave Trade*] was propelled into history by the European contact. African history was therefore presented as an extension of European history, such disparaging accounts had been given of African society and culture as to appear to justify slavery and slavery posed against these accounts seemed a positive divergence of African ancestry. When the slave trade and slavery became illegal, the experts on African yielded to the new wind of change and now began to present African culture and society as being so rudimentary and primitive that colonialism was a duty of Christianity and civilisation."

---

[35] Matthew 10:24 and John 13:16.
[36] 1 Corinthian 7:22 and Galatians 3:28.
[37] Eph 5:58, Col 3:22, 1 Tim 6:2, Eph 69 and Col 41.
[38] EPH 2:19 1 Cor 4:1, Tit 1:7, 1 Peter 4:10, Rom 1:1, Phil 1:1, Galatians (5:1).

Chapter 2
Religion And Slavery

Definition of slavery

A biblical definition of this enormous subject is important as a foundation. The New Bible Dictionary, Second Edition 1992, defines slavery in the Old Testament as follows:

> "Under the influence of the Roman law, a slave was usually considered to be a person (male or female) owned by another, without rights and like any other form of personal property to be used and disposed of in whatever way the owner may wish".

Slavery is attested from the earliest times throughout the ancient Near East and owed its existence and perpetuation primarily to economic factors. Captives, especially prisoners of war, were commonly reduced to slavery[39]. Claimed by the King of Sodom,[40] slaves could readily be bought from other owners or general merchants[41]. The

---

[39] Gen. 14:21.
[40] Numbers 31:19, DT 20:18 and 21:10, Judges 5:13, First Samuel 4:9, Second King 5:2, Chronicle 28:8.
[41] Gen. 17 12-13 2:7.

law allowed Hebrews to buy foreign slaves from foreigners at home and abroad[42]. Medianites and Ishmaelites sold Joseph to an Egyptian official.

The enslavement of Africans and African descendants was worse, a crime against humanity and a unique tragedy in the history of humanity, because of its abhorrent barbarism, its magnitude, long duration, numbers of people brutalised and murdered, and because of its negation of the very essence of the humanity of its victims – the brutal removal and the largest forced migration in history that caused the deaths of millions of Africans, destroyed African civilisation, impoverished African economies and created the basis for Africa's underdevelopment and marginalisation that continues into this millennium. Slavery and the slave trade were based on economic exploitation, doctrines of racial supremacy and racial hatred and subjected Africans and African descendants, indigenous peoples and many others to the most horrific denigration including classification as sub-human and cattle, subjugation to rape, forced labour, branding, lashings, murders, maiming, destruction of their languages, cultures, psychological and spiritual well-being resulting in structural subordination which continues to the present day. There is an unbroken chain from the slave trade, slave colonisation, occupation, apartheid, racial discrimination and the contemporary forms of racism that maintain barriers to the full and equal participation of the victims of racism and discrimination in our public lives – globally. It is an historical fact that slavery was a global institution. This historical fact is that geographical, racial, cultural, economical, sociological categories produced deep differentiations. It is documented and acknowledged that domestic internal slavery was a common practice among different tribes ruled by Kings and Chiefs within Africa. The practice was mainly economical and a symbol and tool of political power. There is no evidence as perceived by European and American Scholars that domestic slavery was brutal. Their findings may actually be based on their scholastic attempts to

---

[42] Leviticus 25-44ff.

appease opponents and to justify the gravity of the Atlantic Slave Trade.

The period of the Atlantic Slave Trade or Middle Passage is between 1492 and 1870. This was the time of the most blatant and morally repugnant exploitation of the African race. It was racial, demographic, irreligious, and socially immoral. Castigation must logically be meted out to Africans as well as to the white intruders due to the very practical and active participation of African Kings and Chiefs in the Atlantic Slave Trade.

Hugh Thomas has certainly described accurately this historical side of the trade. He says that between 1492 and 1870 approximately 10 million or more black slaves were forcefully carried from Africa to the Americas in inhuman conditions not suitable for dogs and pigs. The figure of 10 million is a very contentious figure. Indeed, there is no agreed figure. Scholars' estimates of such figures differ radically, but I shall concern myself with the shipment and transportation of the slaves. It should be noted that Europeans considered that Africans were cattle and treated them as such with the approval of European Christianity culturally expressed by the major denominations, especially the Anglican Church, the Roman Catholic Church, Baptist, Methodist, Presbyterian and Moravian churches.

The slaves were forcefully uprooted to work on tobacco, sugar, coffee and cotton plantations to fuel the economies of Europe and the Americas. The slaves were forcibly put to unpaid work in mining gold, silver and other minerals, in agriculture in plantations and farm and as domestic servants in homes.

At the apex of the slave trade in the 1780's, the French and English were trafficking slaves in great numbers. The captives were procured by barter with the African monarchs or merchants. The passageways for the trafficking were the great rivers of Africa that flowed into the gigantic Atlantic Ocean. Dr. Walter Rodney postulated the view that Europe underdeveloped Africa by forceful dislocation of physically fit Africans from their homes, This was one way of depopulating Africa and this depopulation has impacted tremendously on Africa. Here I must say although Dr. Walter Rodney's postulation held water for a long time, I radically disagree with his concept. I would say that Europe consciously underdeveloped Africa, technologically and scientifically. It is in these two specific areas that we must, examine and accept Africa's underdevelopment.

The African monarchs and chiefs sold into slavery their families, neighbours and captives through their internal slave practice. This was done mainly to obtain some of the most common items from Europe and America and it had no significance for the economical development of Africa, particularly scientifically, educationally and technologically. Slaves were exchanged for textiles, copper, iron, guns, alcohol such as wine, whiskey, brandy and small items such as beads, hats, shaving bowls, knives and even chamber pots.

My vexed argument is quite blunt and simple. What did these basic items have to do with the enlightenment, progress and development of a continent of black people ?

Painful as it is to say, it has to be admitted that thousands of Africans participated in the slave trade for personal gain and materialistic accumulation of goods and property. This took place in the kingdoms of Ashanti, Dahomey, Benin, Loango and Kongo, now Angola, Mozambique, the Gold Coast, which is now Ghana, and also on the island of Madagascar. These countries participated in the capture and domestic enslavement of millions of persons destined for the European ships and the slave markets of Europe, Britain, the Americas and the Caribbean.

European Christianity has a deep racial culture embellished in religious language, namely the words of the Bible, and which was disseminated through their respective missionary movements juxtaposed with European, Christian slave traders and the physical presence and involvement of European Christian churches throughout Africa and the Caribbean.

The historical physical involvements of the churches are visible today at Elmina Castle in the Gold Coast in Ghana, West Africa, where there are Methodist, Baptist, Anglican and Roman Catholic churches. They all deserve eschatological and apocalyptic pulverisation alongside the most powerful and profound moral repugnancy that one can articulate.

The Roman Catholic Church even placed a replica of a communion table on top of the dungeon where the slaves were held below sea level in the most appalling and inhuman conditions. Slaves were living and many dying in the most deplorable conditions that the English vocabulary cannot equal in its evilness and grotesqueness. My point in both evaluating and castigating the physical presence of the major denominations are at the heart of the slave trade at Elmina Castle is simply this – the question is poignant. What I must ask is what were the churches doing there? This is a question that no historian of substance in dealing with the Atlantic Slave Trade has attempted to answer. I claim with temerity and audacity that the churches' purpose was to affirm slavery as theologically correct and justified. The churches had no other reason. The churches had no moral theology. Indeed, they had no theology. What they had was a racial cultural Christianity. The theology of brotherhood, humanity, love, peace, justice, salvation, freedom, freewill, reconciliation, liberation or Manumission, human personality, equality, compassion, mercy, goodness, generosity, holiness and righteousness never entered their vocabulary or their so-called Christian cultural faith on this topic.

As the slaves were considered as cattle, preaching to them in the missionary programme was primarily to cultivate submissive non-beings and inculcate a feeling of inferiority into the minds and psyche of the African slaves. All this they did in the name of European Cultural Christianity. The slave's submission was to be an act of obedience to their slave masters. Indeed, a significant function of the churches was to induce fear into the slaves and to justify the denial to the slaves of their God-given human rights. By their practice of the religious culture of mendacity and rapacity, the missionaries sought to enslave the minds of the African slaves.

The churches were thus a central psychological force at the heart of the Atlantic Slave Trade. There can be no historical reduction or denial of this incontestable fact. Paradoxically, the churches were the main pistons and generators of the Atlantic Slave Trade. Professor Cornel West has provided us with massive data from his research, proving that Europeans of all ranks, from politicians to philosophers were big investors in the business of the Atlantic Slave Trade. We have documentation that shows clearly the historical tribal and Kingship links with Africa and the custom of the internal slave trade.

Hugh Thomas equally recorded the involvement of kings, princes and prelates in the slave trade. These include the following:
(1) Henry the Navigator, whose captains looked for gold, but found slaves (1440);
(2) Pope Pius the Second (Piccolomini), who had declared that baptised Africans should not be enslaved in 1462;
(3) Charles the Second of England, who backed the Royal African company on a golden sail to Guinea;
(4) Ferdinand the Catholic, who as regent of Castile was first to approve the despatch of African slaves to the Americas in 1510.

Religion

Professor Gayraud S. Wilmore in his forceful articulations in his book *Black Religion and Black Radicalism, an Interpretation of the religious history of Afro-American people* claimed that the centrality of the African concept of a cosmological relationship with a monotheistic force was the dynamic driving force that kept the Atlantic slaves alive in the midst of their hellish lives during their oppression and bondage. I wish to move Dr. Wilmore's concept further and to say that the African cosmological propinquity with the universal Supreme Being was profoundly deeper than the European concept of a God that the Europeans claimed they had but who had no purpose or relation with Africans. The specific aspect of religion that the Europeans used to truncate, oppress, brainwash, inculcate and psychologically damage the Africans was nothing more than a European Cultural Christianity. Rather it was a semantical Christianity.

European Christianity

It is an historical mendacity to say that the Europeans took Christianity to Africa. Rather it was African missionaries who took African Christianity to Europe. St. Augustine is an example with his unmatchable linguistic and methodical scholarship. There is incontestable evidence of paganism surviving today throughout Britain and Europe.

European Christianity and the Atlantic Slave Trade: A Black Hermeneutical Study

The Europeans first received Christianity from African missionaries, especially Catholic missionaries. They acculturated the African concepts of religion, the cosmos and a monotheistic God and then this Christianity, transformed by European culture, was exported back to Africa as a religion. Paradoxically, this Bible-based European culture was not practised by Christians prior to the Atlantic Slave Trade. Indeed, Europe never had anything resembling Christianity in the content of theology, theodicy, and Christo-centricism.

European Christianity was used without any moral conscience as a tool to subjugate the African slaves through an act of oppression, exploitation, and dehumanisation, economic and political rapacity defined equally by Professor James Walvin as morally repugnant. Africans were looked upon as animals and they were treated as animals. Defined as animals. They were non-beings. Africans were created by the European God as economic commodities for Europeans to exploit, to fuel the European economic systems, culture, industrial development and political powers of the day. And the majority of Atlantic Slave Traders were so-called European Christians, but we must not fool ourselves about the ultimate purpose of these European Christians because it was not a religion, but rather, a self-serving political religious mendacity.

Reverend John Newton is a good example of the disconnection of Africans to the majority of European and British Christians. The inculcation of European Cultural Christianity was to extirpate the religious beliefs of the African slaves and to replace African religion with a white man's version of Christianity. Christianity to most liberation theologians is liberation, a ministry based on liberation[43]. "The blind received their sight, and the lame walked, the lepers are cleansed, and the deaf could hear. The dead are raised up and the poor had the gospel preached to them". European Christianity was a so-called religion of the most heinous exploitation of Africans during the Middle Passage which lasted for 400 years. The Atlantic Slave Trade period of forced migration of Africans to Europe and

---

[43] Matthew 11 4-5.

the Americas was conducted in the name of Christianity, the name of religion, in the name of Almighty God and in the name of Jesus Christ. The slaving of Africans was justified by Europeans with their cultural Christianity. European Christianity was designed specifically to strangle the spiritual, psychological and emotional aspirations of Africans. It was meant for Africans to become dysfunctional human beings, but robotically functional for the so-called master race as defined by Herbert S. Klein in his imaginative scholarly book *The Atlantic Slave Trade*.

Dr. Klein is right in seeing European Christianity as the vehicle or method used by the slave masters to divide the slaves particularly and to force them to deal with each other in the common language of the white man, because it was the white masters' language and religion that mattered. The slaves were forced to accommodate the dominant Christian culture of the master class and later, of the plantation class.

According to European Christianity, the slaves were denied any sense of self, of community, self-worth, or self- being and the African place in the larger cosmological universe which was so fundamental to the survival and adjustment during their acculturation in the new world of slavery. The Atlantic slave population was a mixture of African peoples deliberately placed together randomly in such a way as to keep them in confusion, linguistically and socially, and ultimately to control their minds, souls and total being.

Having raped, dehumanised, criminalized and amputated and imposed upon them a slave mentality and culture without any sense of manumission and under the total control of the master white race, the minds of the slaves were psychologically and spiritually under the cultural and Christian omnipotence of the mythological master race.

What held the African slaves together? This is both a serious and fundamental question that demands a veracious answer. With temerity and audacity, I declare that the sempiternal propinquity between the African slaves was the Atlantic crossing experience. It was this Atlantic crossing experience that forced or made them become symbiotic as Africans.

European Christianity and the Atlantic Slave Trade:
A Black Hermeneutical Study

How did European ethnocentric Bible culture manage to be transported to Africa? This is a question that I shall tease out later. However, I must reiterate that the churches were the basic fundamental piston of the entire Atlantic Slave Trade. The late Pope John Paul issued in the late 1990's a powerful ecclesiastical apology to the world. In his apology, he apologised for the Roman Catholic Church's reluctance, hesitation and consciously turning aside from a number of major human atrocities and especially the Jewish holocaust. Pope John Paul made a grave and serious ecclesiastical mistake or perhaps I should say a conscious and deliberate oversight. Nowhere in his apology did Pope John Paul mention the Atlantic Slave Trade, which was the greatest and gravest unchristian, irreligious and immoral atrocity ever committed by man, especially by so-called Christians.

CHAPTER 3
DEFINITION OF SLAVERY

Defining the Slave Trade

According to Professor James Walvin of York University, the slave trade or Middle Passage has come to mean one particular slave system, which is the enforced movement of Africans across the Atlantic into the Americas. Professor Walvin goes on to say the slave system which established itself in the public mind is certainly the Atlantic Slave Trade. It would be vacuous to criticise James Walvin or to apply a critique to his postulations here. However, the Atlantic Slave Trade has created a degree of indescribable impressions in the minds of academic historians, especially demographic history. It is of scholastic significance to point out those theologians and philosophers who do not share even a modicum of concern about the devastations of Africa by the Atlantic Slave Traders. Theologians and especially philosophers consciously ignored the Atlantic Slave Trade as an immoral, social, political, historical, philosophical or theological issue.

Dr. David M Thompson, reader in modern church history and director of the Centre for Advanced Religious and Theological Studies at Fitzwilliam College, Cambridge, is very much precise and correct when he says in a correspondence to the writer of this thesis:

"One of the things which is striking about the theology of the European churches in the early modern period is that for the most part, they did not see slavery as a problem, and therefore do not mention it in formal theological works".

One may ask the question why? Because the slave trade was not important in philosophical, moral or theological discussions concerning theodicy, monotheism, theology, systematic theology, process theology or Christianity itself. That is the reason.

I once challenged as an ex-student, Professor John Hick with the penetrating question: Your outstanding book *Evil and the God of Love* traced evil from theodicy, theology and monism, St. Augustine type of theodicy, the aesthetic theme, Catholic thought, the problem of evil in reformed thought, Karl Bath, Eighteenth Century optimism, theological themes, the Iranian theodicy in Schleiermacher's teleological theodicy, moral evil, suffering and the Kingdom of God. But, Professor, you never mentioned Africa or the Atlantic Slave Trade once? Professor John Hick had no answer, but the logical answer lies within the thesis of his own book. Black experience as evidenced by the magnitude of the slave trade had and has no relevance to European and British theologians and philosophers alike.

Laconically, the same is true with history. History for white scholars only relates to and is validated by white contributions and experiences. Professor James Cone told of an interesting dialogical encounter he had with a white American historian. The historian was telling Professor Cone enthusiastically how he was teaching history to his class of students and his methodology. Cone noted that during the period of history he was going over, the Professor had never once mentioned African Americans. Cone said "How can you teach American history or the History of America without mentioning African American contributions, to its history, economy or theology." The Professor replied that the African American contributions are not important. They have no significance in American history.

I personally experienced a similar situation with a young historian, Professor Hugh Mcloud at Birmingham University. Professor Mcloud was teaching history over the period from 1517 to the present day. When I asked him how about the history of the black churches, I was told it was not significant to church history in Britain. This kind of academic and pedantic isolation, rejection, prejudice, racism and denigration of black history in academic institutions is dangerous and especially repugnant and reveals the lack of authentic and veracious scholarship.

Recently, there has been the germination in awareness of the historical and cultural importance of the slave trade. But this awareness and new importance is not for the good of ontological, sociological, historical importance, or philosophical, theological, economical and political. Is it for ethnocentric intellectual satisfaction? A more challenging and pertinent point should be the ontological interconnectedness of the human race both biblically and genealogically, including the cosmological connections between the cosmic Supreme Being or force or energy and the human race. It is illogical to continue to maintain that the Atlantic Slave Trade was just a phenomenon of history. It cannot be because the economic development of Europe and America through the Atlantic Slave Trade is endemically attested in the sociological, cultural, political and theological bloodstreams of Europeans and Americans today. It is particularly significant because of the demographic underdevelopment of Africa and technologically and scientifically as well. I shall argue as a specific thesis on the deliberate underdevelopment of Africa by Europe, Britain and America technologically. In this thesis I have to point out that Dr. Walter Rodney and Dr. Eric Williams both had not pinned down specifically the fundamental reasons for the underdevelopment of Africa. My readers must wait for my theory and postulations in a later chapter.

There are powerful converging forces giving impetus and verve to the awareness through socio-cultural changes in black history on both sides of the Atlantic since 1945. In the USA and the Caribbean and recently in Britain genealogically the offsprings of slaves today seek a political, cultural and social voice. The voice of new hermeneutic history is not still strong enough, but it is a symbiotic voice speaking out of the collective past of black people. The past 30 years have produced new beginnings in the development of scholarship devoted to the slave trade. I emphasise the relevance of interaction between theology and theodicy. The same applies to the radical interaction between the black hermeneutic of the slave trade and black theology. I assume therefore that the world has the right to hear the slave trade voices. This gives it potency and socio-cultural significance.

Appropriately, Professor Walvin says there is a mass of scholarship for the general reader. The significance of the slave trade lies not simply in the story of Africa or even when enlarged to the diaspora in the Americas, but rather in the way Western Europeans rose to unprecedented economic and political power and material well-being on the programme of philosophy practiced on the back of the Atlantic Slave Trade system.

Informed historical scholarship must focus on issues of contemporary social, economic, political, educational and cultural concepts of the relationship between the historical slave trade and our world today. Theologically, at the junction of public memory and scholarly research, there is always an uncomfortable meeting point that chronological history of the slave trade reveals something uniquely terrible about the oceanic slave trade closely linking Europe, Africa and the Americas. This is best described as the triangular trade, a trinity of slavery, suffering and profit.

The slave trade had a geographical economic complexity that was extraordinary, despite many, many attempts by governments and scholars to play down the role of the slave trade; we are constantly confronted by an overwhelming historical period and a unique experience in man's history. The continuation of the magnitude of the slave trade up through the 18th, 19th and 20th centuries was that the great majority of people who had forcefully been taken across the Atlantic not to settle and labour, but also that Africans and their descendents born in the Americas had to live in slavery without any hope of manumission. Professor James Walvin, Professor Herbert S. Klein, Hugh Thomas, Dr. Sydney W. Mintz, the contributors in *Caribbean Slavery in the Atlantic World*, acknowledged that whilst the treatment of Africans during the Middle Passage was what Walvin called "moral repugnancy," the Europeans were congenially treated by their own people, while the Africans were stripped of their humanity and categorised, defined quasi-scientifically as sub-human and slaves. They were slaves and were even categorised as cattle. They were non-beings. They were looked upon as the oil or grease that lubricated the wheels and engines of economic prosperity and development for Europe and the Americas. All this was done in the name of European Christianity by the missionary movement and pagans from Europe. They culturised Christianity to dominate and control Africans.

Through scholarly eyes and intellectual surgery, it is quite clear that the emergence of slavery had impacted profoundly on Africa and Europe. The deepest and severest devastating consequences were to be found in the damage to societies within Africa itself. James Walvin estimates something in the region of 12 million Africans were loaded like animals onto slave ships on the West African Coast and less than 10.5 million survived the Atlantic crossing.

Dr. Vincent Harding

In Dr. Harding's book *There is a River*, he estimated that the grand total of Africans transported across the Atlantic was in the region of 100 million. Dr. Harding's estimate seems exaggerated. In any case, the racial and economic purpose was not only the symbiotic participation in a pandemic slave trade primarily to rape and depopulate the continent of Africa of its people, it was aimed at fracturing African. The figures released of those who survived the diabolical crossing in conditions which the Oxford or Cambridge dictionary cannot provide us with an adequate word to describe or define accurately the inhuman conditions of their passage.

Colossal losses in addition were also sustained in the interior of Africa as slaves were forcefully moved from inland villages to enslavement in the palaces of African potentates and fortified posts of European traders on the coast. This is what Herbert S. Klein and others called domestic slavery, to which I shall explain later.

However, Elmina Castle and others on the Gold Coast were the major depots of slavery. With massive ramifications in Europe, the Atlantic Slave Trade was conducted by Europeans who claimed to be Christians. and this historical fact is evidenced by the presence of the Methodist Church, the Anglican Church, the Catholic Church and Baptist Church found at Elmina Castle. They are both monuments and hard evidence of the churches' involvement and participation in the slave trade. Indeed, I have to say vehemently that the European churches were the major pistons of the Atlantic Slave Trade. The churches were the driving force of the slave trade. In this involvement, there was no theology, no morality, no conscience, no humanity, no Jesus, no medical science. Much later in the slave trade, slaves were shipped to the Americas from the North and South, but Africans were shipped primarily to the Caribbean. They were bought and traded for goods imported and transported through Europe. Goods such as sugar, whiskey, wine, tobacco, jewels, chamber pots, clothes and firearms.

The economic profits of the slave trade came back to Europe. Indeed, all major European maritime fleets fought to create their niche in the European slave trade, even countries as small as Denmark. The volume and abundance of wealth created, profits and general commercial attractiveness of the slave trade were immense. Accordingly, Europe was intimately involved with the development of the slave trade, which indeed was paradoxically, essentially European. To put this into context bluntly, chronologically, the slave trade was first African, then European and lastly American. Christian influence and involvement was central in the high drama of the slave trade. I reiterate the slave trade was not just one single oceanic phenomenon, but rather was formed by a chain of prolonged and protracted movements of African people in forceful enslavement, and it took months and years before the slaves planted roots in the Americas.

This barbaric slave trade in human beings included one of the oceanic experience in which the slave ships formed a most fantastic factor; the crossing had extraordinary and fundamental repercussions for the nature and developments of slave societies right across the Americas. Herded into the slave ships, the Africans experienced deep psychological and cultural scars that we cannot possibly begin to understand, imagine or comprehend.

The biblical exodus is narrated in language and depictions with dramatic force. Three things are of sociological and theological significance here, (a) the Supreme power of God told in anthromorphic language; (b) the irrepressible impression the exodus made and the experience of the exodus people; (c) the translation of the exodus experience to what they had become throughout history to this day.

European Christianity and the Atlantic Slave Trade: A Black Hermeneutical Study

The covenant relationship formed between God and his people. The imprints of God's love, mercy (*hesed* in Hebrew), liberation and of providence is all compelling.

Juxtaposed to the Atlantic Slave Trade was the biblical exodus and it is clearly exoterical that in the Atlantic Slave Trade the slave traders' God was seen as important. God's importance was seen as due without any measure between European Christianity and was projected and practised as an inclusive dominating and oppressive culture wrapped up in the language of the Bible to brainwash and to control the faculties of Africans ethnologically and ontologically.

On the other hand, the Africans, through their cosmological ties with the monotheistic faith they had already held before European missionaries arrived in Africa, which survived their shared Atlantic Middle Passage experience, although spiritually and psychologically truncated by the European bible-based vacuous cultural Christianity that had not even any resemblance to a religion. That was rather a weapon to exploit, oppress, rob and to rape the continent and its indigenous human population.

Professor G. Wilmore made the profound claim that the Africans had a more developed and superior concept of God than the European missionaries, without any theodicy and theology. The black man through his history spiritually in touch with the cosmos and nature has maintained an exceptional link with the cosmic power throughout his sufferings, oppressions and injustice, which the white man can only observe on Sunday, but cannot fully understand between Monday and Saturday. The Jesus Christ of the black experience cannot be encountered or understood through the quest for the historical Jesus, which is a perception of European culture and slavery postulations. The Jesus Christ of Africans is a black brother; he is a brother who knows how to reach out in the process of bonding with his black brothers and sisters in a language of singularity with his oppressed brothers and sisters. This Jesus who was on the Atlantic slave ships, a Jesus who was in the dungeons at Elmina Castle with the slaves, a Jesus Christ who was at the centre of the Middle Passage. Wiping the tears, sweat, bandaging the faint hearted and psychologically wounded of the African slaves. He is the Jesus Christ who in Revelation

21[44], John says "I saw a New Heaven and a New Earth and God himself shall wipe away all tears". The sermon which came from the pulpits of the Methodist, Catholic, Baptist and Anglican churches were not sermons of the Jesus of the black experience, but rather of European ethnocentric Bible-based culture. The communion table in the Roman Catholic Church at Elmina Castle, the bread and wine could not have been the consubstantiation of the body of Jesus who said, "Do this in remembrance of me, this is my Body, this is my Blood." It is at this juncture that hermeneutic and experience become co-terminus in essence and purpose. It is an hermeneutic experience beyond words, synonymous to the unspoken love, yet the human chemistry and inner-feeling is all compelling as in St. Augustine's hermeneutic experience: "My soul is restless until it finds its resting place in thee, O Felix culpa." The most appropriate conjecture at this point is to say emphatically and categorically that the European churches at Elmina Castle were there for the following reasons:

(1) to affirm the European legitimacy of slavery;
(2) to affirm that theodicy and theology does not include African people;
(3) to condition the minds of the Africans that slavery was appointed by the European concept of a God and not the African concept of the cosmological function of God to the Africans; and
(4) to demonstrate the link between European Christianity to the European economic, political, commercial culture.

Professor Walvin once again in his brilliant statement has profound meaning here. Walvin says:

"Large numbers of Africans entered the Americas with physical and mental illness caught by conditions aboard the slave ships"

---

[44] Revelation 21

Even descendants of those on the ships were haunted by the spectre of the slave trade, which reformed in collective, folkloric memory, paradoxically united and recollected by the chronicles of the slave culture.

The slave trade had profound effects on the formation of the Atlantic World, especially on the dislocation of Africa. The demands for African slaves were remarkably fuelled by the desire for trivial goods. Building the economic power base was of paramount importance in which process the Africans supplied the Europeans and supplied the Americans. It was pandemic and morally repugnant, to say the least.

The slave trade was a mindless business, both from the African perspective and the European perspective. There was remarkable African appetite for European goods and the Europeans needed African slaves for the Americas.

CHAPTER 4
RELIGIOUS COMPLEXITIES

The complexities of Religion
Are religious emotions attached to morality? Or
is religion spiritually attached to morality?

I want to examine religion within the context of Africa and its people.

Professor James Walvin again in his acclaimed book *Black Ivory, a History of British Slavery* made the following observations that the planters in the West Indies feared the brutal physical proximity of their slaves, but what they fundamentally feared were African religions. To whites, Africans were pagans worshipping in ways different and beyond the pale of European understanding and intelligence. Africans had no beliefs that Europeans could recognise as religion, and thus there was no need to have any moral conscience in justifying Africans to the condemnation of a lifetime of bondage. Professor James Walvin has touched a serious nerve here, in which we should see the vibrations in the preceding development of this thesis.

There was a deep myth cemented in European ethnocentric culture, and there was also a great polemic that was unexplained. How could the planters justify the continuation of slavery of African slaves who had been brainwashed into Christianity? The slaves who pretended to or actually accepted European Cultural Christianity to mitigate their sufferings – how did the planters justify this situation? The slaves were not converted as properly understood by religious psychologists. They were brainwashed to accept a foreign culture unknown and dissimilar to their African culture. African slaves were castigated physically and the power of fear imposed on them. It was used on them for the pulverisation of their religious beliefs and customs. In other words, all that symbolised or marked as African religious customs were obliterated or extirpated. When Africans became Christians, not by spontaneous choice, but through brainwashing, they were then accepted by the major churches not on religious grounds, but for their loyalty, obedience, rejection of rebellion or obedience to enslavement and oppression. The churches' acceptance of African slaves was not on the basis of equality, beliefs, customs or traditions.

James Walvin continues his elucidation of slave religion and European Christianity. The idea that slaves might share equality was a dangerous one to the slave owners and the planters. Slaves were therefore not perceived as co-religionists to Europeans and the British. In simple non-technical vocabulary, there was racial segregation within the context of European Christianity. The religion that slaves left in Africa hinged on a belief in a supreme being or a supreme intelligence philosophically unlike the European Christian God. This being is the great Creator, but not the great law giver of Moses.

Ancestor worship was looked upon as primitive and barbaric by Europeans, but European Christians forgot that when Christians from Europe used phrases and acknowledgement of Abraham, Isaac and Jacob biblically, they too are practising worship of ancestral figures. For the Africans, their ancestors were their mothers, fathers, brothers and sisters. This has an ancestral ethnological and deep religious validity within the context of the African situation.

West African religion believed in magic and the capacity to use supernatural powers to achieve good or bad ends. The Obeah man or woman was looked upon as a powerful person on the plantation. They were feared by the slaves and the slave planters. John Steadman testified to the fact that the Obeah man or woman encouraged the slaves to question their lot and to challenge their bondage of slavery.

The Christian missionaries sought to condition the slaves' minds to believe that slavery was appointed by God or divinely appointed by God for them and that in Heaven they will be rewarded abundantly with milk and honey. In my opinion, this was damned rubbish. Why did the slave traders not accept sufferings for themselves and wait for Heaven to put their sufferings right with milk and honey? It is an undeniable fact that European Cultural Christianity used the Heavenly concept of eternity to oppress the black race during and after the slave trade when the Europeans and British were having their Heaven on earth.

This concept of Heaven is a nonsense and rubbish to brainwash oppressed people, especially the black race. I want to call firstly on the urgent needs of blacks within Africa and also in the Diaspora and to apply a black historical hermeneutic to the Bible in terms of theology and theodicy. To deculturalise European Christianity, to de-theologise European theology and to reformulate a theology and Christianity along with theodicy that is contextually fitting for the black context, would lead towards economic, political, scientific and technological freedom of Africa. Equally of use would be to formulate a hermeneutic circle with historical contextualisation.

The power of the Obeah man or woman in the slave quarters of the West Indies was accepted on the plantations, so said Bryan Edward. If Obeah was as powerful as perceived by the African slaves, why did they not use it for their manumission? I can agree to the psychological and spiritual hold and even cultural hold that Obeah had within the African community. According to Professor Walvin, and here I cannot part company from Professor Walvin, that it was the rise of black Christianity, or in other words African Christianity that brought about the full force of the dissipation of Obeah among the slaves. Black Christianity looked beyond the cultural limits of Obeah.

The ingredients or tools for the Obeah man and woman were an old snuff box, several phials some filled with liquid and some with odorous powders, pounded glass, some dried herbs, teeth, beads, hair and trash. In a nutshell, the whole farrago of an Obeah man or woman was comprised in this way. In Jamaica in 1773, a slave called Sarah was tried for having cats' teeth, cats' claws, hair, beads, knotted cards and other materials relating to the perceived Obeah man or woman. Professor Walvin's conclusion is fascinating "A little bag with a few trumpery and harmless ingredients hung up over a door was sufficient to break down the health and spirits of the strongest hearted African". What Professor Walvin is actually saying here is it was basically the cultural and psychological fear of the Obeah man or woman with their trinkets and symbols that affected the minds of the slaves. The strongest of African rebel men who when faced with equanimity excruciating torture and death at the hands of their white captors, crumbled before the Obeah man or woman. This is pure psychological fear juxtaposed with a cultural propensity towards the belief in the cultural power of the Obeah man or woman. This was a degree of cultural psychological fear, in other words, of the simple vacuousness of African cultural, ontological stultification. A similar form of African religion was myalism. Myalism was a form of Obeah that was more feared by the white slave owners. Myal men claimed they had links with the spirit world in 1769. European churches were determined to transform the slaves into Christians. In the mid 18th century the Anglican Church made a conscious and determined systematic attempt to brainwash slaves into the acceptance of Christianity. This Christianity was pure cultural Christianity created by the Europeans and imposed on the African slaves. It was not unpolluted Christianity, but rather polluted European Cultural Christianity and injustice that they exported and inculcated into the African psyche.

The slave masters and traders were without heart or soul or even spirit. They were walking dead people without a conscience. Slaves were the masters' sole property. The slaves were subject to punishment of maiming and unlimbing for insignificant faults. The masters claimed they were Christians at the same time, because in the minds of the slave masters and traders the slaves were not human beings. Thus the systematic programme to convert the slaves to Christianity was not from deep religious motives, but rather to influence the slaves to accept European culture. They were like animals being trained to function at the whim and fancy of the master. The slaves were perceived to be profoundly ignorant of what European Christianity was all about. European Christianity was not based on religious, ethical or religious instruction. George Whitefield, the great Methodist preacher, became illustrious through his preaching to the slaves in North America. He played the right preaching music to the ears and hearts of the slaves. He preached hell and damnation, eternal flames or eternal abyss in the heavenly home.

Moses took his message from God, but not until the enslaved Israelites in Egypt first became conscious. He took his message to the oppressors, the Pharaohs. "Let my people go", then secondly Moses had the tremendous task of motivating and inspiring the oppressed slaves whose mental orientation and physical capacity were those of slaves. Moses therefore gave to the enslaved people the consciousness of their potential, the potential to liberate themselves. Whitefield's theology and preaching were profoundly vacuous. Professor James Walvin described Whitefield's preaching in a succinct way, saying "These were sweet words to the slaves," and this was the psychology that Whitefield and others used to truncate and further assist in the subjugation of the slaves, into total submission to European and British Cultural Christianity.

Rather than preach to the slaves that they were victims of a heinous system, George Whitefield sought not to expose the system of slavery, but rather to buttress it. The slaves were in hell here on earth. Any message or promise to extricate them from slavery to full manumission would naturally work upon them. It was the oppressors who needed the challenge and message, not the oppressed slaves.

The debilitating conditions of the slaves were so great, so abysmal, so clouding of mind and human spirit, that the slaves' minds were susceptible to any external influence with psychological and spiritual placation or whimsical hope. I must reiterate with force that there can be no historical denial that the Christian churches of Europe and Britain were at the centre of the slave trade system.

Here again, the churches played a major influence on the minds of the slaves to get them to yield in submission of slavery. In their book *Black Witness to the Apostolic Faith,* David T. Shannon and Gayraud S. Wilmore remind us that the converted slaves in the Methodist church were taught the Capers catechism. William Capers' text was approved as the official document for use among Negroes by the Methodist

General Conference. The principle upon which this catechism was based was the inferiority of the Negro slaves and was intended to provide a theological justification for the slaves' state of bondage and servitude. This was itself a confession that they were inherently inferior to the white race and it was a major involvement of the Methodist church in the brainwashing process and the perpetuation of the subjugation of blacks as inferior to the white race. I hasten to say that the germ of this heinousness still runs deep in the structures of the churches today. Bishop Othal Hawthorne Lakey in his book *The Rise of Coloured Methodism* makes a brief statement showing the principle upon which Capers prepares this justifying statement. John Wesley's writings and Chapter's Catechism were printed in the same volume and among the questions and answers were:

Question: "What did God make man out of?"
Answer: "The Dust of the Ground."
Question: "What does this teach you?"
Answer: "To be humble."
Question: "What is your duty to God?"
Answer: "To love him with all my heart, soul and strength. To worship him and serve him.
Question: "What is a servant's duty to his/her master/mistress?"
Answer: "To serve them with goodwill and heartily and not with eye service".
Professor James Cone in his book *God of the Oppressed*, said "Sometimes I hangs my head an' cries, But Jesus goin' to wipe my weepin' eyes".

Black Witness to the Apostolic Faith

The missionaries and the slave owners worked hand in hand. It is to be reiterated that European Christianity was first of all economical and political and nothing else. Thus, European Christianity psychologically programmed a specific aim to inculcate and convince the slaves that they had a soul and there is heaven. This soul and heaven were created and promoted by European Christians. At the same time, the slaves were not equal to whites in this life or in the next. This was not only ambiguous, but in a sense a denial that the slaves were human beings and equal to whites.

To be a good Christian was to be obedient to the instructions socially and privately as determined by the missionaries alone. Missionaries, says James Walvin, "tried at all times to stress the importance of obedience and used the Bible to support them." Consequently, rebellious slaves, runaway slaves, slaves who resisted oppression were a constant problem and considered a threat to their slave masters, hence the imperativeness of the missionary. To impress on the minds and the psyche of the slaves that they must surrender in the act of total obedience and subservancy to their slave masters. Again, they used the Bible to brainwash the slaves. However, this dependency on the Bible created a major problem for the missionaries. The slaves began to interpret the world anew; they no longer depended on what the missionaries had taught them. Christian hopes and visions of hell and heaven had a remarkable resonance for the slaves who saw that hell was on earth, hell was external, other worldly promised happiness that was denied them happiness here on earth. This was an integral part of the programme of the brainwashing process by the missionaries to the slaves.

European Christianity as a culture was perceived as bringing morality, family life and discipline into the barbarous slaves' quarters, but this could only be possible where God and Jesus Christ were perceived to offer the same salvation to the slaves. It was only used as a process to bring about obedience and submission to the slave trade. It was not used as a vehicle for the liberation of the slaves and release from the system of slavery itself. As a blatant affront to the rectitude of the Supreme Being we called God and Jesus Christ, it was also European theologians' misleading conviction and denial of Jesus political involvement with those on the margin and oppressed.

The late Dr. Walter Rodney's essay "How Europe became the Dominant Section of a Worldwide System" in Verene Shepherd and Hilary McBeccles Tomb *Caribbean Slavery in the Atlantic World, a Student Reader* is eye-opening. Some pertinent points from Dr. Rodney are worth mentioning here and these are:

(1) Africa helped to develop Western Europe in the same proportion as Western Europe helped to underdevelop Africa.
(2) What was called "International Trade" was nothing but the extension overseas of European interests.
(3) Europeans were able to unload on the African continent goods that had become unsaleable in Europe.
(4) In West Africa and in Central Africa it was the Gold Coast that attracted the greatest attention from Europeans from the 15th, to the 18th centuries.
(5) Europe became the centre of a worldwide system and it was European capitalism which set slavery and Atlantic Slave Trade in motion.
(6) Racism in Europe was a set of generalisations and assumptions which had no scientific basis, but were rationalised in every sphere from theology to biology.
(7) When the French Revolution was made in the name of "liberty and fraternity," it did not extend to black Africans who were enslaved by science in the West Indies and in the Indian Ocean.

Dr. Rodney placed his finger at the right spot of the Atlantic Slave Trade when looking at Europe and Freedom, which was never extended to the Africans oppressed by the hypocrisy of European Christianity. Dr. Rodney concludes: "How else can one explain the fact that the Christian church participated fully in the maintenance of slavery and still talked about saving souls". Dr. Rodney as a demographic historian of great academic eminence summed up the mendacity and hypocrisy when he reminds us: "The slaves and free Africans played a key role in Washington's armies and yet the American constitution with its famous preamble "That all men are created equal" sanctioned the continued enslavement of Africans. Olaudah Equiano's words and experience are something not to be ignored, but to be quoted "in this manner without scruple are relations and friends separated, most of them never to see each other again". "O ye nominal Christians might not an African ask you learned you this from your God who says unto you do unto all men as you men be done unto you". Whatever elucidation or hermeneutical definition of slavery, it is universally accepted by scholars of academic distinction that the Atlantic crossing slave trade was the most irreligious, unethical, unsocial and immoral repugnance of Europeans and Western man. I state without hesitation, but based upon concrete historical facts that slavery was rooted in an economic philosophy and culture of white supremacy.

To this I add that slaves were conditioned psychologically, racially and spiritually. Slaves were slaves embryonically, psychologically because a slave child was defined before birth as a slave to the end of its life. What distinguished the religious experience from European Christianity was that slaves had a powerful, spiritual force and had awareness of a Supreme Being.

I am convinced that the categorical denial of black people by the slave system of European oppression, denial of manumission, dignity could have led the African slaves to the rejection of Christianity as it did Malcolm X, but rather through their ontological and cosmological awareness of God the Supreme Being, they mostly forged forward from enslavement and oppression to confession, from experience to confession. In sum, the slaves were denied equal partnership in the Koinonia of Christ, but had instead the Christ of the enslaved Africans.

CHAPTER 5
RELIGIOUS DIMENSION

Religious dimension

I make the assumption that the slave traders as ethnocentric Europeans did not have a defined theodicy and theology. If they had, it was not exoterical to the enslaved Africans or to the pagan Western Europeans who perpetuated the Atlantic Slave Trade of the Middle Passage in unspeakable conditions. Perhaps Equiano's testimony will reveal the condition of a slave.

> "I would not take it out of his hand. One of the blacks therefore took it from him and gave it to me, and I took a little down my palate, which, instead of reviving me, as they thought it would, threw me into the greatest consternation at the strange feeling it produced, having never tasted any such liquor before. Soon after this the blacks who brought me on board went off, and left me abandoned to despair. I now saw myself deprived of all chance of returning to my native country, or even the lest glimpse of hope of gaining the shore, which I now considered as friendly; and I even wished for my former slavery in preference to my present situation, which was filled with horrors of every kind, still heightened by my ignorance of what I was to undergo. I was not long suffered to indulge my grief; I was soon put down under the decks,

and there I received such a salutation in my nostrils as I had never experienced in my life; so that, with the loathsomeness of the stench, and crying together, I became so sick and low that I was not able to eat, nor had I the least desire to taste any thing. I now wished for the last friend, death, to relieve me; but soon, to my grief, two of the white men offered me eatables; and, on my refusing to eat, one of them held me fast by the hands, laid me across I think the windlass, and tied my feet, while the other flogged me severely. I had never experienced any thing of this kind before; and although, not being used to the water, I naturally feared that element the first time I saw it, yet nevertheless, could I have got over the nettings, I would have jumped over the side, but I could not; and besides the crew used to watch us very closely who were not chained down to the decks, lest we should leap into the water; and I have seen some of these poor African prisoners most severely cut for attempting to do so, and hourly whipped for not eating. This indeed was often the case with myself. In a little time after, amongst the poor chained men, I found some of my own nation, which in a small degree gave ease to my mind. I inquired of these what was to be done with us; they gave me to understand we were to be carried to these white people's country to work for them. I then was a little revived, and thought, if it were not worse than working, my situation was not so desperate; but still I feared I should be put to death, the white people looked and acted, as I thought, in so savage a manner; for I had never seen among any such people such instances of brutal cruelty; and this is not only shown towards us blacks, but also to some of the whites themselves".

"At last, when the ship we were in had got in all her cargo, they made ready with many fearful noises, and we were all put under deck, so that we could not see how they managed the vessel. But this disappointment was the least of my sorrow. The stench of the hold while we were on the coast was so intolerably loathsome, that it was dangerous to remain there for any time,, and some of us had been permitted to stay on the deck for the fresh air; but now that the whole ship's cargo were confined together, it became absolutely pestilential. The closeness of the place, and the heat of the climate, added to the number in the ship, which was so crowded that each had scarcely room to turn himself, almost suffocated us. This produced copious perspirations, so that the air soon became unfit for respiration, from a variety of loathsome smells, and brought on a sickness among the slaves, of which many died, thus falling victims to the improvident avarice, as I may call it, of their purchasers. This wretched situation was again aggravated by the galling of the chains, now become insupportable; and the filth of the necessary tubs, into which the children often fell, and were almost suffocated. The shrieks of the women, and the groans of the dying rendered the whole a scene of horror almost inconceivable. Happily perhaps for myself I was soon reduced so low here that it was through necessary to keep me almost always on deck; and from my extreme youth I was not put in fetters. In this situation I expected every hour to share the fate of my companions some of whom were almost daily brought upon deck at the point of death, which I began to hope would soon put an end to my miseries. Often did I think many of the inhabitants of the deep were more happier than myself; I envied them the freedom they enjoyed, and often wished I could change my condition for theirs. Every circumstance I met with served only to render my state more painful, and heighten my apprehensions and my opinion of the cruelty of the whites. One day they had taken a number of fishes; and when they had killed and satisfied themselves with as many as they thought fit, to our astonishment who were on the deck, rather than give any of them to us to eat as we expected, they tossed the remaining fish into the sea again, although we begged and prayed for some as well as we could, but in vain; and some of my countrymen, being pressed by hunger, took an opportunity, when they thought no one saw them, of trying to get a little privately; but they were discovered, and the attempt procured them some very severe floggings."

The slaves were dehumanised. They were reduced to the animal kingdom. They were treated as animals. They were perceived not to have a soul, a personality, dignity, a purpose or function beyond being enslaved by the whites, who perceived themselves to be Christians. The transportation of the slaves in the various slave ships was done in conditions fit for pigs and dogs. Men and women were thrown together in the hull of slave ships with no sanitation. Equiano described the condition, the language and description similar to a rude savage. Diseases developed at a rapid speed, because such environments were propitious for the incubation for their germination.

It should be compared to a pigsty or cow pen with many animals from which the air is polluted with a smell enough to kill. The additional infliction of pain and suffering was the lack of ventilation. Vincent Harding claimed in his book *There is a River* that thousands of slaves willingly jumped overboard into the Atlantic Ocean rather than endure endless suffering and pain. Many thousands of slaves died from the horrendous conditions on the slave ships. The gravity of these conditions reveals the psychology of the slave traders who were accountable to and for the slaves yet they shared nothing with them because they were convinced that slaves were not human beings. Dr. Herbert S Klein reminds us that the slaves were shackled together at night to prevent rebellion and movement. Mortality and morbidity were extremely high and costly.

I have given this background and preamble in order to prove that the missionary movement and preaching to the slaves was at no time intended to save the souls of the African slaves. Remember, the slaves had no soul, no humanity, and no dignity. The slaves were only animals.

Preaching was not geared to the slave traders themselves. There was no morality, no ethical social conduct. The slave masters' class was superior. They had a soul, they were human. It is therefore clear that the missionary movement was a religious extension of the systematic slave programme or business and the missionary movement joined the monopoly of the slave trade.

John Newton is a clear example. After he is shipwrecked, and he claimed he was divinely saved from sudden death, he wrote his song "Amazing Grace, How Sweet the Sound," he then entered the Anglican ministry and became Chaplain to Wilberforce. But the memory of the opulence of the slave trade continually clouded his mind and eventually Newton gave up the ministry and went back into the slave trading business. "Did Newton view the slaves as human?" No. The slave trade was only a business to Reverend John Newton.

A similar situation arises with Queen Elizabeth 1st and John Hawkins. The Queen on hearing the profit Hawkins made from Sierra Leone, and despite her castigation of Hawkins for his ill treatment and brutality to his slaves, the Queen did not hesitate to engage John Hawkins and even knighted him and appointed him to look after her personal financial investments in the slave trade. The Queen clearly demonstrated her commitment to the slave trade by:

(a) Knighting John Hawkins;
(b) Giving Hawkins her own ship to traffic, loot and rob slaves from Africa. Most astonishing is the name of her ship was *Jesus*. Her ship was not the only ship unique in this slave game.

We now see that the religious had no conscience, morality or ethical conscience and attributes resembling rectitude. The slave trade was an economic strategy, industry and business enterprise from which Europe was built. A graph of the system will help us to understand the situation:

Slave Masters	Slaves
Inhuman	Forceful uprootness
Barbaric	Dehumanised
Extremely Pernicious	Spiritually pulverised
Immoral	Oppressed
Unethical	Culturally traumatised and truncated
Deeply irreligious	Animalised

Uncompassionate	Spiritually raped
Full of brutality without conscience	Linguistically strangulated
Unchristian	Deculturised
Uncharitable	Uneducated
Insensitive	Uncivilised
Unmerciful oppressors	Brainwashed
	Subjugated
	Dereligionised

"Which of these two needed the Gospel to be preached to them?" Certainly it was the oppressors, the slave masters who needed it. The master race, the slave masters needed their sins challenged forcefully for their enslavement of fellow human beings. They needed religious condemnation and judgment. They needed the challenge of justice and liberation. There is no evidence whatsoever historically that any of the major denominations, especially the Roman Catholic, Anglican, Presbyterians, Methodist, Baptist and Moravians, preached this kind of expostulation to the oppressors, while they preached subservancy and obedience and loyalty to the slaves. The slaves needed manumission from slavery. They needed their homeland, their roots, they needed to be "Back ah Yard", they needed their hopes, their parents, and grandparents. They needed their cultural gods. They needed to be near the graves of their foreparents, in other words they needed Africa.

My thesis is not pedantic polemic. The missionary movement and European Christianity were juxtaposed to strengthen the economic and political hold on the slave trade. In other words, European Christianity and the missionary movement were extensions and confirmation of the powerful investments and the driving piston of the slave trade. I am unconvinced of any rational, intellectual or academic possibility of truncating the missionary movement from European Christianity and culture from the powerful motivation of the economical and political purpose of the Atlantic Middle Passage. The religious dimension was enmeshed in the slave trade and European Cultural Christianity was used to oppress, enslave, and condemn Africans to unspeakable suffering. It was a culture, not a religion or religious movement, which would be intrinsically ubiquitous in liberation, salvation, faith, God and Jesus Christ. Rather it was projected as a formal system to demoralise, subjugate with the psychological and reduction of philosophy of making Africans accept that slavery was their lot of this life. It aimed to destroy totally Africa and Africans' mentality, culture, language, feelings and ethnology.

Let me put it laconically, European Cultural Christianity was evil. It was wicked, heartless and stripped of the essence and resemblance of conscience. It was a dead, paganistic culture being used to condition Africans for hell.

Black hermeneutic is imperative as the intellectual and psychological surgical knife to cut through the entangled webs, mendacities, historical facts in order to expose the slave system for what it actually was: the pseudo-religious cover for the haemorrhaging of the continent of Africa during the Middle Passage.

Reverend David Haslam quoting Alan Boesack, along with Boesack's quoting Vincent Harding made the point forcefully:

> "Black theology seeks the God of the Bible which is totally and completely different from the God whites have so long preached to blacks. The God of the Bible is the God of liberation rather than oppression, a God of justice rather than injustice, a God of freedom and humanity rather than enslavement and subservience. A God of love, righteousness and community rather than hatred, self interest and exploitation".

> "We first met this white Christ on slave ships. We heard his name sung in praise while we died in our thousands, chained in stinking holes beneath the decks, locked in with terror and disease and sad memories of our families and homes. When we leaped from the decks to be seized by sharks we saw his name carved in the ships solid sides. When our women were raped in the Captain's cabin they must have noted the great and Holy Bible on the shelves. Our induction

to this Christ was not propitious, and the horrors continued on American soil".

David Haslam in his book *The Churches and Race a Pastoral Approach*, agreed that the church was in collusion in slavery. David Haslam's statement is far too lambent and simplistic.

The church, European Cultural Christianity along with the missionary movement, was at the centre of the slave trade; the church was the piston that pumped life and energy to the Atlantic Slave Trade. This powerful centrality is evidenced by the physical presence of the Methodist, Anglican, Catholic and Baptist churches at Elmina Castle of the Gold Coast in Ghana today. I am convinced that historically, theologically and morally, these churches were there to buttress and to affirm that slavery was acceptable and preordained by God. The practice of the slave trade by Europeans and the British was indeed correct and theologically justified in their minds. These churches were physically juxtaposed in the geography of Elmina's Castle. The churches actively participated and were deeply involved in the building up and expansion of the slave trade, the function of the church and missionary movement was to guarantee the psychological and cultural instruction of the Africans by using the Bible and slave trade method, purely for economic profits. It had nothing to do with God, Jesus Christ, salvation or spirituality.

To summarise briefly the situation from the inner chamber of the Middle Passage, it is legitimate to state that the church had a tremendous involvement and interconnections with the full composition of the Atlantic Slave Trade Middle Passage. The church was an operational dynamic voice and participant in the slave trade.

It was an enslaving connection contiguous to the isolation and alienation of Africans in the displacement act of slavery. It was displacement with the economic philosophy of the Atlantic Slave Traders seeking to apply a hermeneutic philosophy to the slave trade. I cannot understand how historical phenomena esoterically became man's bold thrust for economic power and cultural superiority. The correct hermeneutic must be seen through the eyes and minds without any intrinsic link between European Christianity and the slave trade, but rather intrinsically and symbiotically enmeshed inseparably between the African slave trade and European economics of the slave trade. It might be incomparable, but if scholarship is going to maintain its rectitude it must be faced with academic and intellectual audacity, temerity and a liberated mind. The religious movement and European Christianity were the major forces in the metaphorical card game of economics and politics. It was in this situation of powerlessness, displacement and deep geographical, cultural and religious dichromatic roots that the Jesus of the black experience in an act of solidarity with enslaved brothers became spiritually present to the Africans. The interpretation and translation of the homogeneous experience remained to this day ambiguous, problematic and spiritually unconnected with the seeds of the slave trade master class.

Jesus cannot and had not stood in solidarity with the oppressors. Even dialectical materialism cannot justify a modicum significant measure of contiguity. Black people are biblically, theologically brainwashed with a white European Christianity which enslaved Africans for the economic, political and social empowerment of Europeans. It is of the greatest exigency for blacks globally to deculturise, de-theologise, de-Christianise European Cultural Christianity and to cultivate, create and develop a black theology that is existentially and contextually set for the upward and general mobility of the black race. The essential need is to hermeneutically elucidate theology and Christianity and provide the economic, political, cultural contextualisation for the liberation of black people. At this juncture of black development, the extirpation of the European philosophy of superiority, psychologically and culturally would enter the world which is both teleos and commencement of global brotherhood based on the political, economical, theological, soteriological promise of Shalom. No one can experience Shalom without these essential ingredients which form a natural god-given plan for mankind.

Chapter 6
Perfidiousness And Reality

Veracity and Audacity

The hermeneutic discipline and approach to the Atlantic Slave Trade period must embody the ingredients of histographic veracity and audacity as in the case of Eric Williams in his book *British Historians and the West Indies..* Dr. Williams' academic career is illustrious. However, the Atlantic Middle Passage is the period of this thesis. The intellectual circumvention is the avoidance of intellectual perambulating too far from the Atlantic Middle Passage, a radical and critical focus, must include the state and condition of the powerless enslaved Africans first at the hands of their own indigenous captors, the Kings, the Lords, the Rulers, the Chiefs and leaders for their own domestic purposes.

Second, this was done for audacious personal use. The dualism is best explained by Professor Roger Anstey. Professor of Modern History at the University of Kent, Canterbury. In his introduction, to Susanne Everitts book *History of Slavery* (1996), Professor Anstey says, "A decade ago one would almost have apologised for a book on slavery. For blacks it would have revived memories of their humiliation. For whites it would have bought a recollection for acknowledged sin."

Dr. Anstey goes on to explain: "Slavery is a major phenomenon of human history. It has underpinned major civilisations and in its most recent manifestations accept millions of individuals in a massive transfer of population that established the political, social, economic realities of much of the new world, namely Europe, Britain and America."

From this we can deduce with confidence that there is a tremendous legacy of slavery between developed and developing nations. These nations are permeated with the historic imbalance of whites and blacks, masters and slaves. Slavery was an international or global institution which can be traced back to biblical periods as I have indicated above. Arabs, Greeks, Romans and Europeans. Indeed, the Africans had a well-developed continental slave institution. In other words, slavery was endemic in the fabric of the African personality, geography, religion and psyche.

Most accounts relate the African slave trade as domestic slavery or internal slavery. I shall not allow dissipation to look at slavery for historical substantiation outside of the Middle Passage for the black hermeneutical investigation and expatiations here. Susanne Everett says "one cannot qualify the number of slaves who died as a consequence of the internal African wars, which was the fundamental source of African slaves." The Atlantic Slave Trade has incredible demographic, social, religious, cultural, economical and political implications for Africa and the Americas. The trade had far less significance and implication for Europe. Africa had known slavery and slave trading before the coming of the Europeans. The size and organised economic philosophy of slavery across the Atlantic was a new beginning, encountered and experienced. The volume of slaves and the human suffering caused by the traffic is not quantifiable.

The political, social and psychological impact of the Atlantic Middle Passage of the treatments of Africans treated as less than fellow humans but as beasts of burden was supported by the Roman Catholic Church and the Anglican Church. These two major denominations were at the heart and centrality of the Atlantic Slave Trade. I shall develop this observation later.

Between the 15th and 16th centuries, the oppressions of enslaved people of colours and religions were extensive, especially among Muslims and Christians. In 1551, 12,000 Christian Spaniards fell into the clutches of their Muslim conquerors as domestic slaves.

Earlier, almost immediately after Columbus rapaciously entered the New World in 1492, slavery began there. The impetus and audacity of European expansion resulted in an extraordinary arrangement between Spain and Portugal. In 1493 the Pope agreed to a remarkable appeal to settle the latent conflict between these two great Catholic powers and to divide the world and their colonial possessions outside Europe

Rather than aggravate this conflict, the Pope divided the globe into two. The Eastern half of the globe outside Europe went to Portugal and the Western half to Spain. For the Pope, the line of demarcation was the Atlantic. It is noteworthy how much the Church was involved, economically, politically, geographically and with the population controlled alongside the philosophy and economic power. The Portuguese were not happy and they protested that they would be denied Brazil, which was their colony. The Pope allowed them to remain there with the rest of the Americas given to the Spanish and rule over the indigenous American Indian peoples. Slavery under the two powers decimated the peoples to such an extent that the Catholic Church urged them to replace Amerindian slaves by importing Africans and thus to save the pagan souls of the Africans as well as converting indigenous Americans. The motivation was the compulsion to convert, brainwash the so-called heathen for the purposes of serving the economic motives of the Spanish and the Portuguese and had nothing to do with religion.

What is the important hermeneutic here with the practical participation and involvement of the Catholic Church? This is not a matter of collusion as Haslam conceived lambently. To convert the heathen was to control them and maintain their powerlessness, making the Africans psychologically, sociologically, culturally and religiously impuissant. It was to rape the African mentality of all possible freedoms and to denigrate the Africans' knowledge and awareness of their contiguity with cosmology and history, of the supreme intelligence or energy (God), even if this divine relationship is acknowledged with the ostentations of henotheism, monotheism and anthropology are synchronised with the Africans.

Another aspect of the hermeneutic question is to find a logical dialectic rationale for the Church to programme a strategy to convert the heathen to European Christianity. They were to have Baptism and given Christian names. This is their complete denial and conversion from their roots, history, culture, religion and cultural paradosis or tradition.

To assimilate and acculturate the European Cultural Christianity at the same time of the transformation of the Africans from heathenism to Christianity according to the Roman Catholic Church and European political philosophers and vacuous theologians, the converted slaves remained deep in the bondage of slavery.

This paradox is deeply recondite and needs the bootree of liberation, justice, equality, love and peace, which the Church never had. For the Church with its conscious and deliberate policy, agenda and systematic programme to use the placated force and projection of European Cultural Christianity as a shield for the European economic philosophy of oppression and exploitations of Africans on behalf of Europe. The church was actively placed at the centre of the Atlantic Middle Passage. The essential black hermeneutic must be consistently unambiguous. The Church created, encouraged, participated and perpetuated the diabolical prolongation of the sufferings and of the vocabularyness, use of the slave' conditions. Words are inadequate and probably inappropriate to describe and evaluate the stupendousness and the magnitude of the African slave trade system.

Columbus wrote in his journal on 27 November 1492, "After they understand the advantages, I shall labour to make all these people Christians". In a speech to the King and Queen of Spain a year later, he said "God has reserved for the Spaniards monarch not only all the treasures of the New World but a still greater treasure of the inestimateable volume, in the infinite number of souls destined to be brought over into the bosom of the Christian church". Susanne Everett says "before a slave ship could leave the Gold Coast for Brazil its cargo of Africans were baptised en masse and inside the Portuguese fort of Elmina on the coast of Guinea was a chapel dedicated to St. George". Racism played a major part in the mindset of the Spanish and Portuguese. They would not for a moment contemplate the equality of any slave of the race, whether Jews, Moors, or Mulattoes.

These were to be grateful and obedient converts saved by the true faith from the dark and savage practices of their own heathen lands.

Between 1518 and 1585 the Indian population of Central Mexico was reduced by slave trading between the islands of the Caribbean, which shrank from 6.3 million to 1.9 million. The Church supported the Portuguese and Spaniards in favouring for their ships Congolese and Angolan slaves and palm oil, cloth and ivory.

The English saw everything differently because of the dynamo generating the system without any sound apart from in 1667 when England undeterred began building more forts and in 1672 founded the Royal African Company. Who was the major stockholder? Once again it was the monarch.

The Impact of an Evil Commerce

It has long been held in Europe and the West that it was the European slave traders who imposed the Atlantic Slave Trade upon West Africa, thus corrupting the African leaders and tribal communities from which came the dispersal of the local population. This is culturally, historically and sociologically not correct. Indeed, slavery was pandemic as a result of deliberate pre-planned warfare as a common theme in sub-Saharan Africa long before European slavers arrived in Africa. The pandemics of domestic slavery were common among the African kingdoms. Susanne Everett reports that "The slaves supplied by the King of Whydah were prisoners of war who were sold by the victors as booty". "The most common practice was the enslavement of criminals, debtors or sale of slaves of family members in times of famine, gave way to kidnapping and capturing of tribes in wars". Francis Moore, an English man living at St. James Fort in Gambia in 1730, described his dealings with the King of Basally, when he felt the thirst after his brandy sent a messenger to the Fort asking the governor to supply "a sloop with cargo". In anticipation of its arrival, the King plundered some of his enemy's towns seizing the population and selling them for such commodities as brandy, rum, gunpowder, balls, pistols and cutlasses. "If the King is not at war with his neighbouring Kings he preys on his own, in his own towns and abuses them in an identical manner". Everett added, indeed the King did not hesitate to burn down many of his own towns as he thought expedient to seize the people that ran out of the fire and sell them. Ottobah Cugoano, a freed Fanti slave who records in his memoirs, published in 1787, how he was kidnapped as a child and sold at a European Fort for one gun, one piece of cloth and a small vanity of lead. He was as he said, first kidnapped and betrayed by his own complexion who were the first cause of his exile and slavery, but he added the moralistic rider that "if there were no buyers there would not be any sellers".

In 1768 the English slave trade system was carrying slaves across the Atlantic at the rate of 53,000 a year. The French 23,000, the Dutch 11,000 and the Portuguese trading from Angola annually 8,700.

Professor Roger Anstey wrote that "Anglicans might well feel a sense of humiliation to talk about slavery". Why? Because the Anglican Church were not spectators but active participants by purchasing and enslaving slaves on plantations for themselves, in the name of European and British Christianity. Professor Anstey goes on to say they need not placate or sympathise because African and indeed Africa must accept also the full responsibility of the European slave trade. It goes both ways. It was a tragedy and impacted greatly on Africa, but full of self-castigation, because African leaders as mentioned were involved in the trade pandemic all over Africa. Everett describes the mind-set of African chiefs, Kings and leaders. Two things are of significance here:

    (1) the capturing of the people culminating in the enslavement of the people for self-aggrandisement and culture power.

    (2) The heartlessness of selling people for worthless things. This is mental vacuousness. In simple language, they were damned stupid and foolish.

The internalisation of slavery was by reiteration, pandemic on the continent of Africa. Paradoxically it did not dissipate their population. It was not a pandemic African cancer, it was primarily for numerical volumes and strength mixed with culture and political flagrance. The domestic enslavement cannot fully, demographically, economically and politically compare or juxtapose with European Atlantic Middle Passage slavery. Financial value was not placed on domestic slaves as they were considered as of no financial value whatsoever. It was to weaken the numbers of the King's neighbours.

However, we see that the development of the European slave trade imposed on West African people was different. The cancerous evil, human rapacity, immorality in practice rested on the concept of an economic value for labour. Gradually, the powerful leaders of the various African communities came to recognise their dependence on prisoners of war both in terms of class and especially in terms of worth. The impact of the Atlantic Slave Trade is academic to estimate. There are conjectures, no hard figures. For example the number of slaves shipped to the Americas is 10 million. In the 18th century about 80,000 a year between 55 to 60 per cent of these slaves came from sub-Saharan Africa. West African's total population in the 18th century was perhaps 25 million. This is a conjecture. Nonetheless, with the establishment of the African active and conscious participation in the Atlantic Middle Passage, it is not difficult to see the human rapacity of the Africans for American and European goods in the exchange of human cargo.

The paradox and enigma is this absolute intellectual conundrum. The African kings and leaders sold their people for such useless things, such as rum, whiskey, cloth, ivory, guns, beads, shaving bowls, chamber pots, trinkets etc. The African Kings placed no economic value on human or African labour. On the other hand, the Europeans knew the value because from ancient Greece and Rome into the medieval period white slavery was commonly accepted.

The African Kings and leaders never thought of the economic, and technological development of the continent. What was foremost to them was their ego. Educational development was also foreign to them. According to Dr. Walter Rodney, the Europeans sold the African things or products that were unsellable in the Americas and Europe. The Africans became both dependent and rapacious for European goods that the Europeans themselves rejected or considered inferior.

Were the African leaders thinking of Africa as a continent? Were they thinking of the African continent where civilisation began? It had been the birthplace of medicine, science, religion, methods of tool making and was the land of unlimited natural resources, gold, diamonds, silver and timber. I consciously plagiarise Professor Wilmore when he says "the African had knowledge of

God, cosmology and a monotheistic faith far more developed and superior to the Europeans and it was this monotheistic faith which profoundly surprised the European Christians". Professor Wilmore goes on to say "the idea of a Supreme Being was not foreign to Africa. The Hieratical church of African religion had anthropological and sociological emphasis". "Black religion and black radicalism" in *Introduction of the Religious History of Afro-American people* (page 11).

The concept of the divine or Supreme Being was developed by Africans, yet the enslavement and selling of their people in support of Europeans' philosophy of economics and politics by the use of African slaves transported forcefully across the Atlantic had no theological or moral content.

It was not a matter of selling the Africans into forced slavery, but it was the manner in which the African leaders cultivated, developed and maintained the system. First, they enslaved their own Africans deliberately under very inhuman conditions. Secondly they transported them from the deep interiors of their territories. Thirdly at the market forts along the great rivers, they were literally sold for goods that had no value, or connection with the improvement of the social, political, religious and cultural contexts of Africa. Is there a balance? Is there any equilibrium or responsibility? I wish to examine Dr. Eric Williams, Dr. Walter Rodney and Dr. Herbert S. Klein's *Introduction to the Study of the Slave Trade Scholars.*

Dr. Eric Williams in his book *Capitalism and Slavery* made the profound postulation which has influenced many scholars and students of the Atlantic Slave Trade. For Dr. Williams, European economic development came about as a result of African slavery and the sugar plantations in the West Indies. The historical synthesis of the economic, social, cultural and political history of the Atlantic Slave Trade is informative and comprehensive.

European and British slave trade generated great wealth to the British and Europeans. The slave trade formed a cornerstone and foundation stone of European economical prosperity. There can be no repudiation or disagreement on this historical fact. The essential hermeneutic in this significant point must be accepted. Who supplied the Atlantic Slave Trade? It was the Africans themselves. Take it morally, theologically; sociologically, politically, Africans must face the responsibility. Africans built the Europeans economic system and development.

While supplying human slaves for the building of Europe, Africa remained static economically and technologically. Here lies the problem historically and contemporarily.

Four hundred years of slavery, the Americas considered the supply of foods which Europeans demanded to satisfy the rapacity of the Africans too costly in the trafficking of slaves. To circumvent this economic situation the Americans began to breed home-grown slaves. This multiplied the rapid economic development. Europe continued unabated because the Africans made sure that the monopoly of the Atlantic Slave Trade was in their hands.

Dr. Klein in his book *The Atlantic Slave Trade*, describes carefully how the Africans participated willingly in the slave trade. Klein even makes the significant point that at the time of the abolition movement in Europe by the Quakers and Baptist churches, some Africans rejected the notion and actively resisted the abolition movement. Was the Atlantic trade good for Africa? Certainly not. Rather, it had not helped the individuals who actively participated. It had not helped the continent in any way..

The dominating influence over the Africans were the European Cultural Christianity, culminating in the physical presence of the major denominations, especially the Methodists, Anglicans, Roman Catholics and Baptists. Dr. Williams' thesis is still pertinent for the study of the impact of the Atlantic Slave Trade. Although highly praised for their academic work, Dr. Williams and Dr. Rodney have overlooked the most significant areas of the Atlantic Slave Trade, namely active participation by the Africans based on individual greed and aggrandisement and their disinterest in equality with justice as well as technology and economic development.

Dr. Williams's theory and thesis is forceful, but Dr. Rodney on the other hand took a different approach to Dr. Williams. In his book *How Europe Underdeveloped Africa*, Dr. Rodney's theory and postulation is that Europeans purchased and enslaved the best of the African population. Granted that even on the slave ships, there were medical surgeons whose sole purpose was to protect and help to preserve the human cargo. Medically there was nothing to do with medical ethics or medical morality. The slaves were property to be preserved. Philosophically and mechanically, if an engine is not serviced and kept well oiled, the engine will fail. Take for example the medical function of a doctor. The mortality rate of the slaves was unsustainable. Ships were loaded with salt to keep the slaves alive. It was Dr. Scott who invented the ventilation system. It is said by many historians and medical doctors that high blood pressure among Negroes originated in the slave trade period. Dr. Rodney's postulations are documented in his book *How Europe Underdeveloped Africa* and his remarkable contribution to *Slavery in the Atlantic World* by Verene Shepherd and Hilary Mcbeccles and "How European became the Dominant Section of a Worldwide Trade System". Page 1, *The Atlantic Slave Trade* from page 84-101 on *How Europe Undeveloped Africa*. Dr. Rodney claimed that Europe became the centre of a worldwide system and it was European capitalism which set the Atlantic Slave Trade in full motion. Dr. Rodney is full of castigations of Europeans. In a statement such as "After expansion in slaving in 1730 which placed slavery under the control of the Royal company, the small divisions of African states and the political divisions were made easier for Europeans to make decisions as to Africa's role in the world production and trade". Africa succumbed to the slave trade because of its physical divisions.

Dr. Rodney is correct when he says "Africa provided the link between sugar production by European Christians in the Mediterranean and the plantation of the new world. In the second, the third quarter of the 15th century, plantation slavery was established in Madeira.

Dr. Rodney placed great emphasis on the dialectical relationship between development and underdevelopment. That is to say Africa and Europe could not have created a symbiotic system without each others involvement in the interaction. Africa helped to develop Europe, the same measure as Western Europe helped to under-develop Africa. There is a significant paradox which Dr. Rodney held strongly which by hermeneutic is that the term international trade in the 15th century was that Europe made the move through international trade which was nothing more than the extension overseas of European Christian interests. International trade and production was firmly in the grasp of European power.

The concept of metropole and dependency automatically came into existence when great pieces of African territory were caught in the inimical web of international commerce. The European countries decided on the function of the African economy, while Africa formed a great extension to the European capitalist market. As far as the trade was concerned, Africa was basically dependent on what Europeans were prepared to buy and sell to Africa. He says "Europe exported (dissipated), goods which were being produced and used in Europe". Dutch linen, Spanish irons, English cloths, Portuguese wines, French brandy, Victorian glues, beans, German muskets etc. Europeans were also able to unload on the African continent goods which had become unsaleable in Europe. Items like old sheets, underwear, technologically outdated firearms, and volumes of odds and ends found a very receptive and guaranteed market in Africa. Granted it was a caterpillar practice, but the Africans came to the awareness of the possibility of demanding better imported goods. This great pressure was exerted on the captains of European ships for better goods. At the same time, European goods which left the European ports for Africa from Hamburg, Copenhagen, Liverpool and Bristol was determined by the pattern, production and the consumption within Europe.

There is great justification for Dr. Rodney's thesis because for Dr. Rodney it was Europe that assumed the power to make assertions within the international trading system. An excellent illustration is the fact that the so-called international law which governed the behaviour of Negroes. On the seas, it was basically European laws that governed. Africans did not participate in its making and in many, many instances African people were the victims for the law. Dr. Rodney recognised Africans as transportable merchandise; the power of the Europeans was exercised in the selection process of what Africa could export according to European needs. Because of the sale of African goods especially to the Portuguese, this was given the right priority within Africa and Eastern Central Africa. It was the Gold Coast which attracted the greatest attention from Europeans in the 16th and 17th centuries. The major countries which were involved included the Scandinavians, the Russians, Germans, Britain, Dutch and Portuguese because of the decrease of gold production the next productive commodity for the economy of Europe was human beings.

Although Africa had the capacity to produce many practical things of fine quality – e.g. West Africans developed metalworking and bronzes sculptures in parts of Nigeria, but when it came to the comparison of the European goods, Africa's beautiful bronzes were not as relevant as the most crude but deadly European cannons. Europeans' manufacture of many goods was of poor quality but they seemed much more practical to the Africans.

Estaban Montejo, an African who extricated himself from a labour plantation in the 19th century, recalled that his people were enticed into slavery by the colour red. African chiefs and kings were mesmerised and tantalised by European goods that they used wars to capture slaves and sometimes they even captured their own for sale into slavery for European goods and goods from the Americas. A step back to Eric Williams will add appropriate information to the slave system. For Dr. Williams the connection between slavery and capitalism is well attested beyond questioning. Dr. Williams categorically listed various benefits which England derived from trading and exploiting the slaves. He identified personalities and capitalists firms who benefited from African slaves. These included David Alexander Barclay who were engaged in the slave trade 1756. They used the loot from slavery to set up Barclays bank. In the case of Lloyds from being an insignificant banking house it was transformed into one of the world's largest banking and insurance companies.

In addition to these philosophers, politicians, scientists and royals also invested in the exploitation of the slave system, but of particular contention is the participation and deep involvement of the major churches in the Atlantic Middle Passage. On 8 February 2006 the Church of England apologised for their part in the slave trade. Part of the apology is relevant here. The Archbishop of Canterbury, Dr. Williams said the apology was necessary. He said "The body of Christ is not just a body that exists at any one time, it exists across history and we therefore share the shame and the sinfulness of our predecessors and part of what we can do for them and for them in the body of Christ. His prayer for acknowledgement of the failure that is part of us not just of some distant them". Of course, Dr. Williams' apology comes after he had been criticised in November for saying that missionaries "sinned" by imposing *Hymns, Ancient and Modern* on places such as Africa, but what of the Roman Catholic Church? The Late Pope John Paul apologised in the late 90's to different countries and people for the absence of the Roman Catholic Church in critical times and for turning a blind eye at great human hostility and wars. The Pope deliberately did not mention Africa, the slave trade or how Britain and Europe combined to deliberately under-developed Africa. What of the Methodist, Baptist and others? Apology is not enough. President Clinton apologised to groups of African Americans for serious ill treatment, but an apology must be attached with financial reparations. Quotations of apologies might appear good but their real nature cannot be overlooked or escape the pen and mind of a black hermeneutic thinker. The Enlightenment period was not different because lots of the supposedly enlightened philosophical thinkers invested greatly financially and most were racist scientists and philosophers. Professor Cornel West in his book *Prophecy Deliverance and an Afro-American Revolutionary Christianity* reminds us of two specific things. The significance of dialectic methodology, expatiating on this application Professor West says "dialectical methodology is critical in character and hermeneutic content. Black theologians have for the most part been compelled to adopt a dialectical methodology. They have refused to accept what has been given them by white theologians. They have claimed that all rejections about God by whites must be digested, decoded and deciphered. Rather, stipulate that what theologians said must be challenged from the black rejection and theological arguments. White theologians came from the school and culture of the oppressors and particularly from a European cultural Christianity and not from a Christianity of encounter in the context of suffering, oppression, exploitation and enslavement, physically, culturally, demographically, ontologically, economically sociologically and cosmologically. White theologians cannot logically encounter the claim of black theologians to preserve the biblical truth that God sided with the oppressed and not on behalf of the oppressors. Under a genealogy of the modern racism, Professor West says "the notion that black people are human beings is a relatively new discovery in the modern West". Looking at it epistemologically between the two races West has shown the fundamental difference.

"European. White, Sanguine, Brawny. Hair abundantly flowing. Eyes blue, Gentle, acute, inventive. Covered with close vestments. Governed by customs.

> African. Black. Phlegmatic, Relaxed. Hair black, frizzled. Skin silky. Nose flat. Lips tumid. Women's bosom a matter of modesty. Breasts give milk abundantly. Crafty, indolent. Negligent. Anoints himself with grease. Governed by caprice."

Scholarship and the Slave Trade

Professor James Walvin's *Questioning Slavery, Black Ivory, History Of British Slavery.* Eric Williams's *Capitalism and Slavery*, Walter Rodney *How Europe Underdeveloped Africa)*, Ronald Segal's *The Black Diaspora* and Walter Rodney's *Caribbean Slave Society and Economy. Student Reader* edited Hilary and Beckles and Verene Shepherd. These scholarly work that have all contributed tremendously to the study of the Atlantic Slave Trade and its effects on the economies, societies and peoples in Africa, the Americas and Europe. If the names of Joseph Eu Inikoira and Stanley Engerman are added, it is to say that all these scholars have followed similar approaches to the gigantic subject of the Atlantic Slave Trade. Contributions and scholarship are significantly predicated with articulation in the expatiations on the subject. Dr Albert Schweitzer at the beginning of the last century dropped a bombshell in liberal theology with his quest for the historical Jesus, which cut short biblical theology. In his history of the Atlantic Slave Trade, I believe Dr. Herbert S. Klein has equally dropped a bombshell with his book *The Atlantic Slave Trade.* Most scholars shy away from the ubiquitous internal pandemic domestic enslavement of Africans by their own African leaders. It was the African leaders who consciously caught, captured and kidnapped and enslaved men, women and children for pleasure and self aggrandisement and local power. Dr. Klein faced the

questions of African domestic enslavement with academic courage and intellectual temerity. Klein entered historical unchartered waters and with scholarship and determination to discover the truth, and it is by facing the truth that acknowledgement, understanding, proper evaluation and outstanding scholarship can be in their proper places.
. Klein presented his thesis on the economic, social, cultural, political history of the Atlantic Slave Trade based upon his findings on (i) origin of the Atlantic Slave Trade; (ii) the basic economic structure; (iii) its demographic, social and economic impact.

Finally the Cause and Consequences of the Abolition of the Slave Trade Act 1807

Dr. Klein in examining the European organisation of the slave trade claims that the Atlantic Slave Trade was one of the most complex economic businesses known to the pre-industrial world. For him it was the largest transoceanic forced migration in history. Its promotion and transportation was of people and goods.

The Atlantic trade supplied workers to the Americas because of the interconnectedness; the genesis of this trade was supported by the states which played a major role in the Atlantic Slave Trade. In other words, the maintenance of the Atlantic Slave Trade was conducted by the states themselves.

Africa was a modest source of slaves for Southern Europe until the beginning of the 16th century, when rapid change came as America and Europe became twins in colonisation and then slave trading was turned into a major economic and political business. Slave trading was economically fecund both to America and Europe. The system to the participating states involved state control through taxation, subjugation and monopoly were used by the African states and Europeans alike. The Portuguese stronghold was great at the origins. Controlling as they did the supply of gold, ivory and slaves. The Portuguese were later challenged by France and Britain. After the 17th century slaves became the most predominant export from Africa. Gold, ivory and African slaves reached North America by the 1650s through the Royal African Company, and after the taking of Jamaica by the British, slave trading from their positions in West Africa reached top gear.

The slave trade developed into a great transatlantic business, but who was in control? Klein dropped his bombshell without hesitation. He declared that "In the overwhelming majority of cases it was the Africans who controlled the slaves until the moment of sale to their captors. In all accounts it was the Africans who did the selling of slaves to their captors, not the other way around". A further statement of Dr. Klein's shows the powerful drive of the slave trade. There is little question that the thousands of ships that sailed to Africa to engage in the slave trade did so because it was economically profitable. The colonists in the Americas and Europeans were willing to invest in the slave trade, it is well known that most African regions resisted attempts by the British after 1808 to close their trade. The Africans in other words wanted a perpetuation of the trade.

Klein posed some more questions which are pertinent to the understanding of the whole slave trade system. Questions such as "How profitable was the slave trade for the Europeans?" The polemic has been intense about the overall economic benefits of the slave trade to the Europeans themselves. "Was the slave trade profitable or too excessively costly?" "What impact did the slave trade have on the economic growth of Europe?" "What impact did the slave trade and labour have on American economic growth?"

For most European economic historians, the profits were not extraordinary by European standards, but Dr. Eric Williams' saw things differently. He suggested that there was a linkage between the slave trade whose profits from slave-produced sugar and accumulated capital were used to promote the industrial revolution in England. Dr. Williams' thesis holds weight with many students and many academic institutions and scholars. The discussion will continue for a very long time. However, the admission must be immediate that as in many fields American owners and investors participated with the Europeans in the Atlantic Slave Trade.

Dr. Klein has posed for us the question of the African contribution and participation which differs radically from other scholars. Dr. Klein's position is this. Did a market for slaves exist in Africa and were they purchased in a rational way? The question is innocuous, but as some scholars denied the existence of such a market., Dr. Klein proceeded with scholarly courage, but is Dr. Klein's position correct? Did a market exist? The answer from all known sources is that all African slaves were purchased from local African owners and the exchange of goods for slaves represented a real market by any one's definition. European buyers were totally dependent on African sellers for the delivery of slaves. There is little evidence of European penetration beyond the coast before the late 19th century. Because of the powerful solidarity of the states and the threat of disease, slaves to be sold in numbers sufficient to fill a ship that had arrived at the coast via African merchants willing to bring them from the interior. African traders were powerful people who controlled their own goods and market. There was even a taxation system in place. According to Dr. Klein, both an internal and an international slave trade existed in Africa before the arrival of the Europeans and the Europeans found it convenient to adopt the well established local African market and trading arrangement. In most cases, the Europeans only deepened the existing market and trading networks. The trading goods were salt, dried fish, cola, nuts, cotton, textiles and general European goods. In return the Africans exported gold and silver. Dr. Klein is very serious in bringing about a balance which I find appreciatively helpful. Klein posed further questions of a penetrating nature: African markets existed and slaves were marketed throughout Africa prior to the European arrival and if Africans were definitely not passive economic actors, what about the price they received for their goods? "What did a slave cost on the African coast and did this price change overnight?" There remain the fundamental questions in dealing with the economics of the slave trade. Dr. Klein answers his own questions when he says "The Africans were neither passive actors nor people innocent of the market economy and were unable to deal with the Europeans on the basis of equality". They were well integrated into a market economy and responded to market forces as well as any peoples in Western Europe. Though their demands were comprehensive, they were different from the Europeans and were determined by the specifics of different economies and social organisations.

Whatever their approaches might be despite the importance of slavery, it must be admitted even reluctantly that the end of the slave trade did not bring an end to enslavement in Africa or the West

Indies. Dr. Klein has at no time said or indicated any degree of equality of responsibility between the Africans and the Europeans in their economic relationship in the slave trade. We have seen through the pens and eyes of Dr. Klein the active participation of the Africans in the Atlantic Slave Trade. We have seen the creation and development of enslavement as endemic within the African perspective and culture. We have seen the importance of warfare for the production of slaves for commercial sales, but what of the undevelopment of Africa and the super-development of Europe and the USA? Understanding the Middle Passage or Atlantic Slave Trade is the key to the polemic of slavery in this African slave trade and European Christianity and to understand their relationship and economic pull in the slave trade.

Europe, USA and Africa produced goods that were essential on both sides of the ocean. Rather than the enslavement of Africans what therefore was the purpose of the Atlantic Slave Trade? Professor James Walvin attempted to answer this for us and he said, "The slave trade was morally repugnant". Dr. Klein on the other hand states "Having been purchased on the African coast, market place for the slaves destined for America would cross the Atlantic on the journey that became known as the Middle Passage". The manner in which these slaves were carried across the ocean and the mortality they suffered has been one of the most notorious issues in the study of the Atlantic Slave Trade.

Popular literature has pointed this part of the slave experience as uniquely evil and inherently more inhuman than any other of the sorrows of the slave life.

The entire transportation experience was an unmitigated disaster. The central crossing (Middle Passage) took on average one month from Africa to Brazil. Two months from the West African coast to the Caribbean and North America where most slaves spent up to one year from capture and boarding of the European ships.

There was a moral outrage at the heart of whole slave experience. The European produced the goods, kept good records, under government regulation and indeed it was this requirement to record that provides abundant information on the movement of the slave trade. There is no comparison between the African system and the European system.

Some argued that the slave trade was a misery for seamen as well. Thomas Clarkson argued against this. It was the low cost of slaves that made the business profitable. The cost of the purchase of slaves was low or at most moderate. The African market was well connected to the world market. Africans demanded Asian, American and European goods in exchange for their slaves. The more Europe demanded slaves, the more was the demand from Africa for European goods. There were strong moral and mental ploys. Europe demanded more slaves, Africa charged more for their slaves.

Again, Dr. Klein paid particular attention to the participation that Africans played in the Middle Passage by supplying the Atlantic Slave Trade with greater and greater numbers of slaves. He boldly states his position concerning the roles of both sides in the Atlantic Slave Trade experience of alienation, fear, judgment, oppression and suffering.

I am convinced, and there is documentary evidence to substantiate the fact, that the slave masters on the Middle Passage worked hand in hand in partnership with the Africans themselves. Why then did the slave trade leave Africa so poor and dependent on Europe and the USA?

CHAPTER 7
COMPLEXED DILEMMAS

Reasons for Africa's Poorness and Under-development

Dr. Eric Williams and Dr. Walter Rodney, two great scholars on the slave trade, made claims for the under-development of Africa which are sustainable: (a) Dr. Williams: plantation sugar and capitalism; (b) Dr. Walter Rodney the selection of the fittest and European goods unsaleable in Europe.

Both scholars overlooked the most significant conscious deception of the Europeans and the British, namely, the withholding of science and technology from Africa. Africa has been under-developed until this day because of the lack and withholding of technology and science. In addition, the slave trade was the incubation chamber for racism. These are general arguments which are cornerstones in any thesis on the Atlantic Slave Trade and the active participation of European Cultural Christianity.

The need for closer examination is necessary. Slavery was a powerful river steeped in economic development and enormous wealth in the form of underpaid labour or free labour. The golden age of exploitation, says a Colombian University historian Dr. Eric Foner, was in the reality a commercial enterprise and slave labour made it profitable, because they had their toil which was not paid for.

Most people are of the thinking that slavery was an aberration, but actually it was slave labour which made it profitable. Without slavery, the New World would not have been developed. Slavery systematically stripped captive Africans of their dignity and personal identities and subjugated them to merciless depravation and brutality, disease, malnutrition, injury and abuse like animals. It is definitely fair to say philosophically and hermeneutically that African slavery was the oil, the grease that kept the slave trade system in motion for the benefit of Britain, Europe and America and at no time did it economically benefited Africa. The great demand for slaves was stimulated by the high mortality rate of the Africans. If the African states themselves had cut back the supply of slaves to Europe and the Caribbean, the system would have quickly seized up. Only the incessant and consistent supply of the slaves prolonged the endemic evil system.

The list of the goods purchased by the Africans is well documented, generally, I reiterate, made up of beads, rum, brandy, whiskey, textiles, shaving bowls, pans, clothes and inferior guns and gun powder. There were not only nearly worthless things, says Dr. Rodney, but they served no economic purpose whatsoever. They gave no independence to Africa, no possibility or potential to develop technologically or scientifically. However, without the slave trade, Europe and the USA would not have developed economically and politically. European Christianity played a major part in this strangulation of Africa. The expansion of the sugar plantations in Brazil and the Caribbean region depended upon it and historically the plantation owners and slave masters were all so-called European Christians with a Christian culture of oppression, exploitation, greed and racism.

The European churches especially the Roman Catholic Church presented a Christianity based on racism, oppression, exploitation, immorality and the affirmation of slavery of Africans. Both the religious culture and paradosis or traditions of Africans were perceived as sinful and wrong. African acculturation was viewed as acceptable and good basically because of the presumption of the superiority of whiteness and the domination of whites as the master race. This religious superiority and culture was protected by the Roman Catholic Church with its images of white saints and a white Mary and a white Jesus with blue eyes. A blond Jesus in other words represented a culture of racism imposed and inculcated on Africans who had developed a more sophisticated cosmological religious paradosis springing from African roots and nature. African poverty and under-development was due to the lack of technological capacity. Africa's technological reliance is on Europe, Britain and the USA, but the technological underdevelopment is the singular factor. Christianity from Europe is equally pertinent, as is the lack of technological capacity and underdevelopment. In other words, European religion, culture and philosophy are major contributors to the underdevelopment of Africa psychologically, economically and culturally.

The missionaries and the juxtaposed churches in Africa and in the Caribbean created and supported a slave system purely at the economic development of the New World and the underdevelopment of Africa at the same time.

We see the pre-programmed inculcation of European Cultural Christianity in the manner of the Roman Catholic Church's failure to give credence to black saints such as Saint Anthony of Padua. Black saints were kept recondite and are still kept out of sight today. It follows logically to argue that Africa's underdevelopment and the development of Europe and the West deserve castigation because they were due to racism, oppression and enslavement of Africans and their unpaid labour that brought about the economic development of Europe and the West. In a nutshell, there can be no acceptance of the plea that churches which embodied European Christianity ever freed from their participations in the institution of slavery.

The major slave traders were the Dutch, Portuguese, French, Germans and the British from Catholic and Protestant churches, and they are morally accountable for millions of Africans who died in the Atlantic Middle Passage and on the plantations in the West Indies and throughout the Americas.

European Racial Categories of Race

"White. Sanguine, branny, their hair abundantly flowing, eyes, blue, gentle, acute, inventive, covered with clothes vestments, governed by customs."

"African. Black, phlegmatic, relaxed, hair black, frizzled skin silky, nose flat, lips tumid, women's bosom a matter of modesty. Breasts give milk abundantly. Crafty, indolent, negligent, anoints himself with grease. Governed by caprice.

The purpose of this book is to instigate discussions and deep reflections religiously, culturally and theologically. It is an attempt to send a certain measure of reverberations throughout the major denominations and Christian cultures because for far too long, the Christian churches had been complacent and not radical and ready to acknowledge the dreadfulness and ugliness of their active participation in the most heinous crime every committed by man, namely the Atlantic Slave Trade of Africans. The Church for me cannot be the Church of Jesus Christ unless it is genuinely true to itself. There is no longer any need to continue sweeping under the carpet the legacy and consequences of the slave trade as reflected in the environments of Africans and African descendants. The words of Professor Woodville K. Marshall, Professor of history and Pro-Vice Chancellor University of the West Indies, are germane, as they are applicable to all Africans and African descendants worldwide. The past does have its value and our knowledge of it is precious. By preserving the literary evidence of our past, by preserving the documents, the songs, the stories, by preserving the great town houses, the evidence of the land itself and the use that has been made of it, we preserve an essential link with the past. History depends for its existence on this work of preservation. Without evidence, there is no story. Through history we can know the past, and know ourselves by knowing how we have come to be what we are.

In a country such as ours, where shame about the past too often fills the place that should be held by knowledge, knowledge of the past must play its part in our liberation from the bonds of the past. Our history is not dead knowledge. Its significance to us is vital and immediate.

There are no exact chronological figures of the depopulation of African. The figures vary tremendously. Some are modest, some are hyperbolical, for example we have figures ranging from 10 million, 12 million, 15 million, 17 million and reached in Vincent Harding's figures over 100 million. Nonetheless regardless of the exaggerations and the inaccuracies of the figures, it is to be acknowledged that 400 years of the Atlantic Slave Trade had an enormous impact demographically on Africa.

According to Tunde Obadina, in the slave trade lies the root of the contemporary African crisis due to the total human loss over the four centuries of the transatlantic slave trade, estimated from 30 million to 200 million. Vincent Harding in his magnum opus claimed that approximately 100 million died in the Middle Passage. His figure might be hyperbolical. In any case, these estimates are best settled by accepting as Basil Davidson's statement that the loss to Africa was at least 50 million human beings. What cannot be denied is that millions of Africans were purchased for unpaid slave labour by Europe and the Americas, for their economic development without financial, scientific and technological redress of the highest immoral repugnancy perpetuated by the essential participation and involvement of European Cultural Christianity.

It is universally acknowledged that African slavery predates the European arrival on the shores of Africa. The early relations between Europe and African were purely economic. The European had precipitously set up trading posts, castles and forts on the coasts. Albert Vanvein Dantiz, in his book *Forts and Castles of Ghana*, pedantically listed 50 forts and castles. This should lead us to understand the foundation and the development of European trade and exploitation of Africa.

The number of castles and Forts that were built from the early 13th, century until the 17th century is a clear delineation of the tremendous foothold that the Dutch, Portuguese, Swedish, French and British had created for the exploitation of Africa, especially beginning with natural minerals and gold.

They exchanged goods like brass, copper, and bracelets in return for products such as pepper, cloth, beads and especially for slaves. Nothing was innovative. They became part of an ancient internal African trade. Domestic slavery was common in Africa before European buyers arrived. This is acknowledged by most of the major historians on the African slave trade. Black slaves were captured, kidnapped or bought by Arabs and exported across the Saharan Desert to the Mediterranean and Near East. The British with their churches in front refined or rather perfected the slave trade from Africa to the Americas and the West Indies. The products of European and Western civilisation, which were technologically differentiated from the African, captured the minds of African rulers who were deeply mesmerised by these products. With the Bible in one hand, the eyes on the land, gold and people, the churches participated in this effort. In the words of the distinguished South African Arch Bishop Desmond Tutu, "When the Europeans entered Africa, the Africans had the lands, and they encouraged the Africans into Christianity and also to pray. When the Africans finished praying, the Africans were left with a bible in their hands and the Europeans had the Africans' land."

One African slave in Cuba in the late 19th century described how his people were profoundly captivated by the bright colour of European manufactures, "It was the scarlet which did for the African, both the Kings and the rest surrendered without a struggle when the King saw that the whites were taking out their scarlet handkerchiefs as if they were waving, they told the blacks – "Go on then, go get a scarlet handkerchief" and the blacks were so excited by the scarlet that they ran down to the ships like sheep and they were captured".

Was it trust or naivety, or bluntly gross stupidity? Was it psychological and cultural greed? The African engine of civilisation omits all reality. This is attested by Cheikh Anta Diop in his book *'The Origin of Civilisation, Myth or Reality'*, edited by Mercer Cook for Dr. Diop's historical, archaeological, ontological evidence generated a different impression and conclusion. It is imperative for this thesis to incorporate the significant encounters and slave trade relationships. The findings are equally important. The church and religion, psychologically, spiritually and culturally played a major force in the situation.

African Religion versus European Cultural Christianity

Dr. Yosef A.A. Ben-Jochannan made a major significant academic contribution to this question in his book, *'African Origins of the Major Western Religions'*. He dedicated his book to the recent born and those yet to be born. He was thinking of African and African American infants who must one day take their place in mankind's world as the inheritors of the religions created by their forbearers, in hope that they may become the forces chosen to bring to this world its equilibrium once more.

Dr. Ben-Jochannan claimed that the relationship between slave and master is important to any understanding of Christianity. Africans became enslaved with mental enslavement to Christianity because of the slave trade. European Christianity as a culture forced the slaves to abandon their indigenous religions. Dr. Ben-Jochannan says "Blacks need to know their historical roots and as a person of African origin I feel that it is my duty and obligation to enter this field where so many non-Africans have before entered to speak and write about me". Dr. Ben-Jochannan continued that he wanted, "to delineate that Christianity is African in origin and in no sense whatsoever European or Western". He goes on to say "That Semitic and Hamitic has they are presently applied to the early founders of these religions. Judaism, Christianity and Islam are inherently racist in character and content. The sole purpose of Dr. Ben-Jochannan's claim is in denial of the existence of that which most European and Afro-American call Negro. There would be no Judaism, Christianity or Islam if the daughters, granddaughters and great granddaughters of the African God "Ra" and the mysteries had not emerged from Egypt as attested by the coffin and pyramids.

Serious attention must be given to Dr. Ben-Jochannan's claim "There are people today around the world who have suffered from European and European American imperialism aided and abetted by the leaders of Judaism and Christianity, who also actively engaged in slavery by sanctioning its institution through twisted quotations from their own versions of that which is called the holy and sacred scripture. Through history it is shown that most European and European Americans have consistently used the same information revealed in the Bible, disguised as what they call Greek philosophy and Western

Religion. Dr. Ben-Jochannan says of direct Caucasian-orientated ethnic superiority. The title alone suggested that exclusiveness of European and European American (white) people. I use here my hermeneutic and methodology to revert to this European American ethnic conceptualisation as academic dishonesty. It is said by some people who do not wish to create vibrations knowing that truth is not being served. Dr. Eric Williams in his challenging book *British Historians and the West Indies*, Dr. Eric Williams made a provocative revelations of the mendacities of British historians and the Christian churches, "It has been a most arduous undertaking to emancipate Caribbean compatriots from these historical inhumanities in which they have been imprisoned for these painful deprecating centuries of serfdom and slavery. These sufferings were inflicted by the hands of those who created a covering of civilisation heavily loaded with a preaching of Christianity to justify behaviour that one would not expect even from the animals inhabiting the forests of this planet". Dr. Eric Williams's words are forceful, but they must be understood within the context of his thinking both as a distinguished historian and politician within the Sitz im Leben of the West Indies. Dr. Williams as an historian of eminence, distinction has shown how as a people, black people, were relegated to permanent inferiority, even in the comparison with the beasts of the fields. Those who owned enslaved Africans thought it necessary to debase them in every conceivable way. They consciously misused the words of the Bible attributed false claims with signings, publicised alleged genetic deficiencies, perverted morality, turned intelligence upside down even using chronologists to prove themselves. To the slaves of their consciousness that they were dealing with half men and half women but the property which could only be motivated by the whip, hound dogs chains and guns. British and European enjoyed speaking about the period of the enlightenment. In terms of science, philosophy and technology, but there is one essential pertinent aspect of the Enlightenment period which is of enormous importance and relevance to the arguments being put forward in this thesis and that is the enlightenment period. They sanctioned and affirmed their legitimacy of slavery itself and the slave trade. The Enlightenment period based on its own affirmation of slavery and slaves. This in itself has shown the depths of intellectual deception. Prevarication and conscious preconceived attitude culture and conduct of the European and British master race superiority complex. This in itself is abhorrent ethically and morally to the concept of God and religion. At no point whatsoever can religion, theology and God be reflected in this conception.

The thesis and black hermeneutic here being presented is basically of European Christianity and the Atlantic Slave Trade. This is why black people need the exposure of all the mendacities of European Christianity and their active participation in the Atlantic Slave Trade. It is a fact of history that European and British churches are significantly important for the cultivation and activation of black consciousness, black theology and liberation theology.

Indigenous African Christianity, God, cosmology, anthropology have been claimed by Europeans and British to be pagan. With the depths of inferiority and that the only way to see God was for the slaves to abandon African religious practices, customs and traditions and embrace European Christian culture through unquestionable acculturation. In other words anything related to Africa or Africans should be discarded and unconditionally embrace that which is white, British or European. Here we have the genesis of the brainwashing process and the inculcation and superiority of the master race.

The inculcation was the abandonment of pagan Gods and hedonism for European Cultural Christianity, but Europe and Britain had always been itself pagan. It takes the argument much further and more forceful that the commencement and development of the missionary movement was not to convert Africans to Christianity, but was to brainwash them with the European vacuous cultural Christianity and to further the slave trade and economic development of Britain, Europe and the USA. This is why black people are where they are today in this world. They are where they are because of the slave trade, brainwashing and inculcation. The situation of the Black people is because of European Christianity which subjudicated their ancestors, oppressed and brainwashed Africans for four centuries and beyond.

Africans and their descendants worldwide need to defend their traditional religious philosophies. The attestation is that the three major religions of the world, Judaism, Christianity and Islam, often called Western religions have African founders. This is historically factual. These religions existed for thousands of years before the peoples of Europe came into existence. Over the past three to four hundred years indigenous Africans origins and roots have been carefully and purposefully denied. Suppressed and overlooked. In other words, this was a conscious deliberate policy, philosophy and programme to both annihilate and obliterate all features of Africanism and to impose Euro-centric culture and values on Africa and her descendants.

Dr. Yosef A.A. Ben-Jochannan has made a profound assertion that is indestructible and cannot be repudiated. His claim of African origins of the major Western religions with his claim and he makes the attempt to set the record straight in revealing historical facts. For Dr. Yosef A.A. Ben-Jochannan, African people and their descendants in the Western hemisphere of Africa are critically conditioned and affected by this eurocentricism. The destruction of African religious experience has been due primarily to inhuman pressures brought upon the indigenous Africans by European Cultural Christianity, namely by missionaries, by control and influence on many indigenous African societies.

Briefly, it is worth noting that the missionary movements and the major denominations of Europe and Britain came from the concept of a caucasionised God and not from a universal God, certainly not from an African perspective. Marcus Ossiah Garvey was not a theologian or minister of the Gospel, yet it was he who brought a significant different dimension to African American society which made Garvey unique. It was Garvey, President General of the Universal Negro Improvement Association, who started a new Christian philosophy and made Jesus Christ appear black for the people who worshipped him through hell of the Western World. Garvey found his image of Jesus Christ depicted in the Ethiopian Coptic Church, the oldest Christian church in an African nation. An offspring without a spiritual past is a being without an ancestral tie. This quotation of an unknown author is worthy of mention. Marcus Garvey was in many ways technically a liberation theologian, so similar to Paul Bogle, Samuel Sharp, who were also liberation theologians in practice of their faith.

European Christianity and the Atlantic Slave Trade:
A Black Hermeneutical Study

Dr. Yosef A.A. Ben-Jochannan's Contribution

Dr. Yosef A.A. Ben-Jochannan says "Paganism, voodoism, witchcraft, fetishism, black magic, obeah and oledamare are names relegated to a few of the sacred religions of solely traditional indigenous African origin. According to most Europeans and European Americans, educators, theologians and general missionaries who believed within themselves that they had been ordained by some God or the other to some mankind from themselves. These messianic obsessions in themselves are extremely offensive to the peoples of African origin who cherished their ancient traditional heritage that has survived Asian, European and Euro-American slavery and colonisation. The indigenous African peoples were labelled as so-called Negroes, Bantus, Bushmen, and Hottentots. These are labels of supposed inferior status placed upon African slaves by missionaries and their slave masters from Europe. The European and Euro-American Christians' dogmatisms based on their racist philosophy viewed black African, black Negro, Bantus traditional religions as visualistic and idolistic. Indigenous African traditional religions of pre-slavery and of pre-colonial European and American periods that survived the fundamental philosophical and spiritual worlds as so-called idealistic religions.

The indigenous prodigious father of the Christian church St. Augustine felt that a (drink) libation of traditionally African religions is no less sacred in his view than the Christian Holy Communion. St. Augustine, being the most brilliant and erudite Catholic priest in the history of the Roman Catholic church was indeed an African, an Algerian, and was in my opinion theologically sound. We ought to remind ourselves that most of the Christian doctrines especially the Catholic doctrines all came from the pen of St. Augustine, a black African.

I have struggled in every way -- theologically, philosophically and sociologically --to comprehend the minds of those Catholic priests in their celebration of the Eucharist on top of the dungeon at Elmina Castle on the Gold Coast of Ghana with Africans chained and packed like sardines to capacity in the dungeon below. Some were dying, all experienced inhuman conditions beyond vocabulary, be it Latin, Greek, Spanish or English in sufferings, powerlessness, destined to perpetual and endless enslavement in the Americas, Brazil and the West Indies. What theological concepts of love, justice, God or Jesus Christ could have had those Catholic priests? At the same time, in the Methodist church across the road from the Catholic Church, they were singing "All praise to our redeeming Lord", "O for a thousand tongues to sing my great redeemer's praise.". "God of all power and truth and grace, which from age to age endure; whose word when heaven and earth shall pass, remains and stands forever sure". The Anglicans and the Baptists were ,singing "The church's one foundation"; "Happy the souls that joined and saved by grace alone" . "Children of Jerusalem sang the praise of Jesus' name", "Yes God is good in earth and sky", "Thy Kingdom come O God, thy rule O Christ, begin, break with thine iron rod the tyrannies of sin". "Long my imprisoned spirit lay, fast bound in sin and nature's night; thine eye diffused a quickening ray, I woke the dungeon flamed with light. My chains fell off my heart was free, I rose went forth and followed thee". The Roman Catholic, Anglican, Baptist and Methodist churches all saw the African slaves at Elmina Castle as animals and less than human beings. For these church priests or ministers, European Christianity, God or Jesus Christ through their ministries, they were there to affirm that slavery was correct. African slavery had nothing to do with God or Jesus. Apart from the church and the missionary's task to brainwash the slaves into total submission and obedience to the European white masters cultural Christian faith. We celebrate in Britain each year Guy Fawkes Night. I believe the mission of Guy Fawkes was in the wrong direction. Elmina Castle was the right direction for Guy Fawkes. At Elmina who were the pagans? Who were the Heathens? Who were the primitive people? Who were the barbarians? The answer is quite simple it was the Europeans. For European economic philosophy and European cultural prosperity was one of extraction, oppression and exploitation. Elmina Castle at the Gold Coast with its enduring monumental castle and European churches is a timely reminder of the centrality and functionalism of European Christian churches at the heart, at the centre of the slave trade. There can be no repudiation; nothing can be made recondite to hide this blatant atrocity delineated by Europeans in the name of Christianity. I hasten to add Europe was never a Christian country. The historical evidence is abundant, they were always pagans and they used Christianity which was nothing more than a vacuous culture to exploit the people of Africa.

Britain and Europe had a policy of extraction. The only thing the Europeans put into Africa was juxtaposed churches because they used the churches to further the slave trade. European cultural Christianity was deeply irreligious and lacked morality, conscience, spirituality and was inundated with human rapacity.

Dr. Eric Williams' astute findings are helpful to the heuristic thesis in hand. Dr. Eric Williams wrote "David Hume in his essay of National Characters written in 1753 had expressed the view that Negroes were naturally inferior to whites. No civilised nation had emerged among them. Africans had no individual who was eminent either in action or speculation. No ingenious manufactures, no arts, no science. Franklin had refused in his fight of superior beings to darken the people of America. Adam Smith in his writing "Theory of moral sentiments" "There is not a Negro from the coast of Africa who does not possess a degree of magnanimity which the soul of his sordid master is too often scarce, capable of conceiving". Thomas Clarkson saw the slave trade as an immense mass of evil. Clarkson was dealing with the great international problem in which Britain in Clarkson's view was the chief sinner. Thomas Clarkson had hit the nail on the head. The slave trade begun by the Portuguese, Dutch, French and Spanish. The perfectionist in exploitations and oppression and brainwashing of Africans, Britain was the leading player in those acts of human atrocity.

The deliberate inferiority categorisation of Africans was an act of inculcation. In other words, European Cultural Christianity played on the Africans' minds and sought to capture the African psyche. They psychologically brainwashed the Africans and all that embodied Africanism were negated. Nothing African was regarded as noble intelligent or prodigious.

The Europeans lied. They practised the crudest mendacities to brainwash the Africans. The African slaves were treated as cattle. If they were cattle-slaves why were European Christians teaching and preaching to the cattle-slaves? Its purpose was not salvation, justice, liberation, unity and to affirm that they belonged to common humanity.

Dr. Yosef A.A. Ben-Jochannan says "The Europeans tired of the Christian God (Jesus Christ) was different to the Jesus Christ presented to the Africans and to the Ethiopians before they were introduced to the Romans in Rome. "Fear ye well", came from a Negro spiritual that had its origin in the slavery of the Jews and Christians of the slave masters' sadistic cruelty and genocide to the helpless and defenceless African slaves. "Fear ye well, Fear ye well" that's the blows from the master full whip with its metal pellets these words were composed during the world's worst era of genocide by one of the group of mankind's inhumanity towards the other. Europeans and Euro-Americans physical and mental enslavement of African peoples in Africa and the Caribbean islands. European and Christian missionaries afflicted Africa and the indigenous African peoples by condemning their Africanness.

The limbo dance is deeply religious and sacred. As the Jewish Barmitzvah or a Christian first communion, Dr. Yosef A.A. Ben-Jochannan scholarship though brilliant when he said, quoting from pages 21-22 from Reverend Mendelson "What of the Christian missionary movements? It is slow but steady progress into Africa the charges levied against it are both numerous and biting. The missionaries came to us and said "We want to teach you to pray to God". We said we want to pray; we would like to learn to pray, so the missionaries told the Africans to close their eyes. "We closed our eyes; there was the Bible in our hands, but our land was gone when we opened our eyes."

The Reverend continues but they are also with the words – words repeated endlessly across the breadth of Africa. "The Christian missionary movement was an attempt to quench the African spirit. It tried to turn Africans into European Christians. They kicked down our culture to show us which side God is on. Missionaries are unrealistic about polygamy. Wherever the white man still has the upper hand, the missionaries remained strangely tolerant of racial discrimination. The missionaries drag their feet when it comes to training Africans for church leadership and authority. The missionaries have been indifferent, even hostile toward African nationalism. There has been no real sympathy for the political aspirations gripping young Africa".

The missionaries knew that imperialism, colonialism, cattle-slavery, neo-colonialism were and are partners with Europe and European American style of Christianity. The infamous slave trade and political independence in Africa is a fact which too many Christian missionaries cannot yet understand or accept. The force here cannot be denied or relegated because Amos N. Wilson in his column on the falsification of Anglican consciousness pointed out that Eurocentric psychiatry and the politics of white supremacy made the forceful arguments. Dr. Wilson says "the falsification of African consciousness is due to eccentric history as methodology which creates historical amnesia in Africans in order to rob them of their material, mental, social and wherewithal for overcoming poverty and oppression. Secondly, the alleged mental and behavioural maladjustment of oppressed African people is a political-economic necessity for the maintenance of white domination.

If it had been intellectually recondite, now through the consciousness of the Eurocentric economic strangulation it has become elusive. To this I add that every characteristic in the black personality serves an economic function. Euro Cultural Christianity was systematically programmed for the economic foundation of Europe and the Americas. Europe had a powerful European cultural philosophy of economics. Paradoxically, black history is connected to European economics. At the centre of this economic philosophy were Christianity and the church. It is a passing observation that African missionaries transported Christianity to Europe. Historically, it was the Europeans who took Christianity to Africa. Africans at the time of the Atlantic Slave Trade were perceived as cattle, inhuman and biologically inferior, yet in 384 Africa produced St. Augustine from the soil of Africa. A Professor of Rhetoric at Rome University at age 28, St. Augustine's scholarship was so dynamic that he was precipitously expelled from Rome to Hippo where again because of his intellectual brilliance and strong Christian vocation, he was banned from travelling and was forcefully ordained Bishop of Hippo with the clear instructions never to leave Hippo. The point is significant here. Primitive Africa, economically and educationally had scholars trained in Africa who Europe and Rome could not appreciate as the greatest scholar the Roman Catholic church has ever had.

The Atlantic Slave Trade system became twinned with the European Cultural Christianity. Dr. Anaim Akber in his papers on "African psychology" says "the insidious slave system is notorious and the most humanly degraded method of exploitation and abuse in the history of civilised man. From his disharmony he was inculcated in the slave personality of Africans, the Atlantic Slave Trade, European Cultural Christianity, it was made for the slaves. It was tied to the slave master the so-called master race. Whatever the social, cultural, and psychological needs of the slave master, it was destructive to the needs of the African slaves.

Slaves' Recalcitrancy

There is no historical evidence whatsoever that with the Atlantic Slave Trade (Middle Passage) African slaves ever accepted slavery. There is just no evidence to substantiate the jejune concept that slaves had succumbed or accepted slavery.

The biblical period of the Israelites had slaves in Egypt under the Pharaohs is theologically, historically, epistemologically and hermeneutically significant for our thesis here. The important points are that the Israelites in Egypt developed a slave culture. There are three different dates for the period in Egypt, ranging from 400 years to 465 years according to Old Testament biblical scholars. The point here, we need to note is that after at least 400 hundred years in Egyptian slavery it was normal culturally, psychologically that the only culture was that of slave culture. This argument is borne out by Andrew Kirk in his book, *Liberation Theology*. It took the political, and I consciously use the word political and not religious for theological reasons, and redactionary reasons, political leadership of Moses to expostulate and to inculcate his people to come to the point of acceptance that as Egyptian slaves they had a conscious past that they had the key and potential to liberate themselves. Moses took this approach politically before he motivated the people to a theological or religious consciousness.

Even the cries of the Israelites and Yahweh's command through Moses to "Let my people go" meant according to the biblical text, to worship their God. The cry was not a cry for manumission from slavery, but a cry to be free to worship their God. Whether it was a monotheistic faith or theistic or polytheistic no biblical scholar has had the confidence to stipulate. Indeed in the wilderness, the Israelites' rebellion against Moses and Aaron was due to their cultural and slave orientation, the hold through history of the essential place of slavery was so deep in their psyche. I must hammer this point home even much further and to postulate that even in a situation of slave bondage, this could and can only be a physical bondage. It cannot be completely psychological, because in man's nature, is God's gift that man was made to be free. I shall discuss later in this paper, that slaves on the plantations in the West Indies in formulating their rebellions, insurrections and conspiracies and there are several accounts of slaves who confessed that they would rather die than to live in slavery because nature created them to be free.

The domestication of the African slave trade people is colossally dissimilar to the Atlantic Slave Trade in degree of insidiousness and the magnitude of suffering and moral repugnancy of the trade. Domestic slavery grants straight away some humanity and congeniality with comity rather than the brutality which the European Cultural Christian perception of the inherent biological inferiority of Africans to Europeans. Again there were there, and there will never be any biological evidence that black people are biologically inferior to white people. It was of the highest degree of immorality, mendacity and racial superiority complex.

The Atlantic Slave Trade impacted not only on Africans and Africa, but on the whole wide world. The Atlantic Slave Trade had become a pandemic disease of the highest cultural and social malignancy. The legacy of the Atlantic Middle Passage was:
    (a) economically based;
    (b) politically;
    (c) theologically;
    (d) sociologically;
    (e) ethnologically;
    (f) ontologically,

From the early period of my research at New York Theological Seminary for my doctorate, I have held the view based on liberation theology that consciousness for manumission cannot be suppressed sempiternally. God has implanted in man's innate nature or being the appetite for freedom. It is what the theologian Frederich Schleiermacher called "the God consciousness". In his book on Christian faith, Schleiermacher was conducting philosophical speculations. I am dealing here not with philosophical or theological speculations, but I am dealing with the hermeneutical philosophical knife to cut through the myths, multitudes of mendacities, brainwashing of Africans, the biological and economical destruction of Africa is my thesis. This is my point. The cultural inculcation of European Cultural Christianity in order to imprison the minds and oppress the bodies of Africans for 400 years.

The psychological, cultural, sociological, spiritual theological and economical effects of the Atlantic Slave Trade is deep in the blackness and psyche until this very day globally in this 21st century. The scars of the Atlantic Slave Trade syndrome and amnesia are conspicuous among African and African descendants globally.

However, the basic focus now is the slaves' attitudes to the Atlantic Slave Trade -- the plantation slave trade and African slave trade. The slave traders had the following fears:

1. Because of their insidious slave trade, and the oppression of the slaves as property and cattle, the slave trader lived with inner trepidation of the fear of constant rebellion by the slaves. Was this a form of acknowledgement that the slave system was inherent and morally repugnant? For it to be morally repugnant, they would have to have the awareness and consciousness that the Africans were even semi-human. This was not the case. Africans were perceived to be animals and were treated as brutes and dogs. Morality did not come into play. Christianity based on a monotheistic faith and a Christological concept never entered their minds.
2. The slave traders lived in fear of African music, witchcraft, obeah and myalism. Of the two categories of fears there is only one that constitute the potential for manumission. It was a symbiotic rebellion. Nothing to do with magic, music, witchcraft, obeah and myalism, but the African psyche was fragmented, truncated to the core. The inculcated and the

inculcation was so deep that any systematic rebellion took more than ordinary audacity to mobilise and even in the act of mobilisation and the consciousness in planning, the rebellion there was the deeper sacrificial consciousness that death was imminent.. It was psychologically and teleologically a drive for extrication from slavery which was so deeply and spiritually to the slaves that planned their rebellions and conspiracies and insurrections. The sufferings of the slaves could not and cannot be justified especially when civilisation is mentioned. No cosmological elucidation is appropriate. The fundamental affirmation and postulation is that the system was profoundly and endemically evil. Again, morally and religiously repugnant.

Slaves' Treatments

Most historians are in general agreement that the Atlantic Middle Passage was hell for the slaves. What kept the trade in full swing? The driving force was the economical philosophy of Europe, the demand for slave labour and the produce from the West Indies and elsewhere was just tremendous.

The medical provision was not ethical or ethically motivated. It was motivated principally to protect the cargo for the profits of Europe. The cargo was Africans. There are graphic pictures and descriptions of the barbaric conditions in which the slaves were kept. Slave ships were specifically designed for the maximum capacity to carry slaves.

Dr. Herbert S. Klein in his book *The Atlantic Slave Trade* on pages 145 to 147, listed a number of photographic pictures of slave ships with cargos of human slaves.

Conditions were indescribable to the point, the slaves chose the wide unknown Atlantic Ocean to the slave ships condition. We have good and reliable evidence to substantiate the fact that slaves died commonly from diseases, ill treatment, psychological and cultural alienation and sometimes religious alienation.

Much study is yet to be done not only on the physical destruction of the Africans, but the psychological, cultural and religious alienation from their indigenous geographical, social and spiritual environment.

I am of the firm opinion that these areas are equally destructive. Death is the final termination, but those who survived carried deep in their psyche and their souls the psychological scars, the cultural scars, the spiritual scars and the deep religious scars of alienation from their mother country, their families, their neighbours and their environment.

There was a radical decline in the African population also. Demographically, the Atlantic Slave Trade had dire effect on the population growth and future of Africa. This demographic impact is still in full continuation today. Dr. Klein says the impact of the slave trade caused the African population to decline by 2 million between 1700 and 1850. The decline on the Western African population was 25 million in 150 years. This was due to the Atlantic Slave Trade and the cost of the total loss of 16.3 million people. Whatever these estimates of loss, it cannot be denied that the transatlantic slave trade did have a negative impact on the African population growth. Another way of looking at it is that demographically the system created underdevelopment in Africa. This underdevelopment is geographically pandemic in all the human spheres of Africa until this day. Can Africa recover? Will Africa ever recover to its fullest potential?

One significant aspect of the Atlantic slaves' treatment was that the slaves were usually shackled together at nights to prevent rebellion and movement during the day. They would be on deck. I reiterate they were shackled together. They were shackled by the hands of European so-called cultural Christians. They were shackled with the knowledge, support and participation of European churches and British churches. They were shackled because of the European and British church leaders' consent and personal involvement in the Atlantic Slave Trade. On deck they were forced to exercise sometimes accompanied by African musical instruments like animals in a circus. Some captains purchased African drums, so as to force the slaves to dance. All European and British mentality and conduct was designed in a systematic controlling way to subjugate the Africans into total submission to the will and power of the European and British master race. All was done in the name of Christianity, God and Jesus. I agree with many Rastafarians and many African and

African descendants, brothers and sisters that there is justification to argue that the European and British God is bound to be perceived as different from that of the Black Africans and African descendants.

In the Atlantic trade there was no relaxation for the slaves. All were controlled by the slave masters and slave traders themselves. They were a law unto themselves likewise, so-called churches. In St. Dominic, six slaves were purchased at bargain prices and were nursed back to health and then resold at a healthy profit. They were all cargoes. They were animals they were cattle, they were not human beings. Dr. Klein summed up the Atlantic Slave Trade nicely when he said laconically "there is little question that the thousand of ships that sailed for Africa to exchange the slave trade did so because it was profitable". In other words, the motivating dynamo for the Atlantic Slave Trade was economic profitability. Nevertheless I am of the firm opinion that academic veracity should allow us to say that although European and American merchants were happy to invest in the Atlantic Slave Trade , the slave trade was profitable to most of the coastal African slaves exporting slaves. Susanne Everett in her book *History of Slavery* reproduces early photographs of the slaves, images of chained slaves and little children, chained by hands and by neck as well as slave markets, slaves with slave collars and slave auctions.

Slaves' Insurrections

There was always the fear of the slave trade revolt. As noted previously, the slave masters carried with them the constant, incessant inner flow of the fear of slave's insurrection. Between the 18th and 19th centuries there were a number of slave revolts. In 1712 slaves set fire to several houses and 10 whites were killed. Retaliation was paid by 21 slaves who were killed by execution and burning. In South Carolina in 1739 approximately 20 whites were killed and 40 Africans died as a consequence of that. Some 1,800 to 1,822 revolts are recorded.

The most audacious revolt against the oppressions of slavery was that of the immortal Nat Turner in Virginia in 1831. Turner was a charismatic slave preacher. On the 21st August 1831, Turner and his friends swept through Southampton like a hurricane and killed 60 whites within a day. Needless to celebrate the power of the troops sent against them and how they put down the rebellion. The omega of Turner's revolt was the execution of 25 blacks and lynching of 200 Africans.

From prison, Nat Turner wrote his confession and in it he claimed his actions was a result of divine inspiration. No rational person can with spiritual or religious rectitude deny Turner's divine inspiration because the slave traders' treatment of Africans could not have been inspired by a moral God. The slave traders' God and Jesus emerged from a deep Eurocentric and ethnocentric cultural Christianity based on economic profits and enslavement arising from oppressions of Africans for over 400 years. Leaders of the revolt would have had the courage of the biblical Moses and Aaron, because any failure or any failed revolt would have resulted in certain death. Leaders such as Toussaint L'Ouverture of the slave trade, Gabriel Prosser and Denmark Vesey 1800 and 1822 were slaves who were planning against the system and how to resist the seductive and irresistible inner call for manumission. Because of attempted slave revolts and insurrections, slave traders sought by all means to control the slaves. Their first step was to keep the slaves ignorant and prevent them from learning to read. The traders' deliberate and conscious policy was to keep the blacks mentally and psychologically ignorant. They made it an offence to teach a slave or slaves how to read. Even religious instructions were viewed with deep suspicion. Ignorance even of the Sermon on the Mount was regarded as a means of social control. This is where the missionary movement came into full action and where the church played its most important and major role in brainwashing the slaves for the sole purpose of the slave traders.

Everett reminds us of the consistent programme of Europeans and Americans to keep psychological, physical, cultural and religious control of the slaves. Although slave owners tried in 1830 to ameliorate the conditions of the slaves, the owners were at all times and at all levels seeking total control, domination and subjugation.. According to Professor Genoese, these ameliorations were designed to make the South safe for shareholders by confirming the blacks in perpetual slavery and by making it possible for them to accept their fate. Again, this is where the church as the missionary movement came into full play. Paradoxically, their humanitarianism never extended to manumission. Emancipation in 1831 to 1832 was extremely difficult. What was granted was higher social status, better treatment and agreement. Dr. Klein says desperate attempts of the slave holders were made, but the Atlantic tide of opinion was now turning against the trade. I am not too convinced that Dr. Klein is accurate in this matter. He has overlooked or ignored like many white scholars the power and impact of the slaves themselves in the Caribbean and on the plantations to force their liberation, abolition and emancipation.

There was just no justification, economically, sociologically, religiously or politically for the African slave trade. The Atlantic Slave Trade is unique, and we must not lose sight of the uniqueness of the phenomenon of Atlantic Slave Trade. Attempts have been made to make it similar or dissimilar or to equate it with other slave societies, but I reiterate the Atlantic Slave Trade remains phenomenally unique

There has been nothing similar in recorded history of civilised man. According to C.E.M Jode's *Introduction to Modern Philosophy*, 1964, it was Dr, W.E. B. DuBois who postulated the essential differentness of slavery and revealed the real meaning of slavery, different from that we may apply to the labour today. It was in part psychological, the enforced personal sense of inferiority, the calling of another master, the standing with hats in hand ;it was the helplessness of the slaves. It was their defensiveness of family life. It was the submergence below the arbitrary will of any sort of individual. Slaves were seen as cogs in the huge machine of the system of the "peculiar institution."

As slaves died, they were immediately replaced because the level of production for economic profits could not be abated or stopped. The Atlantic Slave Trade generated such enormous economical wealth to Britain and Europe that the engine was out of control in that there was no political machinery moral or religious machinery to stop it rolling with the movement of the economic force of profitability.

Pictures and documents as early as 1860 and ascribed to Solomon Northup on cotton plantation on the Bayou Bolus in Avoye, Louisiana reveal realities of slavery. Although Northup was a paid freeman, he was later drugged and kidnapped by two white men and sold into slavery. Northup described the plantation conditions of the slaves. Slaves were not allowed to rest because they were machines or seen or perceived as machines. Only 50 minutes was allowed to the slaves to swallow their ration of cold bacon. Slaves worked until the middle of the night. The slaves were not considered human, they were only machines. They were turned off not because they were overheated or unwell, but because their oppressors, the traders needed rest. Slaves were punished should they fail to produce the estimated volume in time. In other words, slaves equalled profits and production. Slaves equalled economic profits. Born as slaves they lived as slaves in short lives as a slave and died as slaves. As a slave was a replacement tool used and recorded at random. Slaves were never perceived to have any human attributes. A slave was without a soul. So because a slave was not human and one without a soul, what was the point of the missionaries going to Africa to start preaching to the slaves? The slaves were already considered like animals and had no souls. A slave was without a God, and the slaves were without a God because the slave traders and the missionaries had conditioned the slaves and forced them to abandon their ancestors; their indigenous religious roots. Slaves had no soul, therefore what was the point in preaching God and Jesus to the slaves? That was not the focus of the missionaries. The missionaries focus was to brainwash the slaves into accepting subservancy, subjugation, oppression and exploitation. To slave with this European God, Jesus and Christianity was nothing more than the acceptance of European cultural religion or Christianity. A slave with the European culture was fully acculturated in the psyche of the Atlantic slave Africans. The slaves were replaceable tools in a systematic slave trade because of the supply and demand from the African domestic slave trade system of Africa. Slaves had no freedom. Slaves were property owned by the slave masters.

    This enslavement and ownership by the slave masters dominated and permeated even the sexual encounters between the slave traders and the slave women. John Newton and William Cooney in 1755are extremely good examples of this bestiality with the slave women. Slave women were treated like female beasts used at random on the plantation in conspicuous view of other slaves. There was no respect for human dignity.

The unbridled and aggressive white sexuality with slave women was ubiquitous, yet Africans were seen as immoral, wanton, lascivious and devoid of social attributes which distinguished Europeans as civilised people, but this was deeply racial and mythological perception. Investigation and study reveal that all corruptions, disrespect of the sanctity of women, of black women in particular. were the result of contaminations with Europeans. I take the point sociologically further. Within polygamous society, there is no evidence of rape and there is no evidence of promiscuous immoral social conditions. Yet these social immoralities were transported and exported to Africa and the plantations by Europeans, who claimed that they were civilised yet their conduct and philosophy were that of barbarians and pagans. African black women were treated in a despicable way. As James Walvin described in his book on the slave trade, the slave masters on the plantation climbed off the back of their horses and grabbed any slave woman of their choice and sexually used her in an act of bestiality in the presence of other slaves. With this conduct, they claimed they were civilised.

Their normal relationships was the result of colonial slavery. In other words, the slave trade produced sexual exploitations of a great kind. Slaves' sexual exploitation was part of the fabric of slave society. Slave women were reduced to nothingness. They were reduced to the animal kingdom. They were powerless. Psychologically they had no choice. Slave women were subjected to the libidinous desires of the slave owners, Slave women were at the mercy of the slave fathers, sons, brothers or friends of her masters. They had a freedom of choice to sexually use the women. The slave woman was the property of her master. She had no freedom, no choice, no dignity. She had nothing. She was a tool to pick and choose whimsically at random. James Walvin is worth quoting here to drive home the slave masters' culture, "When other friends visited a neighbouring estate on Sundays, it was the common practice to have women selected early in the week from the various properties of the various estates for the sole purpose of sleeping with their visitors, their white friends after a meal or a supper". In other words, mundanely and bluntly African women were the afters of the white masters' and their friends after their drinking and meal session. Thomas Thistlewood expected to be provided with his favourite slave woman to complete an evening of drinking and eating with his friend. Thomas Thistlewood had a choice, he had his favourite slave woman as his afters to complete his evening out. Europeans destroyed African cultural paradosis or tradition of polygamy. Polygamy was endemic in African culture and historically and ontologically where polygamy existed as a custom and practiced, there is no evidence whatsoever of rape. Put it into a biblical context, we find that polygamy was permitted in the Old Testament.

Slave women were degraded by European men who felt no constraint and demanded sexual gratification as well as labouring services from slave women as well. The whites sought to justify this aspect of the slave trade by alleging it based on the supposed sexual rapacity of slave women and, with illogical European cultural mendacity, to have been caused by the promiscuity of African men. Widespread violence existed in the colonies because of the sexual environment of the trade and the animalistic conduct in ubiquitous and persistent violation of slave women by white men who were sexually attracted to their slave women, because of the sexual convenience and the powerlessness of African women. At the same time, black men were commonly castrated for a variety of reasons such as rebellious behaviour, wandering away or physically striking a white person. Once again, James Walvin sums up the slave trade sexual culture when he says "sexual relations between black and white were created in the main by the behaviour of white males (p223) *Black Ivory the History of British Slavery*. Thomas Thistlewood's journal records his sexual conduct with slave women from March 1754 to 1758. In 1759, this feature of the slave trade culture was reflected in law. Children from slave black-white relations were legally defined as superior to the slaves, but inferior to the whites. Children were given their mothers' status, but not their fathers' racial status. What can be said of this. There was biological racism and this biological racism emanated even from and through the Enlightenment. Biological racism was also perceived and practised by theologians, scientists, sociologists and politicians, hence the cultural and social aggregates were:

(a) the chronological;
(b) the economic philosophy;
(c) the theological philosophy of blacks not having the divine presence in them.

Africans were stripped of all African religious paradosis, tradition, and acculturated to the acceptance of European Christianity, which was basically a pernicious and vacuous culture, far removed from humanity, God, Jesus Christ, devoid of honesty, justice, goodness, righteousness and morality, but inundated at the same time with insidiousness and senseless rapacity for women and economic profits.

The 1831 Morant Bay rebellion of the Maroons led by Paul Bogle and James Walters served as a paradigm and was a great inspiration to other slave insurrections. Paul Bogle gave thanks to God. for a successful mission. On 17 October 1831, Bogle and Maclaren signed a declaration which reads:

> "It is time now for us to help ourselves. Skin for skin, the iron bars is now broken in this Parish, the white people send a proclamation to the Governor to make war against us, which we all must put our shoulder to the wheels, and pull together. The Maroons sent their proclamation to us to meet them at Hayfield at once without delay, they will put us in the way of how to act. Everyone one of you must leave your house, take your guns, who wont have guns, take your cutlasses down at once. Come over to Stonygut that we might march over to meet the Maroons at once without delay. Blow your shields, roll your drums, house to house, take out every man, march them down to Stonygut, any that you find in the way takes them down with their arms, war is at us, my black skin, war is at hand from the day to tomorrow. Every black man must turn out at once, for the oppression is too great, the white people are now cleaning up their guns for us, which we must appear to meet them too. Chairmen, in heat we are looking for you a part of the night or before day break."

This declaration was a declaration of war because in the declaration it says clearly "Every black man must turn out at once, for the oppression is too great". Again, the oppression is too great. The ontological cry from the psyche of the slaves through the mind of Paul Bogle and Maclaren was for their complete manumission. The Europeans' slave trade system was one of oppression and exploitation. The cry was extrication from oppression of European so-called Christians.

In the book, *The Killing Time, the Morant Bay rebellion in Jamaica* by Gad Henman and Vincent Harding's *"There is a River"* (the black struggle for freedom in America), Harding's information on black rebellions is widely appreciated as a significant contribution. Harding lists spectacular and historic rebellions and their leaders, such as Nat Turner, Frederick Douglas, Harriett Tubman, Sojourner Truth, Martin Delaney, Denmark Vessey, H Ford, Douglas and David Walker, Cudjoe and many others. Walker and Turner presented their theological arguments challenging the Europeans and Euro-American whites and their white owned God. One can draw both a theological and philosophical conclusion that the slave trade whites did not know the ontological cosmological God. It is therefore correct for these immortal and illustrious slave pioneers and liberationists to have questioned European moral, religious and social foundation. Africans had an ontological, cosmological and theological God consciousness of the powerful energy and power that keeps the world and cosmos in motion. Scholarly juxtaposed to Vincent Harding is Hugh Thomas *The Slave Trade:, The History of the Atlantic Slave Trade 1440-1870,* Thomas presented a thesis encapsulating kings and princes of the slave trade ranging from Henry the Navigator (1440), the King of Benin (1686) and the powerful slave merchants, figures such as Tegbesu of Dahoney (1750) who made £250,000 per year by selling Africans into slavery. He too claimed that he was a Christian. King Alvare of the Congo who provided slaves to the Portuguese in 1686. "Look at the shipbuilder who bent over his desk determined his pen in hand, how many armies he can make occur on the coasts of Guinea, who examines a ledger the number of guns he will need to obtain a black, how many chains he will need to have him guaranteed on his ship, how many strokes of the whip to make him work," said Guillaume Raynal, *historien philosophique et politique des idées* (1782). According to Hugh Thomas, the slave trade was basically a government enterprise, the correct deductions from this endemic and argument is that the Atlantic Slave Trade's prime mover was the state. The state was in control of the slave trade and not the individuals, but the state.

In different ways, the French, the English and the Dutch had aggregated a similar financial interest in the Atlantic Slave Trade. These include the Dutch crowns, King Louis XIV of France, King George I of England, the King of Sweden and Denmark. Companies were formed with the Royal African Company leading the show. Again, the Royals and the state were involved.

Historical records and books are very clear, and therefore free from any measure of irreconditeness to the part that by the 16th century, obligations were laid down that Portuguese traders to West Africa in search of gold and slaves should abate from anything moral or religious in Lisbon and especially help in the upkeep of the clergy. Again the clergy were at the centre of the Royal slave trade. The church and the clergy were the centre of the state control of slavery. In these spectacular situations of the trade, the merchants were powerful figures. They had economic influence. This is demonstrated by Thomas Leyland who died in the historically important year 1807, the year of the alleged Abolition of the Slave Trade Act which happened only on paper, but not in practice and enforcement. Leyland died leaving the gigantic sum for those times of £600,000 in his account. All were made out of the Atlantic Slave Trade.

Hugh Thomas had no hesitation in discussing the European Cultural Christianity proclamation of active participation by the Christian churches, clergy and state in the Atlantic Slave Trade. Thomas said bluntly "all Christian dominations were involved in the slave trade". This is Thomas' firm conviction based on incisive scholarly examination of the Atlantic Slave Trade. To consolidate my passionate hermeneutic of the Atlantic Slave trade system and the churches at Elmina Castle, namely the Catholic, Anglicans, Baptist and Methodist, Hugh Thomas' thesis has helped with my postulation and hermeneutic "that usually the dominating religion vis-à-vis European Cultural Christianity in the part of Africa concerned decided the religious complexion of the Merchants". In Liverpool, London and Bristol, the proliferation of slave merchants were Anglicans. The regions such as Nantes, Bordeaux, Lisbon/Seville, Bahia and Luanda were Catholic

The Quakers in England in the 18th century, especially in Newport with the Wanton family, were still trading in 1705. The Friends were deeply involved also from Pennsylvania, the American "Quaker State," and they carried slaves from the West Indies to the US. In Brazil the slave merchants were the Brachia and their religious brotherhood organised religious processions at the church of San Antonio Da Barra.

The Bishop of the Algarve in 1446 was a prince of the church and still sent out a caravel to Africa. Several so-called spiritual pretenders were definitely shareholders in the insidious and pernicious Atlantic Slave Trade.

In the 17th century, the Cardinal Infante Enrigu Ipiological, brother to King Philip III of Spain, developed a formidable trade in slaves. Also deeply involved were the Jesuits. The widely spread slave institution escaped no-one from the religious circles and the freemasons were in the main, merchants. In Spain and Portugal the slave trade was dominated by the Jews, but these were converted Jews attached to the Cathedral of Seville. In Portugal most of the cathedrals symbolised the power of the slave trade and the Roman Catholic participation in the slave trade.

Both served deep psychological and spiritual needs of ancient Man. Myalism and magic/obeah were common among the slaves. For the slaves, evildoers were the whites or slave owners or the master slavers. Myalism was basically the vehicle for resisting the evils of slavery. We can assume that myalism took its directive from Africa. What of Christianity? The majority of slaves had tremendous difficulty in recognising Christianity as presented by the white Europeans. Their difficulty was that European Cultural Christianity was not religious; they felt that it was not a religion, but a culture of oppression, exploitation, dehumanisation and colonisation imposed on the psyche of African people. Both the slaves and the white planters looked at each other with deep confusion.

Africans did not divide the world into sections. The secular or sacred whites went to church on the Sabbath and for the rest of the week, they lived a secular life. Ministers of the Gospel had very little interest in the slavers. The ministers also forced resistance from the planters because they did not want to complicate their relationship with their slaves by introducing Christianity. In other words, there was a tremendous tension that existed between the vanguard and the promulgators of European Christianity and Christianity in its entirety without any co-mixture with the slave trade.

Among the Anglicans was a significant debate concerning a theological justification for converting the slaves, but it is noteworthy also, that the debate did not include any economical justification. Moreover, the debate was driven by the belief that any conversion should be modelled on the Christian assumption of the mental inferiority of the slaves.

With all the clarifications and substantial information, it is important to say that the religious revival in the 18th century was to urge the need to convert the heathen world that was the basis of their revival in the 18th century. The missionary movement was an attack on slave quarters and on the slaves' acts of paganism. By the time the British finally freed the slaves in 1838, Christianity had become a major force in the slave quarters in the British West Indies due to the success of the preaching of the missionaries.

The missionaries used Christianity to brainwash the slaves, their mission was specifically and systematically aimed at the slaves and not the slave traders themselves, and the slave owners. In other words, they were not against the oppressors, the planters but this was not Christianity, it was an act of oppressive culture. European Christianity had nothing to do with liberation. It was not an act of oppression; it was not an act of subjugation. Subjugation, socially and morally repugnant at the same time. It was a Eurocentric culture carefully covered up to exploit, subjugate, inculcate and to psychologically and spiritually truncate the will of the slaves.

CHAPTER 8
RELIGIOUS INVOLVEMENTS

Abolition and Emancipation

We have looked at the development of slavery, the expansion of slavery and the involvement of the major European countries, such as France, Holland, Denmark, Spain, Germany, The Netherlands and Britain in the web of the economic transatlantic experience. The European Cultural Christianity was imposed on the Africans. There is a falseness of the claim that Britain abolished slavery. From the concrete evidence, British and European abolition of slavery was a paper gesture only. Abolition was not on moral grounds, ethical or theological grounds. Any claim to the moral, theological and humanitarian is with a grip or power by virtue of the prolongation of 400 years of slavery. Dr. Eric Williams' thesis is even more forceful and substantial. It was from the economical profits of the colonial plantations that financed the industrial revolution. Dr. Richard Hart's learned conclusions on slaves must be carried further.

1. Historians consistently fail to acknowledge the power of the slaves in their insurrections and non-violent actions, which logically precipitated the abolition of slavery. In other words, the concept of abolition promulgated by Britain on humanitarian grounds was a lie.
2. It was the slaves themselves who secured their manumission. Historians again deliberately ignored the slaves' valour.

I now wish to distinguish briefly the fundamentals between abolition of slavery on paper and positive emancipation. I have given appropriate accounts of the abolition movement and their participation and contributions to the abolition movement. We have seen the measure of co-mixture of persons who were far from being modest, especially on the part of the African and West Indian slaves.

After 1807 and 1808, slavery itself continued for another further 30 years. In the colonies of the West Indies and Africa and in the USA, it was alleged by different historical schools that the slaves were better off under slavery than after the Abolition. I shall give some attention to linking in the USA much later. This is both controversial and highly ambiguous, and therefore special research or enquiry is needed to unearth what lies behind this assumption or claim. Maybe sociologically, educationally and politically they were better off. I shall give some attention to linking in the USA later and to black ex-slaves who were involved in the slave trade.

Black Religion and Missionaries

The result of Christianity was beneficial to the slaves from St. Vincent, according to a planter, who maintained: "The national result was cleanliness, good health, propagation in well-contented family lives". This was continuance of former tricks and thefts intended to increase loyalty to their masters or master slavers. The London missionary society wrote "...it is neither your business nor in my power to deliver from the bondage the slaves of men." Here we see again that the missionary movement was an integral part of the dehumanisation and subjugation of the slaves. Reverend John Smith, when he was despatched on his mission to Demerara in 1816, was told "Not a word must escape you in public or private which might dislocate or render the slaves to be displeased with their situation. You are not sent to relieve them from this servitude condition, but to offer them the consolation of religion." In time, these consolations were psychological, temporal as much as spiritual. They were part and parcel of the brainwashing process. By the end of the slave trade, the slaves on that island provided work for 63 Moravian, 58 Methodist and 17 Baptist clergymen.

The slaves were deeply brainwashed with the consolation and infusion in their psyche that all would be well in the here after, namely in heaven with milk and honey. I hasten to add that even this legacy of brainwashing is still with the majority of African and African descendants worldwide today. The slaves thought much of their dreams of salvation. Fear of damnation and hope for redemption was the infusion of spiritual opium used for the brainwashing of Africans. Religion was the basic tool that impacted on the psyche of Africans and African descendants.

Religion from the Old Testament perspective is based on liberation, justice and complete manumission. Indeed, Shalom does not mean sociologically and politically peace. Peace is only one definition of Shalom. Shalom means intactness, prosperity, long life, economic freedom and development. Shalom does not have any meaning in relation to oppression, dehumanisation and exploitation. Religion was used by the missionaries and Europeans to exploit and to oppress black people. The psychological legacy is with blacks today. Religion for the oppressed was the vehicle for blackness, like Africanness, it was a state of liberated consciousness.

Concerning the biblical exodus in the covenant and Sinai, the wilderness experience of the Promised Land is meaningless without recognising the gigantic task of Moses that made him almost unique. It was the raising of the ontological consciousness of the oppressed people to create and utilise their own liberation that was of paramount importance.

The Church and the Plantation Environment

The churches offered salvation to the enslaved people, but salvation with submissiveness not liberation. The churches offered hell here on earth with the prospect of a superior life later in heaven. The planters claimed superiority over the slaves and called themselves European Christians. Here again by virtue of reiteration, Hugh Thomas' claim is substantiated. The churches or rather all the major denominations were integrally and actively involved in the slave trade. One can argue that Christianity was presented to the slaves and the manner in which Christianity was carried by missionaries to Africa and the West Indies was strongly ambiguous and hypercritical. It was a psychological and cultural Christianity without any theology, doctrines and morality, indeed it was a Christianity of vacuity. It was without any degree of spirituality, justice or manumission for the slaves. It was the culture of the master race. It was the culture of the master enslavers. It had no relevance to the slaves, being a foreign religion, an alienated religion, a religion that made Christianity a problem for the slaves to understand. How could the slaves understand? Their sufferings, exploitations and oppressions came from a religion that imposed all these conditions on them. To a God of justice and equality something was clearly missing. The language, apologetics, religion and meaning of life were fundamentally different both in terms of context, present and future. This was the place where inculcation and brainwashing took place. It was in the incubation chamber of the enslavement of Africans. This meeting point was dichotomous. The slave leader of enormous eminence and valour, Cudjoe uttered in his valediction these immortal words "I rather die on yonder gallows than to die a slave because nature made me to be free". Nature to Cudjoe the slave was the moral God, which was the omnipotent God, the ubiquitous God without the philosophical, cosmological relevance, but the God in Jesus Christ of the black experience that is of slavery. The slaves were expressing deep awareness of ontological freedom. It was this ontological freedom that the master slavers, missionaries and European churches sought to destroy in the psyche and soul of the Africans. However, this ontological freedom was something indestructible in the soul of the oppressed Africans.

Chapter 9
Situational Involvement

European Christian Cultural Involvement in Slavery

The universality of slavery is never in any realistic doubt, even people in geographical, contiguous continents engaged in intercontinental slave trade. The global dimension was real. However, only Africa has seen the racial, oppressed and enforced migration of peoples across the Atlantic in the West and the Indian Ocean in the East by West African traders and East African slave traders to Asia and the Americas. In medieval and early modern Europe, Europeans bought and sold one another as slaves. Both sides were engaged in the ubiquitous practice of slavery. In the 18th century Britain enslaved the Irish. Sometimes they disguised it as indentured servitude. These were transported to the West Indies and the Americas. In other words, Britain enslaved its own people. Europeans enslaved their own people especially in Rome and other European countries. In order to grapple with the magnitude of the slave trade and the integral involvement of European Cultural Christianity, one must acknowledge that in the transportation of Africans across the Atlantic no other race was forced into such large scale slavery by the multitude of so-called Christians, including Royals, philosophers and scientists. There is no comparison on record. There is no historical evidence that anything of a similar magnitude took place elsewhere. Therefore, the Atlantic Slave Trade or Middle Passage continues to remain a unique experience and not a one-off phenomenon.

The diabolical slave trade existed across great distance with the subjugation and exploitation of one continent of people, primarily because of their ethnicity, by people of another. What is significant is the fact that the principle agents for the continental distribution of African slaves were white people, namely Europeans and the British. The transatlantic demographic rape of Africa has generated much academic debate and writings, and some in which jejune scholars likened the mild force of African domestic slavery or the "unfreedom" to the rapacious and more inhuman exploitation of Africans on the plantations of the West Indies and elsewhere in the European-colonised Americas.

A second school of thought sought to counter the first school by proclaiming that the European Christians initiated the Africa slave trade access to the Atlantic when institutional slavery was already an established custom in West Africa. Historically, African domestic slavery and domesticated slaves cannot be compared.

The context of West African history on Slavery and the Slave Trade published in 1969 in *The Journal of African History* by J. D. Fage, who claimed that as early as 1500 the Portuguese were selling slaves on the Gold Coast. These slaves were mainly war slaves from the internal domestic slave system of Africa.

The Dilemma and Paradox

The African kings and chiefs were now faced with a tremendous dilemma. This dilemma was not an uneconomic, scientific, technological or sociological dilemma. To keep their slaves or sell their slaves because of European demands, the chiefs and kings obviously decided to sell their slaves for guns, items for personal use, such as clothes, garments, jewellery, shoes, trinkets and gun powder for their guns.

Selling the slaves served no purpose for economic or for technological development of Africa. Rather it served as the fundamental area for the dissipation of Africa and the states of the continent.

Of the five continents in our world, Africa is the most ancient. Africa is also the most exploited. Africa is the most raped continent on earth. A good comparison is with Australia or North America where some form of democracy has existed for 200 years.

Dr. Walter Rodney makes a useful observation. He noted that it has long been claimed that "....slaves formed part of African society and that consequently it was not difficult for African chiefs and kings to begin selling their own slaves." Rodney goes on to say that no convincing evidence has been bought forward except to support this view or theory. On the contrary it appears that the sale of human beings was a new experience to most African societies and came about as a direct reaction to the presence and activity of the European cultural Christians, their doctors and scientists. Sir Reginald Coupland has made, like Dr. Rodney a useful contribution, arguing that the inauguration of the earlier export of slaves from East Africa to Asia, especially by the Arabs. According to Coupland, the Arab slave trade began before the Christian era and continued unabatedly into the 19th century. Coupland's thesis could well be the result of an uneasy conscience of Christian Europeans for perpetuating the atrocities of the Atlantic Slave Trade. One should always bear in mind that Britain and other European governments and churches had always sought to find ways to minimise their atrocities and the evilness of the slave trade.

There can be no historical denial that European cultural Christians and the missionary movement was at the heart of the slave trade. Resistance was powerless and therefore ineffective because the Christians with British and European genealogical history kept the system oiled and serviced. Dr. Moses De Nwulias' careful postulations can help our understanding and they therefore are worth referring to here. For him, it was whites who specialised in the division of humanity into distinct races and who formed the principal exporters and distributors of African slaves. Both in the preliminary and later stages, the development of the external trade in East African slaves was due to those enterprising peoples. The significant point is that slaves were extracted in small numbers from some parts of Europe and Africa and transported home by merchants who belonged to the white master race. In other words, they were the masters enslavers.

CHAPTER 10
RELIGIOUS CULTURE AND SLAVERY

European Christians and the Slave Trade

It is with a degree of fascination to note that by the middle of the 19th century, African slavery seriously engaged the attention of Britain, and we must not lose sight that Britain participated in the slave trade fully, comprehensively and in a controlling manner. I state with temerity and audacity, Britain perfected the slave trade professionally, economically and politically. Economically and politically, Britain began with a modest role in the slave trade. From this humble beginning, Britain rose to the apex of the lists of white buyers, enslavers and exploiters of Africans by the end of the 18th century. Britain consolidated and expanded her grasp on the slave trade. And Britain even perpetuated the slave trade for over 35 years after its Act of Parliament and lip-service to the ineffective Abolition of Slavery in 1807

CHAPTER 11
DESIDERATION AND THE APPROACH

Abolition - The Appetite

The Abolition of Slavery Act was passed in Parliament in 1807. A similar Act was passed by the U.S Congress in 1808. The requirement was emphatic, that all British citizens and their subjects in the colonies were required to abstain from this economically lucrative trade. Lord Scott, the British Prime Minister at the time, had said most emphatically, that "Slavery was an economic necessity for Europe". Now this economic necessity had become a hellish reminder for the slaves. In 1811, the British Parliament also declared that slave trading by British subjects was a criminal act and, subject to great penalties. We must remember here that the British Magna Carta exempted slavery and piracy as not illegal. The Enlightenment period also affirmed slavery as God given.

This was a critical time for Britain locked in combat with Napoleonic France for the political and economic dominance of Europe. Britain competed with France and sought to dominate not only Europe, but also the continent of Africa, holding colonies within Africa and colonies across the West Indies.

It was at this time that the Abolitionist Movement is said to have pricked the humanitarian conscience of Britain. It was thought that this might be a good weapon with the British economic powers. In the Treaty of Paris on May 30th 1814, France and Britain agreed that the slave trade was repugnant to the principles of natural justice and the enlightened age in which they lived. This was only lip service, but was not really a part of moral, social, spiritual or theological consciousness. The two countries agreed to unite their efforts at the approaching Congress of Vienna to induce the Christian powers to proclaim a universal cessation of the slave trade.

The Abolitionist Movement message was delivered to the Congress. The Congress listened tentatively to the humanitarian garb now being worn by Britain and eventually the Congress decided that each country should choose the appropriate time to abolish slavery. Britain was deeply disappointed at not carrying Europe collectively into this action. But says Nwulia, "The sagacious Europe could see through Britain's deceit while declaring the slave trade a crime against humanity a morally regenerated Britain did not dare to condemn slavery itself, nor did Britain refrain from collecting the gains of slavery in her Empire and elsewhere." This dichotomy between moral idealism and cultivated self-interest would continue even after Britain had formally emancipated the slaves in her colonies. Britain's basic purpose was self-interest and nothing else. To demonstrate this crucial point, Dr. Moses D.E Nwulia asked "If the slave trade was so abhorrent to the principles of humanity, why was the status of slavery not included in the general ban". Dr. Nwulia reminds us correctly, "White Christians fervently wished that the day of liberation will never dawn for the heathen slaves". No one can make any statement recondite enough to obliterate the historical fact that white church people never saw their slaves as equal human beings. Let me put that fact another way. Britain was the heathen and paganistic country itself and Britons went off to preach to black slaves. Giving sermons not about salvation or liberation, but rather seeking to ensure that the slaves were comprehensively brainwashed with a white religion that was designed to subjugate them and make them accept the inferior station of being slaves. This was deliberate, conscious and preplanned. White Christianity was politics and economics, wrapped nicely and neatly in a parcel to truncate the lives and minds of black people throughout Africa and the West

Indies. This is why I argue forcefully for the decolonisation of white Christianity. A black decolonisation of European theology and philosophy is required and furthermore a thorough deaculturisation is imperative for the African race.

We agreed by virtue of the abundance of historical records that the slave traders and planters were British and European, cultural Christians. These wicked whites, so-called Christian planters, were assured of one thing; it was the paramouncy of servitude. In order for them to survive and prosper, the African slaves should be made to work always as slaves. They were not to be removed from the station of slavery and enslavement. Their minds, their emotions and their psyche were to be controlled by their slave masters.

The British could not resist acting surreptitiously because there was sub-optimisation in their humanitarian God of stultification. Faced with this situation, the British circumvented their response to the substitution of humanitarian rhetoric with a position for cheap labour through extensive resort to slave smuggling. Again, the Christian influence was self-evident. The Christian planters believed seriously that their economic self was bound up with the constant stream of cheap slave labour.

The British humanitarian concern was prompted by the British Government deciding that its prosperity that was becoming threatened by the increasingly uneconomic slave trade. In any case, the slaves gained nothing. They earned their freedom by their own struggles for manumission and emancipation. The slave planters gained economically over 400 years. At the time of Abolition, they were paid £20 million. How could this be justice or righteousness? For 400 years of the most heinous crimes against a single race of people because of their genealogical and ethnological origins and epidemically because of their pigmentation. The £20 million paid to the Christian planters remained in the British banks and economy. Nothing, not even an apology to this date has been made for the racist evil deeds of British control of Africa and its people.

Sligu's message to the apprentices was "You have been slaves and lately acting as apprentices, this decision made you absolutely and unconditionally free."

I cannot forget the Catholic communion table with the Eucharistic equipment on top of the slave dungeons at Elmina Castle. However, the Jews were not inconspicuous in the slave trade during the 18th century, and played a modest part in the slave trade in Brazil where they gained a reputation for sadism. They were even accused of stealing children to sell as slaves. Hugh Thomas continues his radical account, by making his point so chronologically persuasive and informative. He points out that many slave traders were members of Parliament. Among these Parliamentarians was William Wilberforce, who was actively involved in the slave trade. In the 18th century the list of Parliamentarians included Humphrey Maurice, John Sergeant, Sir Alexander Grant, Henry Cruger, Charles Holme, John Hurdman, and Sir Thomas Johnson, Mayor of London. They sent off a ship with their blessing in 1700. The list is long of the European and British Royals, politicians and statesmen who were deeply involved in the Atlantic Slave Trade. What is most paradoxical in European Cultural Christianity is that a significant number of merchants were looked upon as philanthropists in Europe and Britain. Foster Cuncliffe is recorded on a plaque in St. Peter's Church, Liverpool as a Christian committed to public duty, mercy, an enemy of vice. Brian Blundell of Liverpool was a founder member of London's Bluecoat School. Philip Livingston of New York founded a professorship of divinity at his university at Yale. He also helped in the establishment of the first Methodist society in America. All these, despite their philanthropic practice were involved in the slave trade, because they did not perceive the slave trade to be morally repugnant and deeply irreligious and biologically repugnant, ethnologically repugnant and sociologically repugnant.

John Brown in Providence founded the university which bears his name. Abraham Redwood's library in Newport is a monument to the slaver traders and monument to their munificence. The long list provides no contradiction. but it does present a moral, spiritual, theological and economical dilemma. Despite the injunction of biblical charity, the slave traders saw no reason to make a charitable contribution to their slaves.

It is like the preamble to the American constitution, says Dr. Walter Rodney, declaring all men are created equal, while at the same time reinforcing African slavery. In other words, in the eyes of the American framers of the constitution all men are created equal, but that did not include Africans.

The gigantic slave trade from Angola to Brazil was by the 18th century well organised by African, Britain and other European countries. Slaves were held in barracoons before Brazilian captains purchased them from Rio de Janeiro.

Paradox and Ambiguity are Coterminous to the Slave Trade

During the 1780s and 1790s, there was a widely spread views that the pernicious slave trade was better for the Africans, than allowing them to be free men. Sir Dalby Thomas in 1709 claimed that people in Africa had no religion or laws linking them to humanity. These views held by white Europeans with European Cultural Christianity beliefs. Denigrations of Africans originated out of a conscious premeditated racist super-race beliefs and opinions and they drew on their Eurocentric, ethnocentric racism in defining and categorising Africans. In other words, they enforced and inculcated a European concept in order to force the Africans to perceive themselves as inherently biologically inferior. This was a significant essential function not only of the slave trade in its entirety, but of the missionary movement, which was totally integrated with the slave traders in the search of the economic profitability and prosperity of Europe, Britain and the Americas.

William Chancellor Surgeon in 1750 wrote, "The Slave Trade was a way of redeeming an unhappy people from inconceivable misery." This is codswallop. This is rubbish. Williams Chancellor Surgeon's statement deserves total condemnation. The greatest misery man has ever faced in any ultimately genocidal situation is that of the Atlantic Slave Trade. Let no one be fooled, that there is no historical record anywhere in this world to compare with the magnitude of sufferings of slaves in the Atlantic Slave Trade and in their treatment on the plantations. William Chancellor Surgeon is trying to put forward a case that slavery was morally justified to redeem the Africans. He was not only morally sick ,he had no conscience. This definition of William Chancellor Surgeon was defined and measured by European Cultural Christianity. His statement was in keeping with the European Cultural Christianity. The late Dr. Walter Rodney is correct when he said the treatment of Africans was proof that European colonists were hypocrites. How else can one explain the fact, says Rodney, that the Christian church participated fully in the maintenance of the Atlantic Slave Trade and still talked about saving souls. The first martyr in the American Revolutionary War of Independence against the British in the 18th century was an African descendant named Crispus Attucks. Some merchants paid lip service to the ethics of the slave trade. Some Quakers questioned the ethics of the slave trade. In 1763 Henry Laurens, John Ettein and Bishop declared that they wished the economy and government were different. He also lamented and praised the American constitution that became the measure of rectitude for the actions of the majority of the Christian community. It is important to interject at this point that the contributions of blacks throughout history has never been acknowledged by scholars ranging from historians, scientists, sociologists, anthropologists, theologians and philosophers to educationalists. The contributions of black people in university libraries and other spheres are always placed under the literature section as fiction, rather than history. For example, the writings of Equiano and Ignatius Sancho.

The powerbase was the extraordinary economic commitment, justification and neglect of human consideration. Extrication from this psychological cultural hold was difficult. Both Hugh Thomas and James Walvin agreed that there were more black slaves than admitted from 1780 to 1788 in England, especially in Liverpool, Bristol and London. Some slaves were held in the political and economical ambivalence of both liberty and bondage. Black communities existed in the 18th century, in Middleburg, Zeeland, Holland, as well as in Lisbon and Seville.

The geographical regions linked were mainly Brazil and Angola, Cuba and Africa, Lisbon and Africa, Benin to Elmina, Europe and America. One can hypothesize these vessels as having been given names of women and also biblical names such as *Jesus, which* was given to John Hawkins by Queen Elizabeth I. These ships were also blessed by the Church. The captains of some slave ships throughout the slave trade were very cunning, such as, for example,

Hugh Crow, who wrote, "The observation of slaves to our colonies were a necessary evil." Crow acknowledged the evilness of slavery, but pleaded that it was a necessary evil. Similarly, Lord Scott, leader of the House of Lords in London, told Wilberforce that slavery was an economic necessity for Britain and Europe. Thus the Atlantic slave trade had no moral attributes. In other words the system was without a moral conscience.

Captain Williams of Bristol at the beginning of the 18th century felt remorse and remarked "… Nor can I imagine why they should be designed for the colour being what they cannot change. I cannot think there is any intrinsic value in one colour more than another. That white is better than black, only we think so". Here again, the culture and the perceptions were all intertwined within the Eurocentric cultural Christianity of the day.

Reverend John Newton, captain of The Duke of Argyll belonging to the Manestry Brothers of Liverpool and the future vicar of St. Mary's Woolnorth; unlike Crow, Newton did not seek to justify his involvement in the Atlantic slave trade. Newton wrote, "I know of no method of getting money, not even that of robbing for it upon the highway which has so direct attendance to face the moral sense". It is noteworthy that John Newton had no qualms, no compulsion, no sense of guilt, no conscience in putting the slaves through hellish treatments and conditions to beat and to whip the hell out of them and to condemn them to unspeakable conditions and suffering. On arrival in Liverpool he would crepitate halleluiah, praise the Lord. He would bless the Lord God Almighty for a safe return and a profitable voyage. John Newton did all of this not as a layman, but as an Anglican priest. In addition, Newton only abandoned the slave trade because of poor health. If good health had sustained John Newton, he would have continued his involvement in the slave trade without any moral scruple.

It is therefore misleading to prolong the myth that many historians and sociologists and even Christian theologians are promulgating that John Newton became a Christian through a shipwreck after which it is claimed he wrote the song "Amazing grace how sweet the sound". "Amazing Grace" was psychologically and spiritually John Newton's praise of the profitability of his involvement in the slave trade and its human cargo. It is said John Newton had a vision of becoming a clergyman. But when he was a slave captain, Newton was already a Christian. What do we mean by Christian? What canon do we use to determine whether John Newton was a Christian? Certainly there is nothing on record in terms of theology, ethics, morality, sociology or theology to justify John Newton's situation. John Newton even wrote to his wife when leaving Africa on a ship loaded with slaves of being inundated by dangers and difficulties which without a superior protection no man could escape or surmount only by the goodness of God. Immediately after writing to his wife, John Newton faced a slave rebellion. Newton added, that he "overcame the emergency with divine assistance." The God of liberation and the God of the Old Testament is a God standing without any reservation always on the side of the dispossessed, the marginalised, the voiceless, the oppressed and the powerless. There is no evidence biblically or historically that the monotheistic God of the Old Testament had ever sided with the oppressors. John Newton is said to have read prayers twice a day. He read Virgil, Livy and Erasmus while still commanding a slave ship. Even when Newton wrote his famous hymn "How sweet the name of Jesus sound in a believer's ear, it soothes his sorrows, heals his wounds and drives away his fears. It makes the wounded spirit whole, and calms the trouble breast. 'Tis manna to the hungry soul and to the weary rest. Dear name the rock on which I stand, my shield and hiding place; My never failing treasury fills with boundless stores of grace. Jesus my Shepherd, brother, friend, my prophet priest and king, my Lord, my life, my way, my end accept the praise I bring. Weak as the effort of my heart and cold my warmest thought, but when I see thee as though art I'll praise thee as I ought. Till then I would thy love proclaim, with every fleeting breath; and may the music of thy name, refresh my soul in death. Amen." John Newton 1725 to 1807.

This is one of the hymns that I believe any conscious person, be he black or white, should never sing. It was written by a slave trader without any regard or conscience of his involvement in the Atlantic slave trade. Indeed, for John Newton the Africans were without soul. They were not human beings; they were cattle; they were property. African slaves were tantamount only to economic profit for his personal pocket and for the economy of Britain.

Any simple theological hermeneutic investigation of Newton's concepts of right, wrong, evil, goodness, God and Jesus will not find the remotest philosophical similarity with African cosmic propinquity with nature and God. Newton had only a European Cultural Christianity, and Newton was not exceptional. Captain Carassous in 1791 in the Canary Islands, expressed sympathy for the poor Spaniards. He also expressed hope that the French Revolution would liberate the poor from burden of their poverty. Carassous then set off for Mozambique to buy more Africans for Santo Domingo as a medical doctor on a slave ship where he was in charge of all matters relating to the cargo of the slaves. There were other physicians of slavery, such as Alexander Fulconbridge and Thomas Trotter who in 1750 declared that he found beauty in Africa, but despised the Africans. He found Africa and its environment and nature wonderful and beautiful, but loathed the indigenous inhabitants of the continent. What a double standard. What these people had both in terms of culture, Christianity or religion was nothing more than vacuity.

Jean Barbot pleaded in the 1680s to those officers tempted to castigate slaves brutally, to consider those unfortunate creatures as men as well as themselves, although they were of a different colour and were pagans.

Richard Watt and Gregory of Liverpool had their lives saved by a slave and both later became blind while treating slaves suffering from ophthalmia. Becoming an abolitionist, poet and book-keeper, he called on God for "the power to make these tyrants bleed." John Newton was convinced that the slave trade damaged the sensitivities of the slave crews themselves. In other words, the barbarity, inhumanity, cruelty and sufferings of the slaves transformed the nature and the mind of the slave crews so that they became emotionally, mentally, psychologically and spiritually dead. But vehemently added with conviction that the dead sensitivities of the slave crews was also symptomatic and shared by all who were involved in the Atlantic Middle Passage or the Transatlantic Slave Trade.

The real or supposed necessity of treating the negroes with rigour gradually brings numbness upon the heart and renders those who are engaged in it to indifference to the sufferings of their fellow man. There are instances where crews were treated just as bad as the slaves. Crews lived and died on decks, although this was largely due to the inimical climatic conditions and the environment, and were not as a result of the direct brutality in any way similar to that of the slaves.

This will be dealt with at greater length when we come to what is called the Abolition Movement, but for now it is worth noting that most of the religious leaders, denominations, ministers and members of Parliament were financially involved in the Transatlantic Slave Trade with few if any exceptions. Therefore, one wonders if there was really any substantial moral drive behind the rise of the Abolition Movement or did it come about because slavery was on the decline and no longer served to promote the prosperity of the traders. The decline of the slave trade meant a rapid decline in the purpose of Christianity and European Cultural Christianity. European Christianity was an integral function of the slave trade. One could not work or function without the other. They were metaphorically inseparable twins. Church and slavery, Christianity and slavery were integrally bound up with each other. We should never forget that South Africa's system of apartheid was instigated by Britain and America and sustained by Britain and America. Moreover, the central organ of the apartheid system was the Dutch Reformed Church, whose justification for apartheid was theological. Another point of paramount importance is the need to separate the Abolition Movement from emancipation. Both British European and American Abolition was paper abolition. The slave trade continued into the 19th century without any significant tangible abatement. In other words, abolition was not a moral conscientious desire, but rather a placative disguise for the furtherance and expansion of the slave trade.

There was no immediate end of the slave trade immediately after 1807 and 1808. Even in West Africa, Britain held to the Gold Coast, modern Ghana, for 100 years after agreeing to free the country from British colonial rule. In Accra, there is a statue of the Unknown Soldier and a monument of 100 steps symbolising the extra 100 years that Britain kept the country under the grip of colonial rule.

The significant addendum to this important aspect of black history, African history, the slave trade history is emancipation itself. With emancipation once again, it was the slaves who created their financial basis for emancipation. White scholars deliberately ignored the valour of the slave warriors and fighters. The slave leaders' validation still rings today. "I'd rather die on yonder gallows than to be in slavery". I'd rather die than to continue in slavery because God made me to be free".

The greatest fear among the slave owners, the master enslavers, was that emancipation would cause great loss to the whites. The evilness of the slave trade was not realised immediately. The manumitted slaves were spiritually intoxicated by brainwashing. They were mentally and psychologically entombed; intellectually stunted; socially dislocated; spiritually redundant and emotionally amputated.

Chapter 12
Culture And Religion

European Religious Intentions

I return here again to the impact and influence of a foreign religion and the minds of the slaves. What conflicts there were, and how the European churches used their religious beliefs of superiority and religious culture to psychologically and spiritually strangulate and amputate the lives and minds of black people. This legacy is ubiquitous with Africans and African descendants worldwide. I hasten to point out that European churches had a programme of destruction of the African religious beliefs, traditions and practices. They replaced the African religious beliefs by the implantation of European churches and European Cultural Christianity.

European Christianity

The linking of the Baptist church with Christianity where myalism was incorporated with white religion, namely the Holy Spirit, baptism by emersion. Baptism therefore took place in rivers and seas which in parts of Africa were considered the homes of the spirits.

We cannot make any exoterical postulations of theological importance between Christianity and myalism. The only rational elucidation is that Christianity was perceived to be rather worldly, while myalism was towards this world. For the slaves, myalism was far more important than the Christian concept promulgated and inculcated in them that the Christian other world was a better place. It was not only a form of tantalisation and memorisation, but in many instances it was used as a tremendous mythological concept to brainwash the slaves, to accept through endurance their enslavement with the hope that in the hereafter they would be compensated with milk and honey. This was total rubbish. If that was the case, why didn't the master slavers have it the other way round? The slaves endured suffering, oppression, alienation and exploitation knowing that they would reap milk and honey on the other side. There are deep cultural similarities between Christianity and myalism especially in times of spirituality. Religion and magic also shared some degree of commonness in the ancient world. Both myalism and magic served deep psychological and spiritual needs in ancient man. Myalism and magic or obeah were common among the slaves.

The word abolition should be removed from history, literature, economics, and theological, philosophical and political vocabulary of the British. Such abolition never existed or effected; it was just vacuity. It is impossible to concede that the British would act in any way moral or religious. The economic magnet of slavery was powerful. This situation was an act of prevarication and procrastination. Slavery had never been seen by the British government as immoral or irreligious for the removal of slavery on humanitarian grounds. Rather religious leaders provided theological conceptualisation as injustice, immorality and equality. Black people were believed to be placed on this planet under the domination of whites. This is why Christianity had never presented openly superior master race culture. Christianity was always used to enhance the British domination of the world.

British and European Cultural Christianity should be extirpated from the minds and lives of Black people, psychologically culturally, religiously, spiritually and theologically, by dropping it into the middle of the Atlantic Ocean with one million tons of concrete to make sure it will never lift up its head to damage the minds of black people, namely African and African descendants anymore. Laconically, my postulation is a call for a radical de-Europeanisation of Christianity and theology. I declare that the Sitz im Leben of black people and Africa today is the legacy of European and British Cultural Christianity and slavery. Metaphorically, the Bible is still in one hand and the gun of economics and technology is in the other. This is in the spheres of racism, powerlessness, economics, politics, racial injustice, alienation, structural strangulation of adults and sexism.

I must not leave out Aids and HIV in Africa which is pandemic. It is the cancer destroying the continent of Africa today. For the prolepsis of whites, completing their philosophy of economic domination from the Atlantic Slave Trade, Africa is in a state of precipitous decline because of the impact of Aids and economic and technological strangulation by the West. IMF loans and other loans to Africa will never regenerate the economy of Africa because the interest rates and strings attached are designed to further strangulate Africa and to keep Africa constantly underdeveloped. Lack of free trade and a free market with Africa is also another damaging legacy to Africa today.

Africans and African descendants must exigently develop their own hermeneutics simultaneously and contextually without fear, politically and economically. The starting points are:

1. the theological and spiritual;
2. the psychological;
3. the emotional;
4 the sociological;
5. the political;
6. the economical;
7. the educational.

This list is not fixed. A simple approach and philosophy is this; black people need to stop seeking to become whites, culturally and otherwise. Paradigms are powerful influences. This is a deep cultural and genealogical blockage. Gus John's comment is both helpful and powerful for blacks to swallow mentally and psychologically, and to keep it inside.

According to Gus John, black consciousness had its day. That in itself makes the social, gregarious and cultural identity even more necessary for reintegration to redeem the prodigality of the black race from complete transfiguration socially, culturally and religiously, into a people without rootness, genealogically and ethnologically. The black race needs a philosophy of collectiveness and self-consciousness, rather than to be a people in need of a collective psyche.

Mahara Umba Marimba Ani in *An African Centred Critique of European Cultural Thought and Behaviour* says "Religion is integrally related to the development of ideology in the West. For that reason, and because of the unique nature of European culture, it is critical to make clear what I mean by "religion". This is important because what is identified formally in the European experience as religion often has very little to do with what is understood generally as the "religious". In a phenomenal logical sense, this discussion focuses on the European experience of religion as a formalised institution existing in relation to the other institutions of European culture, as opposed to religion as the expression of beliefs about the supernatural world and as the basis for ethical behaviour or as an African centred critique of European cultural thought and behaviour.

A significant graph which is of importance to illustrate the psyche of the Europeans.

European	Christianity
European Ideology	European self image Cultural other Religious moral cultural being Heathen Non religious Immoral
Idea of Progress	Progressive, modern, cultural being
Evolutionism	Backward Primitive Object Civilised Cultural being
Scientism	Scientist, knower

European	Christianity
White supremacy	White racial being, Pure Human Black, dirty Non human
Cultural Other	Must be saved, developed, advanced Civilised Studied Known Control
	Avoided, treated enslaved destroyed

Dr. Ani goes on to say it must be understood that the idea of "saving" "advancing" "developing" "civilising" or "studying" do not indicate an identification with the cultural other or a desire to make her into a European. They all translate into the idea of "control". They symbolise, primarily and essentially a power relationship in which Europeans are supreme.

Finally says Dr. Ani, "The difference between the militarist and the missionary is only one of modus operandi, the blows of one are more physically apparent, those of the other leave battered souls and cultures in their wake".

Chapter 13
Elucidation Of The Slave Trade

Defining the Slave Trade

It is historically and academically misleading to attempt to equate any other slavery system or society to the Atlantic Slave Trade or the Atlantic Middle Passage because the Transatlantic Slave Trade is "unique". The Atlantic Middle Passage enveloped historically the continent of Africa and its people. The African Slave Trade of the Middle Passage impacted on the whole of Europe and the West economically and politically. These are the fundamental distinguishing historical facts which cannot be separated from the old Europe to the New Europe and the Americas today. The uniqueness is best encapsulated in this phrase, "British and European so-called cultural Christians dehumanised Africans".

Slavery was a worldwide institutional practice, but Hugh Thomas expatiated on slave societies within Europe and especially Rome. What distinguished the Atlantic Slave Trade beyond any comparison was that Africans had no rights, no freedom; they were defined as cattle. They were dehumanised; they were owned and were properties of the master enslavers. They were non-beings; they were singularly economic tools for the economic machines of Europe, Britain and the Americas. Africans were (economy slaves); they were expendable parts of the economic machine. The profit culture and profit driven motive. This has no morality or religious consciousness. I am here using religious consciousness according to the definition of Dr. Ani. Indeed, European Cultural Christianity was used psychologically to make the Africans efficient grease for economic wheels of the slave system. In this state of affairs the European churches were conspicuous active participants engaged particularly and religiously in the function for the economy for Europe and the Americas. It is imperative and pertinent to identify the psychological legacy of Africa and African descendants. The first admission must be that black people globally have been "messed up" "mash up" "wreck up" "topsy turvy" "broke up" mentally and educationally, sociologically and especially theologically "confused up".

A major cause of black people's situation economically, politically and sociologically is the white man's European Cultural Christianity which has been oppressive and truncative psychologically. "Blessed are the poor" (cod's wallop) rubbish. If blessed are the poor is good medicine or tonic economically for black people, why the hell did the British and Europeans not absorb this myth. Instead, they used Christianity to oppress, exploit and expand their culture of domination and control of Africans.

The black man's paradise is futuristic heaven. "Which heaven?" Are the socio-economical, socio-political and socio-theological shalom existential among the white race? But for the black man, his future glory is in heaven.

The colonised are told by the colonisers that their happiness is to come in the future, which no one has ever been to look at and come back with a report, except that which had been inculcated in the minds of the slaves, the spiritual and psychological are coterminous. Slavery was hell on earth for the slaves. There can be no semantics to circumvent this existential reality. The slaves had been through hell across the Atlantic, through the Caribbean and on the plantations in Brazil and America. The promise of "heaven" and drinking "milk and honey" was endemic in the brainwashing process to keep the minds of the slaves bound to unrealised transcendental spiritual imaginations. George Wakefield and many others played their part in this brainwashing process in preaching hell and damnation to the slaves while the master slavers were not challenged on any moral, ethical, biblical or theological grounds.

God's kingdom of justice, peace, equality, joy and brotherhood must be realised physically, economically politically and educationally in this life. Malkuth is in the heart and the existential Sitz im Leben of the oppressed.

The apartheid system in South Africa lasted for over 400 years with Britain and the USA - the major props in the raping and extractions of the resources along with the imprisonment of a brother, Nelson Mandela. All was conducted in the name of European Cultural Christianity. In the above abbreviated vocabulary of the enslaved African people the oppressed, the marginalised, the powerless, the voiceless African descendants and the impuissant Africans are "f.....-up". They are "f.....-up" with the European Cultural Christianity, because of the missionaries' movements. They are what they are because the bible and European Cultural Christianity. The bible was presented by European Christians, slave owners to the Africans for one single purpose, to "mash up" their brains, captivate the brains with the most preposterous nonsense of future glory and happiness and milk and honey in heaven. Accept slavery as preordained by God. Preaching and teaching that their salvation was on the other side, handing the bible to enslaved people racially while Europeans possessing the African lands and the West Indies. European Christians never made any attempt to educate or to remove oppression and exploitation from Africans, rather European churches preached to the enslaved people sermons well thought out, well defined to mess up the black people's brains about God, Jesus, Angels, Salvation and heaven, all defined by whites for black people. I reiterate all definitions were white orientated. Furthermore, European Christianity was the opium for the slaves. Jesus was presented as white. Total rubbish. Angels were presented as whites. Rubbish. Saints were presented by the Roman Catholic Church as Whites. Rubbish. They even presented St. Augustine as white. St. Augustine was a black African, an Algerian. Because of St. Augustine's intellectual and unmatchable academic scholarship as Professor of Rhetorics at Rome University at age 28. St. Augustine was presented to black people as a European. I personally was taught in British Universities by Professors of Philosophy that St. Augustine was a European. Damned lies.

I praise Dr. Eric Williams in his splendid book (British Historians and the West Indies). Dr. Williams showed chronologically and historically and tabulated the conscious mendacities of academic scholars. They prevaricated the truth and facts. Dr. Williams pointed his theory of action that inferior races were raised by living in political union with races intellectually superior. Dr. Ani is worth quoting here. She says the Europeans did not emulate Jesus (the Christ); such behaviour would have been, as it was for her, suicidal in the context of European culture. The Christian statement instead functioned to sanction European imperialistic expansion by giving moral status to the European concepts of (universalism) and evolutionism and progressivism. The church in this way performed a vital function in the creation of the Western European Empire. Because of this objective ethic, it was directed not toward the European, which have been in direct contradiction to the imperialistic objective and to the cultural other, and did indeed complement the imperialistic objective.

The Slave Trade and British Scholars

It is to be acknowledged first and foremost, that European Cultural Christianity was basically the opium for the African slaves. Europeans, and especially the British had a major problem with the slave trade middle passage slave traders. The economic fecundation of the slave trade was so fantastic that the monopoly became the key factor between the European nations and the African suppliers. The Africans made sure they held on to the monopoly of the slave trade. To this monopoly Dr. Eric Williams wrote "…it was the profits from the African Slave Trade and the ancillary colonial trade which provided a great part of the finance for Britain's industrial revolution. It was Britain's industrial lead which generated that supreme confidence among its capitalist pioneers which ultimately extended Britain's economic perspectives beyond the restricted boundaries of the colonial empire".

Adam Smith believed, "That slave labour was a great dissipation, unproductive and hyperbolically expensive". But Adam Smith went further by postulating that the slave trade was the result of injustice and rapacity for the possession of Africa and its congenial people. Africans had never injured the people of Europe in any war, commerce, or politics. The Africans displayed generosity, kindness and hospitality.

Adam Smith had a modicum appreciation for Africa, while David Hume had the opposite views. Hume in a special essay in 1753 on national characters expressed his conviction that "Negroes (blacks) were naturally biologically inferior to whites. No civilised nation had emerged among Africans. No individual imminent either in action or speculation. No ingenious manufactures; no arts, no sciences". But Adam Smith's opinion was based on pity, rather than conviction. It is to be remembered that Hume also invested financially in the slave trade. What a paradox. Not only Hume, but all the British philosophers like the Royals had in fact invested their money into the slave trade. But rather I would say what a dichotomy of imperialism and "solid ignorance". It is what Dr. Luther King called in his book, Strength to Love, sincere ignorance David Hume is best stationed to that of academic diffidation of human value and a perception that biblically there is one Supreme creator. Anyone looking at Hume cannot hesitate to believe that his academic intelligence would not allow him to deny man's ontological and theological equality.

Thomas Clarkson carefully reminded David Hume that the Negro race, even in servitude had produced distinguished people such as Phyllis Wheatley and Ignatius Sancho. People call them illustrious prodigies, but they were only prodigies as would be produced every day if they had equal opportunities as the British or Europeans.

Dr. Eric Williams also confirmed with a laconic critique of Hume that he was unable to examine, elucidate or expatiate on the subject from any broad point of view. The summation of David Hume is best said that he was jejune and vacuous in his theory. His theory, perception or postulation was nothing more or less than intellectual vacuity and racism. Scientific racism and racist theories of the 1850s provided a justification for African slavery by Europeans for the harsh treatment of people in the colonial world. Hume and his colleagues had overlooked biblical anthropology because of their racial propensity.

Sidney W Mintz in a collection of essays on "Slavery, Colonialism and Racism" said it was economic motives which prompted the

European conquest of Africa. Mintz added, "Britain had ended slavery in the West Indies and had done much to suppress the Atlantic Slave Trade but that Britain allowed South Africa at the same time to become independent with full power in the hands of a minority of overseas Europeans and racial oppression continues in South Africa until recently". Britain at no time acted without an ambiguous message. Dr. Eric Williams' approach and insights are well established amongst scholars of distinction and students with enormous intellectual potentiality.

Dr. Williams' views are also useful in the process of defining the British concepts of the Atlantic Slave Trade and their economic profits. Dr. Ani is also helpful. For her Europeans were successful in their efforts to economically and politically control others, namely Africans, because culturally they were able to force Africans to assimilate their definition of their inferiority into their own self image of themselves, while at the same time gaining support for the image of themselves as superior. Another graph by Dr. Ani is helpful.

Europeans are rational	**Others are irrational**
Critical	Non critical
Scientific	Superstitious
Logical	Illogical, magical
Civilised	Uncivilised
Advanced	Primitive
Modern	Backwards
Lawful	Unlawful
Orderly	Unruly
Responsible	Irresponsible
Adult	Childlike
Universal	Parochial
Energetic	Lazy
Active	Passive

European Christianity and the Atlantic Slave Trade:
A Black Hermeneutical Study

Europeans are rational	**Others are irrational**
Enterprising	Apathetic
Creative	Imitative
White	Black/coloured

Europeans are	**Others are**
World Saviours	Objects to be controlled/manipulated
Conqueror	
Organiser	
Peacemaker	

James Baldwin describes the European image of others in this way. "In the case of the Negro... his shameful history was carried quite literally on his brow. Shameful, for he was an heathen, as well as black and would never have discovered the healing blood of Christ had we not braved the jungles to bring him these glad tidings. Shameful, for, since our role as missionary had not been wholly disinterested, it was necessary to recall the shame from which we had delivered him in order more easily to escape our own. As he accepted the alabaster of Christ and the bloody cross in the bearing of which he would find his redemption... He must, henceforth accept that image we then gave him of himself having no other and standing moreover in danger of death should he fail to accept the dazzling light thus brought into such darkness". Dr. Ani goes on to say "The European Americans' conceptual self as separate from others, and therefore in a position to others, is an extension of the European ontological conception of the human being as being against or in opposition to nature. In isolating himself from nature, he succeeds in constructing the illusion of a despiritualised world of which he has complete control, because he can control and manipulate the material within it with his science and technology".

Throughout the study of the Atlantic Slave Trade, modicum attention has been given to the slave women, especially the barbaric and brutal ways in which they were treated with denigration, indignity, despiritualised and de-souled. The slave women were looked upon by the master slavers purely as sexual fantasies for sexual gratifications only. Motherhood is sacred and the dignity of women had been distinguished throughout history by men. At times it is cultural, political, professional or educational. Polygamy has been with men for centuries including biblical times and some of our societies today practise polygamy. In societies of polygamy there is seldom any record of rape and many of the social defects and social conducts of male and female are sharply defined. These can best be explained by examining the different cultures and religions.

The enslavement, powerlessness, dehumanisation and animalisation of African women during the Slave Trade, Middle Passage and Plantation system and culture by the perceived superior class, viz Europeans. This needs scholastic examination. The level of critique must be:
1. cultural
2. psychological
3. spiritual
4. physical genealogical, biological
5. economical
6. sociological
7. political

These strands are all interrelated because they form the basis and conception of the whole person created in the image of God.

The slaves, masculine and feminine genders were owned by the slave masters, the master slavers. They were merely a sexual curiosity. They were abused physically, emotionally, morally and spiritually and were reduced to the animal kingdom.

Professor James Walvin gave a graphic and detailed account in his book (The Slave Trade of a Slave Woman). "A slave woman was working on the plantation as she bent with her backside turned to the slave master on his horse, the slave master jumped from his horse, grabbed the slave woman and sexed her on the plantation in the presence of her husband and the other slaves". Two things are significant here. First, she was the complete property of the slave master. He had all the powers over her. She had no choice, because she had no freedom. To sex her at his choice and location was his power over her. She had no right in the physical encounter; no choice, the bestiality was dreadful. In this situation, the woman lost everything pertaining to her womanhood. She was his property to be used according to the slave masters whim or mood. She was psychologically, culturally and spiritually controlled by the white man. Secondly, male and female slaves were the properties of the master enslavers. The slaves had no rights. They were totally conditioned to slavery. They themselves witnessed the pernicious black experience of humiliation, powerlessness and degradation to the level of pigs, dogs, goats and sheep. They were stripped of anything relating to human beings. Professor Walvin goes on to say "For slave women, they were the after meal pleasure of their slave masters, brothers, and colleagues". Women were also whipped for refusing the advance of the slave master. This was the condition on the farms and also on the plantations. It was claimed that the African slaves ruined the industry of white people who have seen a rank of poor creatures below them, detest work for fear it should make them look like slaves. In other words, white slaves and white people resisted anything that resembled that of a slave on the plantation.

It was the African labour power that became the main ingredient of an extraordinary international exchange of people and goods. The Atlantic sugar economy hinged on the African slave labour. Remove the Africans and the trade would collapse immediately. The inundation of slaves kept the trade going incessantly for the New World. Again, Walvin is clear about the sexual conduct of Europeans with African women. He wrote further on page 220 of "Black Ivory a History of British Slavery". "When whites visited friends on neighbouring estates on Sundays it was common to have women selected for the purpose of sleeping with these visitors". White friends visiting Thomas Thistlewood expected to be provided with their favourite slave women to complete an evening of eating and drinking.

Profession Cornel West in his challenging book 'Prophecy, Deliverance and Afro-American Revolutionary Christianity' made the following observations and statements. "The notion that black people are human beings is a relatively new discovery in the modern west. The idea of black equality in beauty, culture and intellectual capacity remains problematic and controversial". Professor West questioned the epistemological basis for this discourse. West also supplied us with information of the degree of racism within the enlightenment among the philosophers such as Jefferson, Emmanuel Kant, David Hume and Voltaire.

Hugh Thomas writing in his book 'The Slave Trade – The History of Atlantic Slave Trade 1440-1870'. Thomas' accounts of the treatment of African slave women are narrative poignant and graphically gripping in its content of abuse. Slave women were at the mercy of their slave masters' brothers, friends and sons. It is important to constantly remind ourselves that African slaves were not seen as human beings. They were animals. From this Eurocentric racist culture and religion, cultural Christianity was the source of sexual pleasures. At times sexual power over the women was a psychological and racial demonstration that the slave master controlled both men and women simultaneously and sempiternally. Both were his properties. The slave master had the right to the slave woman without the husband's consent. The husband could not even imagine that he had a voice. The women on the plantation were sexed in the presence of their husbands. The husbands were only in name. They were both owned by the master enslavers.

The degree of bestiality began with the crossing of the Atlantic Ocean. Men and women were dumped in the hull of the slave ships, naked. The women were available for the captain, the crews and the slave men.

At Elmina Castle there are quarters to this day where the slave women were taken for sexual pleasures by the slave traders, captains, missionaries and crew.

Professor Walvin's writings on sex in the slave quarters reminds us of slave conditions. White slave masters violated their dealings with slave women. Thomas Thistlewood's journal records his personal sexual rapacity and concupiscence. Thistlewood even allowed his friends and visitors to sleep with his slaves.

The male slaves found that their wives were taken from them at random. Sometimes temporarily or permanently for the sexual pleasure of local white men. Those who resisted male or female faced a range of punishments. For the men whipping and castration and also execution. Walvin's summation is worth quoting in full. "Africans were described as immoral, wanton and lascivious, devoid of all sexual restraints which Europeans viewed as distinguishing qualities of civilised people". We must again acknowledge the pertinence of Dr. Marimba Ani in her tomb on African centred critique of European cultural thought and behaviour. She reminded us that the categorisations and descriptions and definitions of Africans were all based on Euro-centric cultural Christianity's definition of black people.

A quotation of pertinence from Dr. Ani will suffice. "The relationship of Christian ideology to European imperialism to the way in which Christian thought has contributed to European nationalism by intensifying the we/they dichotomy on which it depends and by providing corresponding images of Europeans and majority peoples that mandate the unlimited expansion of Western European political control. The essence of the Christian tradition is its assumption of theological and moral evolution laid into the superior and humanly proper conception of one God (pure spirit)". The ultimate abstraction. The Christian mandate to impose this conception on other peoples represents the epitome of the European Utamaroho. Essential to this proselytising mission is an invidious comparison in which the non-European described by Chinweizu in 1978. "The Rest of Us", comes out not only "the loser" but is dehumanised as well. The "pagan, heathen, adulterer or polytheists" have no religion in terms of European definition; yet these are all terms used to describe European spiritual conceptions. Africans are 'cultural other'. They were morally inferior. They were less than human. Therefore, whatever was done to Africans with the objective of making them more human (e.g. giving them religion) was justifiable. Catherine George also provides us with an example of the Christian image of the cultural other. She demonstrates the way in which Christian ideology enable Europeans to behave as they do towards people of other cultures. She speaks of Christianity's influence upon the civilised views of the primitive. One can even take to a much higher level the degrading and bestiality treatment of African women. An avid link to the Europeans' anthropological discipline and description of Africans. This anthropological description is entwined within European Christianity. For example, European anthropologists defined the primitive, the savage, always in opposite to Europeans. For them the primitive was non-critical, non rational, non-scientific, uncontrolled, immoral, irreligious and most of all incapable of creating civilisation. As a result of this anthropological understanding, definition and conception of African women and men, Europeans so-called Christians treated them as inhuman. They therefore demoralised and dehumanised them to the level of bestiality.

Walvin says, "It was increasingly clear that much of the corruption evident in African life and society was a result of the centuries of their links with Europeans". In other words, it was the Europeans who exported and transported their incorrigible corruptions and immorality to Africa and beyond. It was also especially caused by the damage wrought by the burgeoning slave trade.

It is impossible to contemplate anything normal or natural in terms of relationships in such situations of abnormal standard. In a world as that of the economical slavery of African men and women.

The experiences of sexual exploitation were of the beastliest kind imaginable. Parliament and the so-called humanitarian movement and the non-conformist churches began to question the climate of sexual laxity. They were appalled. Slave women unable to resist the blatant advances of their masters, slaves continuing to be provided for their visiting friends without any voice or rights. Beating and punishments to the extreme and sometimes death from beating when sexual advances were spurned. The dreadful stories of sexual exploitations became part of the fabric of slave society.

Cornel West is not afraid of relating racism and the evilness of treating slave women to the endemicness of racism in European culture. In an attempt to understand the application of hermeneutical penetration of insights, critiques of cultural Christianity and the deeds of the Christian slave traders must be questioned; it must be looked at with scholastic rectitude. Nothing should appear or left to be recondite in this sphere of history.

Equally, Professor James Cone in his latest book *Martin and Malcolm and America – A dream or a nightmare* made the point of Malcolm's rejection of Christianity. Look says Malcolm X at the deeds of Christianity. I agree without reservation with Malcolm X's questioning of Christianity. European Christianity was basically a vacuous culture, devoid of conscience, morality, ethics, the lowest form of human decency and profoundly and deeply irreligious.

We should remind ourselves that the conduct, behaviour and deeds of the master enslavers' treatment of African women were in the main labelled as European Christians.

A reasonable knowledge and experience of the Atlantic Slave Trade along with the treatment of the slaves, was bound to impact on the minds, psyche and the posing of legitimate questions. Why did black people become Christians? Black people were conditioned to a tremendous process of brainwashing. The inculcation was psychologically, culturally, spiritually and sociologically damaging to the image and psyche of the slaves. The process was the forceful stripping of all forms of Africanism, African culture, African religion and African religious beliefs, and especially deep African cultural paradosis. The forceful renaming process of Africans, names to the adaptation of the slave masters names. In other words, Africans were forced to abandon their family names, family ties and adopt the names of the slave masters.

Professor Cornel West's questions are very apt. He asks "Why did large numbers of black people become Christians? What features of protestant Christianity persuaded blacks to become Christians? The British separatists used the Methodist religious decentres in American religious culture gained the attention of the majority of slaves in the Christianising process. West answered his own questions from his context. He answers by stating emphatically and academically "Black people became Christians for intellectual, existential and political reasons". Christianity is as Frederick Nietzsche has taught us and liberation theologians remind us, is a religion especially fitted to the oppressed. In other words, European Cultural Christianity was designed and formulated specifically for the enslaved Africans.

Christianity, says Cornel West, is first and foremost a theodicy, a triumphant account of good over evil. Conversion experience played an essential role in the Christianising process. It is democratises and equalises the status of black people before God. In other words, European Christianity laid the demarcation and equalisation stratification before God. There is a deep cultural, psychological and social legacy also which is very deep in the psyche and culture of black people or rather of African and African descendants. Many black women today continue the slave mentality of interracial relationships. Most of these relationships cannot be based on knowledge or awareness of the history of the slave trade. Even personal consciousness of the slave trade brutality and sexual exploitation of African women. In a nutshell, people with a profound knowledge, awareness and consciousness of the European anthropological definitions of Africans' treatments, expectations and conditions would no doubt think again to enter into interracial relationships. Professor Gus John has expanded this significant point.

These treatments I have already tabulated, thus, there is no need to enter into any form of reiteration here.

The slaves were acknowledged religiously and scientifically, even philosophically as animals. They were not fully human; they were not human beings. But they were sexually accepted for sexual gratifications without emotion, spontaneity, dignity or bearing the ontological image of the Supreme Being, force or energy we call God.

A particular disturbing aspect of the churches' practice, psychology and theology was the admission in the slave trade and the demoralisation of Africans. The churches never questioned the institution of slavery; rather the churches supported and identified alongside the Atlantic Slave Trade. Not only did they not question the theological justifications for slavery, but they did not perceive or encourage "manumissio in ecclesia". The church enslaved the Africans because the church was a significant partner in the slave trade system.

It must be admitted that brainwashing, false inculcation, psychological and cultural raping of the slaves' religious and social beliefs along with the destruction of African customs and practices and was replaced by European customs and cultural ethnological traditions.

The African slaves were defined, looked upon, and treated always as inferior, dehumanised, de-Africanised mentally, socially, destabilised demographically by Europeans by so-called European cultural Christians. It was programmatic, it was systematic, it was pre-planned and deculturised. African women must use their monopodium as unique Africans and descendants. Restoration of the African dignity linked to the African genealogy is significantly important and exigent for Africa and African descendants.

The deduction that is being made by the author here is that the African diaspora is fragmented throughout the world. This fragmentation is numerically, economically and technologically dysfunctional for Africa and African descendants. Restoration of fully Africanised conscious people with respect and dignity is exigently needed. The absence of collective consciousness is part of the legacy of the slave trade.

One can experience extrication from the endemic racist treatment of African women. African women stem from the concept of being an African woman with cultural, physical and psychological stratification, removing the label stamped on the minds and impinged on the complexion with negativism must now be embraced with love and respect for being black.

Extrication from the psyche and brain that enabled European categorisation and definition of the African. Let us look at the definition of African briefly. African equals black, phlegmatic, relaxed, hair black, frizzled, skin silky, nose flat, lips tumid, women bosom a matter of modesty, appearance - give milk abundantly, crafty, indolent, negligent, anoints himself with grease, governed by caprice (Winthorpe Jordan).

"One wonders when will the chronos be when African men and descendants will see in every black woman's eyes Mary the Mother of Jesus, "Mary as a black sister, the Mary who cried at the announcement of bearing the worlds saviour - "My soul doth magnify the Lord"". To see in the eyes of black women the Spanish Black Madonna. The African man has taken on the function of the slave masters. Thomas Thistlewood, "He polluted African women with the syphilis disease. African men are now polluting African women with HIV and AIDS".

To be truly effeminate was extraneous to African women because they were captured and kidnapped by African chiefs and kings and sold as slaves for total rubbish, or rather, nothing of value. Later claimed by European males as brutes, savages and sexual deserts after eating and drinking on a Sunday evening.

The myth of the Obeah man/woman as religious servants had no potency as claimed by the Africans themselves. The enslavement conditions was apocalyptic and gave to the enslaved sexual females, with only the sense of existence to be used and abused, condemned without manumission and rights of being human. To be reduced to the degree of numbness, body with physical, emotional or spiritual living the sexual violation of the man was tantamount to a total rape which must have left the African enslaved woman useless and without any inner feelings. Without a sense of self worth because of complete dehumanisation by the slave masters. This historical, psychological legacy is still permeating African descendants today. The slave women were sold and transported from slave farms like donkeys, goats, mules and horses. An animal to be used without mercy. In other words they were only numbers.

Chapter 14
Ecclesiastical Involvement

Christianity

Dr. Robin Walker in his recent academic book (When we Ruled) said on page 350, "As in North Africa, the enslavers used religion to pacify the enslaved".

The bulk of my concentration in this thesis is to see the relationship between European Cultural Christianity and the Atlantic Slave Trade. I go one step further to say that the Europeans and the British used Christianity ruthlessly to enslave Africans. Indeed, European Cultural Christianity was a systematic economic philosophy entwined in religion or Christianity that was a religious belief or philosophy of immense and phenomenal vacuity. European Christianity had always been a religious missionary movement to enslave Africans which was a religious programme according to King Alfonso I of the Congo. For King Alfonso it was a religion of vacuity which was morally, ethically, theologically and sociologically useless.

European Christianity actively participated in the enslavement of Africans; the destruction of many African kingdoms such as the great Congo Kingdom with the co-operation of some chiefs, and some kings. On the other hand, Christianity has been presented as free from the most heinous crime recorded by man, namely the Atlantic Slave Trade. The disguises used were all based on mendacity and cultural superiority. The major protagonists in the slave trade at the beginning of the 16th century were the Portuguese and the Spaniards. They did most of the enslavement activities. By the 17th century, other European nations became deeply involved such as Holland, England, France, Denmark, Sweden and Prussia. It is a general historical belief that with the involvement of all these European countries, Britain became the dominant force in the enslavement of Africans. At the same time it is to be acknowledged by the prescriptive record of Europe and Britain that the process used by European countries and Britain were that of European and British Christianity to enslave the Africans.

European Christianity and British Christianity has never been a pedigree religion, as perceived and presented to the world by Europeans and the British. The Baptist church saw the coming of Christianity led by the Baptist myalism as incorporating some aspects of white religion, i.e. the Holy Spirit and the practice of baptism by emersion. Baptism took place in rivers and seas which in parts of Africa were the home of the spirits. They saw Christianity as worldly, while myalism was towards this world. In other words, there was contiguity between the cosmos and Africans. According to myalism philosophy, evil-doers were the whites or slave owners but basically myalism was a vehicle for preventing the evils of slavery. Myalism took its full direction and dynamics from Africa and the indigenous Africans.

The majority of slaves had tremendous difficulty in recognising Christianity as a religion. Christianity as a European religion and British religion was one of oppression, exploitation and dehumanisation of Africans in the name of religion. The white planters and traders and the slaves themselves gazed amazingly at each other's religion in an uncompromising way. For the slaves there was no social stratification for them, only hell here on earth and European Christianity made sure that the slaves were held in that situation. Suffering, oppression, alienation, pain, dehumanisation and indignity were the disseminating ingredients of European and British Christianity.

The African slaves did not truncate the world or divide the world up into sacred or secular. Whites went to church on the Sabbath and for the rest of the week they were enmeshed in secular living.

Some ministers forced resistance to the planters and traders because they did not want to complicate their relationship with the slaves by introducing Christianity. The real difficulty was the introduction of European Cultural Christianity into Africa and the use of European Christianity in the enslavement of Africans in the West Indies and the Americas.

The Anglican Church

The Anglican Church had a remarkable unbelievable debate about the theological justification for converting slaves. Conversion of slaves or the inculcation of European Christianity was not for any moral, ethical or deep religious reasons. Conversion to become good obedient slaves to their slave masters; to accept slavery without any human dignity, humanity and the spirit of God. It is indeed a timely reminder, that the slave traders perceived that Africans were not human beings. They never had a soul, a heart; they never had a God, they were only cattle. They were pagans, they were barbarians. They were even seen as incorrigible pagans. With this contention and belief, what therefore was the purpose in seeking to convert the slaves to what? European and British Christianity was a religion of oppression, exploitation and dehumanisation of the Africans. Another way to look at the European and British history is that they came out of the dark ages; they must have forgotten their dark ages. Dr. Basil Davidson in his book 'The African Slave Trade' made the point abundantly clear that upon until the late 17th century "Nobody talked as yet of any civilising mission". Nor was the slave trade based around ideas of Negro inferiority. Professor Du Bois noted that during these days of the Muslim rulers of Egypt they were buying white slaves by the tens of thousand in Europe and Asia and taking them to Syria, Palestine and the Valley of the Nile. Writers began fabricating a literature for the general public that portrayed Africa as a land of savages to give the impression that the transatlantic enslavement system was beneficial to the enslaved. In addition, enslavement became explicitly linked to a civilising mission. Professor Arnold Tony of Oxford University wrote a very famous book 'A Study of History' where he informed his readers that the black race had never built a single civilisation. In the 17th century however, the literature written for traders, government officials and geographers contained little of the dishonest nonsense says Dr. Robin Walker aimed at the masses. Similarly says Dr. Walker in the 20th century, few scholars tried to keep the truth alive in around the same period as Tony such as Professor Frobenius and Churchward. Left wing and liberal scholars have continued the character assassination of Frobenius and Churchward. This is how the absurd notion that Africa had no history became the dominant view. Images of jungle savages eating missionaries in cooking pots were also fabricated to make the propaganda stick, but as Lady Lugard that excellent authority on West African history pointed out "Two slave traders Barbot and Bosman were much disturbed by a widespread belief among the natives of Africa that we buy them only to fatten and afterwards eat them as a delicacy". Barbot tells us that natives infected within this belief will fall into deep melancholy and despair and refuse all sustenance though never so much compelled and even beaten to oblige them to make some nourishment, notwithstanding that they will starve to death. And though I must say I am naturally compassionate, yet have I been necessitated sometimes to cause the teeth of those wretches to be broken because they would not open their mouth or be prevailed upon by any entreaties to feed themselves and thus have forced some substance into their throats".

Dr. Robin Walker says, "The term dark ages only apply to Europe. The rest of the world was not necessarily in a dark age. The dark age period of European Christendom actually corresponds to the golden age of Islamic civilisation."

The Anglican Church did not debate the theological conversion and place of the slave traders in God's scheme of salvation. Slave traders acted without any morality or religious consciousness. Slave traders who perceived the slaves to be animals or none beings.

It is of hermeneutic significance that the Anglican Church sought a debate for the theological justification for saving souls, the souls of slaves, but not the slave traders. It was assumed that the slave traders were already Christians like the Reverend John Newton. The Anglican Church did not debate any economical justification. Why should they? The church's purpose was to brainwash the slaves into total submission; submission with the acceptance that Africans had no soul. If Africans had no souls, if the slaves had no souls, what was the purpose of the missionary movement and the missionaries? Their purpose was never meant to embark on soul saving for God's kingdom. Their mission was to make sure the slaves accepted their state and condition in this life as ordained by Almighty God. In other words, the church and the missionary movement went hand in hand with the slave trade movement.

The theological debate took off with great speed and impact. The assumption was that for a specific drive towards conversion and that it should be tailored to the inferior mental capacity of the slaves. Again, it was part of the European Cultural Christianity programme to sub-divide and to create divisions between Africans, European and the British. European and British were perceived to be a master race of intelligence and superiority. Inventors, engineers, scientists etc. While the slaves were perceived to be barbarians, illiterate, ignorant and pagans, we must remind ourselves that these categorisations and definitions were purely made by Europeans and British as part of their cultural racism and their cultural racist Christianity.

This was the area for brainwashing. Inculcate inferiority into the slaves. Make the environment of the slaves as that of an animal. Slaves you are cattle. Slaves you are inferior, and so inferiority was backed up scientifically, sociologically, economically and theologically. Slaves were perceived to be inferior by complexion, history, sociology and demographically.

European Cultural Christianity was used and seen as narcotic. In other words the opium of the people. It was widely held that suitably converted and fed suitably with an appropriate diet of quiescent theology, blacks could become perfect slaves, complacent slaves, accommodating and socially tranquillised. Despite this well thought out and socially systematic programme and claim, Christianity as the Baptist saw them was equally blamed for this. Christianity at the time possessed slaves for their own use. Myalism was assiduous to ward off evil and to keep the triumph of good over evil, to allow slaves' strength to win against the evils of the slave system and its perpetuators. It is a strange paradox that the slave traders did not make any drastic or radical attempt to eradicate African religion, the religion they feared and disliked so much. They changed African religion by a simple process of conversion and baptism. This is where the danger was. Dr. Robin Walker in his book *'When we Ruled'* saw it differently. For Dr. Walker, it was acculturation versus Christianity.

The missionary movement was highly competitive in numbers. The more slaves they converted the more they believed the slave trade would be stable. Once again, the missionary movement was contiguous to the slave trade.

It is clear to see therefore that the relationship between the economic philosophy of Europe and Britain alongside European Cultural Christianity has its attestation and appellation in the forts and the castles of Ghana. The forts and castles were built by Europeans and British royals and the Christians basically for economic and political monopoly. For example:

(a) European and British expansion
(b) For economic exploitations of Africa for the economy of Europe and Britain.

Political and economic rapacity with inundation played into many wars and conflicts. According to Dr. Albert van Dantzig in his informative book 'Forts and Castles of Ghana' said "Indeed the Portuguese were quite active in their missionary zeal, and converted a large number of Elmina's inhabitants to the Christian religion". Second, Holland was a sugar producing colony and to work the plantations which they had conquered from the Portuguese, the Dutch needed great numbers of slaves. In this respect their voltric face is remarkable. At first, before they had any plantations colonies the Dutch Calvinists had maintained a holier than thou attitude strangely condemning popish practice of using slave labour, but as soon as they themselves realised the vast economic profits which could be derived from it they readily discovered the appropriate text in the scriptures to justify slavery.

With European Christianity, the missionaries and churches were the force behind Europe and Britain's economic expansion and domination. Beginning with gold which they found less profitable than the slave trade, the slave trade became the economic backbone and cornerstone of the economic philosophy of the slave trade period for Europe and Britain.

European Christianity and the Atlantic Slave Trade: A Black Hermeneutical Study

According to Karl Bath, in his book, 'Church Dogmatic', Bath defined theology by stating the claim "theology is a function of the church". If this is true, then the Atlantic Slave Trade was upheld by the church and therefore such theology of the church was an act of antinomianism which made European and British Christianity vacuous of any moral law. I do not agree with Karl Bath's concept. Theology is a function of human experience of God. In their context of suffering, alienation, oppression, exploitation, dehumanisation and the amputation of human manumission, economically, sociologically, ethnologically with the God of consciousness fully realised and the dignity of being fully and truly human. Conversion of slaves never meant manumission or the restoration of the slaves' dignity. It meant the slaves' admission and surrender to their so-called imposed and inculcated inferiority complex. Slaves should be submissive to their slave masters. Thus conversion was not spiritual or theological. It was the imposition of a foreign white culture on the minds of Africans.

It was a psychological weapon; it was pre-planned. It was programmatic. It was cultural Christianity challenging Africanism. It was Europeanism seeking the complete extirpation of all the sociological, cultural, spiritual and historical properties of the Africans. Next to conversion was a method of baptism. Baptism was the changing of African names to Christian names which were the slave masters' names. Daniel, Brown, James, Adam, Jacob, Smith, Ingram, Gilroy and McCarthy etc. These were slave masters' names.

It was the changing of African names to European names that the cultural and sociological identity came under the greatest destruction by European Cultural Christianity and Christian influence. Baptism was the affirmation that Africans now have a new name. They took on the slave masters' identity. It was the extirpation of the slaves' African roots, ancestry, religion, paradosis and history. It was the obliteration of their Africanness. It was the embracement of European Cultural Christianity which promoted and disseminated oppression, dehumanisation, non-being and inferiority among the slaves. Baptism and conversion were spiritually and psychologically juxtaposed as the slave traders, plantation owners and the missionaries worked hand in hand to recreate the African as nothing but a slave designed by God for European influence and redemption. Thomas Cook in his book *Methodist History of the West Indies* believed that God had created the Africans to be slaves for the Europeans to redeem the Africans. Cook was making out that God is involved in cosmic dissipation, should it be apocalyptic or eschatological. Africans were not included. They were animals, non-beings, inferior creatures and beasts of burden. Whites had nothing in common with the slaves, not even biological similarities. This appearance was not significant, because Africans are black. Although racist to the foundation, whites were seen to be omnipotent; blacks had no rights, no dignity, no humanity, and no freedom. Conversion and baptism were vehicles used to transform the Africans into Europeans, robots, machines. In the words of Lord Scott "Slavery was a basic necessity for Britain and Europe". This necessity was purely economical and a cultural domination of British power in the slave trade and the economic philosophy for Britain and Europe.

Whipping and grave punishment were integral components, and the conversion and baptism were brainwashing techniques of the slave trade. The reiteration is significant that Europe only had a racial culture of oppression and exploitation of Africans. European Cultural Christianity was the tool used to truncate the minds of the Africans culturally and spiritually. Conversion and baptism of the Africans was a visible sign that ancestor worship, polygamy and other voices determined by European cultural Christians were kept by the African slaves to the hilt.

These extraordinary cultural ambiguity was that there was no preaching or expostulation of the slave traders and masters regarding the treatment of the slaves. Subjugation, whipping, punishment, oppression, raping of African women, sexual and emotional abuse of the slaves, women and children aged 2 years were sent to work on the plantations were all acceptable by the missionaries. The missionaries therefore had no moral crusade, no theological or ethical crusade; they were concomitant with the slave traders.

There was no moral, ethical, social, psychological, spiritual or theological challenge to the slave masters. Their conduct was perceived to be right. For them it was justice and righteousness. In other words, they made the games and they made the rules for the games. Judge and jury combined symbiotically.

Let me repeat the essential points: the Anglicans debated the theological justification for slavery. They never debated the economical philosophy of the slave. The economical philosophy was interlinked to the theological justification of the slave trade. With conversion and baptism, the European Cultural Christianity was basically a Christian slave religion. It was a religion that denied Africans their rights, justice equality and freedom. It was a basic culture based on exploitation, oppression, injustice and evilness of the highest criminal immoral level. Laconically, it was morally repugnant according to Professor James Walvin.

European Cultural Christianity

Before 1750, Christianity was not a prominent force among the slaves in the Northern colonies of Africa but Africans survived over the Caribbean region. However, by the mid 18th century, systematic and powerful efforts were made to convert the slave to Christianity. Was it because the slaves had at no time accepted slavery? Is it because the slaves were consistently rebelling and conspiring? Their intention was to convert the slaves to European Cultural Christianity. Once again the church was at the centre of the Atlantic slave trade and plantation slavery. Anglican ministers had baptism for the slaves' children, wives and married parents too. There was nothing worse than slaves who were living in a state of profound ignorance of which Christianity was presented as redemption for them. How could they know what Christianity was all about? Christianity was forced upon them as a European cultural religion wrapped in religious languages. Bondage, philosophy and theology, were a Christianity of oppression and enslavement of Africans because of their ethnic origins, genealogy, history, cosmology and geography.

Anglicanism

The English colonies from the inception were doomed to be Anglican when the Virginian Company was established in 1606. It was desired that it should provide true word in service of God according to the rights and doctrines of the Church of England. Let's examine the words "The true word and service of God". These are Anglican words. These are not enslaved African words. These are British words designed to brainwash the Africans to accept British theological and liturgical words. The words have nothing to say about Gods liberation of the oppressed people. By a demonically possessed Euro-centric and ethnocentric race called the British and Europeans.

In the context of the Atlantic Slave Trade Middle Passage, it was theologically and philosophically impossible even to conceive of a God of justice, love and liberation as morally good and perfect. A God who was inactive to the sufferings, exploitations, inequality, brutality, dehumanisation and indignity of Africans. Quite bluntly, it was this ambiguous recondite European cultural racist Christianity which really messed-up Africans until this day. In fact, it has messed up black people's brains, lives, ambitions, aspirations and Africanness. Relationships between the local people and the Bishops were always problematic. The ministry soon fell under the power of the planters. It was a slave lobby which controlled the local church. Ministers were not independent of the planters. Most ministers were deacons with limited influence. They could not effectuate control over the plantacratic lobby. The Church of England's office was concerned about the need to convert the slaves. But, their fears were based on the knowledge of the Roman Catholic Church. Conversion of slaves were the churches goal, indeed ultimate goal. We know that the slaves' bondage, oppression and alienation, demographically and sociologically brought about their dehumanisation.

In 1515 the first batch of slave grown West Indian sugar was shipped to Europe. Three years later, the first Africans were shipped directly to the Caribbean and the Americas. These developments marked the beginning of the triangular trade. The credit for this system was in no small part due to the activities of the Reverend de las Casas, a Portuguese national. In the year 1680 King James I gave a charter of monopoly to 30 London merchants to deal in enslaved people.

Bishop Fleetwood said, "No man living can assign a better and more justifiable cause for God withholding mercy (Hesed) from a

Christian than from a fellow Christian, and also withholding of Christianity from an unbeliever". Professor James Walvin of York University says "This was precisely what the planters in the English colonies did. Who were the unbelievers; the slaves or the slave masters?" We must remember it was not a religion that was inculcated into the Africans but was basically European Cultural Christianity and for the British it was the British customs of perfidiousness, ambiguity, exploitation, oppression and blatant racism.

Planters and Conversion

I have with other noble scholars established that the church was always at the centre of the slave trade. The Church of England faced the objections of the slave owners to see their slaves baptised and converted. Some slave owners disliked the theological prospect of seeing their slaves in the afterlife. "Is it possible that any of my slaves could go to heaven and I must see them there?" This was the question the slave owners posed. They too claimed that they were Christians, but Christianity for them did not envelope the slaves. The slaves were animals, sub-human, they were cattle, and they were animals without a soul. For the slave traders, the African value and worth was to be slaves and nothing more. They had no soul, they had no God spirit. They were discardable. They were the cog of the racial oppression machine. The attitude of the slave owners were psychological, sociological, biological and blatant segregation. The slaves whom they claimed were converted to Christianity were not converted from their African religious beliefs as witnessed by the slaves in Haiti. They were outwardly converted to the appearances of European Cultural Christianity, but at heart, they were Africans believing in African religion.

I remain convinced that the slaves found European Cultural Christianity vacuous, vapid and meaningless. The missionaries impressed on the slaves to endure the suffering of slavery "because in heaven they would enjoy milk and honey". Two things are important here. First, psychologically and spiritually the brainwashing was simple. Any oppressed and exploited people would reach out for some form of spiritual desideration for a better future, a better life to come. Second, God's kingdom is here and now. The slave traders and spiritual leaders professed to the slaves a religious Christian belief that they themselves had subscribed to believe in or even to practice. Why had they not as slave traders, masters and missionaries give up enslaving God's people? If heaven is the place for all prodigal people, all suffering people, all oppressed people, why did the slave masters refuse to accept the reality of time? They need to give salvation, mercy and righteousness to all of God's people. In other words, both the missionaries and the slave traders ruthlessly used European Cultural Christianity to thoroughly brainwash the slaves. The slaves were forced to endure oppression, dehumanisation and suffering in the hope of reaping milk and honey in heaven. This was the most blatant diabolical evil act of brainwashing the Africans who had a superior culture and concept of a monotheistic God than the British and Europeans.

Chapter 15
Religious Paradosis

What is Conversion?
I am hesitant to believe that the conversion method and expectation of the missionaries and ministers of religion during the slave trade, was theologically based on sincere religious ignorance. European Cultural Christianity had been polluted by the philosophers, scientists, the Royals and definitely the theologians had no developed theology for the slave trade. The Anglicans had asked about the theological justification for slavery but there were no defined theology. Conversion meant the acknowledgement of God's grace, mercy, forgiveness, love, justice and equality before God. The slaves were looked upon as a soulless people with ignorance, barbaric, uneducated and uncivilised. What of the slave masters? They were so-called Christians without any moral conscience. The slave masters and missionaries were culturally imperious to the slaves. Inculcation by European and British Christianity was nothing more than the extension of an imperial culture and power. It was the church acting as a political arm of the Government to dominate and perpetuate the culture of slavery.

There were conflicts between the slave traders and the missionaries, but the fundamental point is that the missionaries did not point the missionary cultural Christianity to the slave traders' and masters. It was automatically admitted that being white made good

Christians and Africans with black skin meant everything negative and having full impersonalisation and conversion for the missionaries was the replacement of everything African to the full acceptance of Europeanism and Britishism. In the process of conversion, the slaves remained impuissant even when the European Cultural Christianity was profoundly incongruous to the slaves.

It was Christianity without justice, liberation, equality, economic freedom and political freedom. Manumission never meant intellectual and educational freedom with the technological and scientific power for the Africans. Both the subject and predication was that the slaves remained sociologically and economically slaves to eternity.

Christianity was the process through the institution of the church to keep the slaves in their inferior places. It was a controlling of the minds of the slaves. It was oppression and exploitation of the slaves who were made sub-human by the church and the slave system.

The psychological strangulation of the slaves' minds through European Cultural Christianity was incommensurable. The damage is so manifold that it is with Africans and African descendants to this present day.

Present day Christianity need deculturisation, dehumanisation, de-white theologisation and to take its rightful place of black theology which speaks for Africans, black people, the oppressed, the marginalised, the voiceless, God's children and the brothers and sisters of the Christ of the black faith in the context of blackness.

The diabolical and brutal whipping of Kunta Kinte to accept the European Cultural Christianity name and to reject his African name is another clear evidence of the European Christian involvement in the brainwashing process of Africans. The names of slave ships bearing religious names remind us that Christianity was only a culture and bears no theological relevance. Names such as Jesus, Queen Elizabeth I slave ship and the Grace of God.

Slave Christianity According to Some Scholars

There are a number of distinguished scholars who have written on different parts of the slave trade. Scholars such as Zerbanoo Gifford. Gifford's contribution is very significant. For her, Christianity played an important role in the rise and fall of Britain's slave trade. Early slave traders used what they believed was a fact that Africans were pagans, as one of their strongest justification for enslaving them and made attempts to convert them to Christianity. Hermeneutically, this was only a strategy. For the slavers, European and British Africans were perceived to be incorrigible pagans. Why therefore bother to convert pagans? Africans were treated like animals without souls or humanity.

A laconic constructive criticism of Gifford is justifiable. The British and the Europeans claimed that the Africans were heathens, barbaric, ignorant and paganistic. It was a false cultural claim. They had no historical documentary or authentic scientific proof. We must also remember that in the enlightenment period, the enlightenment scientists and philosophers also defined and categorised Africans as barbarians, pagans, and heathens, and furthermore, that scientifically Africans were inherently biologically inferior to Europeans and British.

This perception was mythological, ethnocentrically racist, immoral and had no ontological foundation or linkage to theology or theodicy.

Historians, scientists, theologians, anthropologists, sociologists, all glossed over the historical fact that it was the British and Europeans who were pagans. The medieval period is a classic example. The Anglo-Saxon period equally a good example. These are historical attestations that Britain and Europe has always been paganistic. The British and the Europeans enslaved their own people for economical and political reasons. Britain also enslaved the Irish for over 700 years. What about the period of the Dark Ages? Dr. Robin Walker again in his book 'When We Ruled' has provided some useful information pertinent to the matter we are faced with. How Europeans and British categorised Africans in a derogatory, mythological and historically inaccurate way. In doing this Britain and Europe had forgotten their own history, or as Dr. Walker put it "By 500AD the Western part of the Roman Empire was in decline. This was of some importance since the Romans carried the flame of civilisation in Europe. Europe therefore entered an unhappy period known as the Dark Ages". Dr. Walker has provided us with a quotation from Professor Robert Briffault (a keen student of the development of culture) Professor Briffault wrote "From the 5th to 10th century Europe lay sunk in a night of barbarianism more awful and horrible than that of the primitive savage, for it was the decomposing body of what had been a great civilisation… cities had practically disappeared…They were pulled down and used as quarries to build towers in which a Bishop or a Baron who could afford some protection established himself. In Nimes, for example, the remains of the population dwelt in huts built among the ruins of the amphitheatre. Other towns were completely abandoned…Famines and plagues were chronic; there were 10 devastating famines and 13 plagues in the course of the 10th century alone. Cases of cannibalism were not uncommon; they were manhunts, with a view to plunder but for food. It was on record that at Tournus on the Saone human flesh was publicly put up for sale.

Dr. Briffault was not alone in holding this perspective. The historian Joseph McCabe wrote learnedly on medieval history in his view "None of our modern sophistry redeems this squalor of Europe from the 5th to 11th century. By the year 1000 Europe was reduced to a condition which, if we were not Europeans we should frankly call barbarianism, yet at that time the Arabs had a splendid civilisation in Spain, Sicily, Egypt and Persia and it linked on those of India and China. We write manuals of the history of Europe or the Middle Ages and we confine ourselves to a small squalid area (Russia and Prussia) were not yet civilised and Spain was (Moorish) and ignore the brilliant civilisation that ran from Portugal to the China Sea.

Finally, the term "Dark Ages" only applied to Europe. The rest of the world was not necessarily in a Dark Age. The Dark Age period of European Christendom actually corresponds to the golden age of Islamic civilisation".

The Africans were pagans. The British and the Europeans were Christians and their cultural Christianity was used to enslave the Africans. It had nothing to do with liberation from paganism, but rather for the fulfilment of the economic philosophy of Britain and Europe. From the enslavement of the pagans (Africans) who benefited? Certainly it was not the Africans, but the British and Europeans benefited. The sufferings, deaths and diabolical brutality of the Atlantic Slave Trade people namely, Africans. In other words, they claimed they were civilised but the treatment of their fellow human is beyond the pale.

Dominically and theologically with the biblical evidence from the Old Testament and New Testament especially the synoptic gospels and John's Gospel, Christianity in a nutshell was not used as liberation, salvation and complete manumission of the slaves.

The slaves were claimed to be pagans. By whose cannon, categorisation and definition? It was by Britain and Europe. The deeds of the so-called slave traders' Christianity depicted a mentality of ethical, religious, moral, social and political repugnancy of incorrigibility. It further reflects the postulation that God and Jesus Christ must ultimately be the God of the "Black Experience". Jesus must also be the saviour of the Black Experience. It is utter rubbish, rather dissipation to perceive of a moral God philosophically or theologically with any relevance of theodicy or theology relating to the slave traders. Let's face the hard facts and realities. The British, the Europeans and the slave traders were demons. They were demonically possessed. They embodied demonism. They were inhuman. They behaved and conducted themselves in a manner depicting the lowest strata of the animal kingdom in terms of mentality, psychology and deeds. Again, the words of the immortal Malcolm X rings with verve and not philigmaticism. "Just look at the deeds of Christianity that is European, British and American Christianity". Christianity was therefore perfect opium used to condition the minds of the slaves to accept European Christianity and to accept the inculcation that they were pagans and barbarians.

The capers' catechism was approved as the one official document saved for the Negros by the Methodist General Conference. The catechism was based on a doctrine of inferiority of the Africans to the whites. This inferiority was intended for theological justification for the slaves' state of bondage and servitude. It was not intended for their liberation for the restoration of their human dignity it was intended to psychologically entomb the minds and the psyche of the Africans that they were inferior.

Who enslaved the Africans? It was the royals, the Governments, the MPs, the philosophers, the theologians, the scientists, the engineers, the anthropologists and the sociologists. The immortal words of Lord Scott are applicable here. "Slavery has become an economic necessity for Britain and Europe. The pagans and the barbarians were not considered as important to the economic development of Britain and Europe, but the enslavement of pagans and barbarians were of economic necessity.

The slave traders' European Cultural Christianity had no moral, religious social, human, justice, liberation, spiritual or Theos Christos content. It was a culture of oppression, exploitation and dehumanisation of Africans.

European and British Christianity during the Atlantic slave trade period was essentially integrated with the politics and economics of the day. In other words it was an extension of British and European political ambition and philosophy based on the economic philosophy of the day. European Christianity was profoundly enmeshed with European and British political philosophy of greed and exploitation of Africans' free labour purely for economic gain. It was a practice of extraction from Africa. The perpetuation of underdevelopment without any injection into African, scientifically, technologically, sociologically and economically. Britain and Europe were extractionists, rather rapists.

In the 18th century the Methodist, Baptist and Moravians were emerged in the wake of the new movement. The Anglicans and Roman Catholics already had a foothold in the slave trade. These churches joined purely for competitive reasons. To convert the slaves into robots for the Christian slave owners. The conversion had nothing to do with spirituality nor a cosmic God, a cosmological Jesus, justice, peace, mercy, brotherhood, humanity or righteousness. It was a vehicle designed only for the enslavement of Africans. It was designed to give justification to the slave owners for the European economic system.

The slave owners were convinced that the slaves should take the medicine of European Cultural Christianity. The penetrative and worrying question for the slave traders was "Is it possible any of our slaves will go to heaven, and we must meet them there?" It was theologically justified to enslave the Africans. It was theologically justified to inculcate and to brainwash the slaves to accept subservancy.

Again European Cultural Christianity was nothing more than a culture without spiritual or religious roots.

Zerbanoo Gifford in her essay on Thomas Clarkson has helped us to understand the reinforcement of the slave traders' culture. She stated that the slave traders believed that to allow the slaves to know the Christian Gospel of brotherhood was a dangerous thing. How could a slave be allowed to think that he was equal to his master? It was purely a racial matter, based on a culture of superiority of being the perceived master race.

The Reverend John Smith was told by the London Missionary Society, "Not a word must escape you in public or private which might render the slaves displeased with their masters or dissatisfied with their station in life. You are sent not to relieve them of their servile condition but to afford them the consolation of religion". Consolation was their opium, namely that they should endure the suffering of slavery in this life and in the hereafter they would reap milk and honey. What nonsense. What rubbish. It was purely a European and British vehicle for the slaves to produce their goods to build and strengthen the economic power and to make them feel they were omnipotent and at times omniscient.

Although religion was the opium used by the missionaries some slaves by virtue of learning to read the bible, used religion and the bible for their manumission in return. Examples of validity are as follows:

Sam Sharpe 1831 is a significant example, and he was a black revolutionary paradigmatic figure of rebellion in Jamaica. Sam Sharpe was a charismatic Baptist preacher in Montego Bay. In that revolution 14 whites were killed but the slave owners took their barbaric revenge and in return killed over 500 slaves. We must remember the preposterous portion here. Sam Sharpe himself was hanged for leading the rebellion. His final and immoral words were "I would rather die upon yonder gallows than live in slavery". We need to draw a distinction between Sam Sharpe and Cudjoe. They both used similar words. Sam Sharpe's confession or conviction had no theological and epistemological consciousness, whilst for Cudjoe, "I would rather die on yonder gallows than to live as a slave because nature made me to be free". Cudjoe was more theological and cosmologically conscious. The British in particular in Jamaica in the 18th century used their cultural Christianity to continue to enslave and ruthlessly oppress the slaves.

The black slave hymn expressed the sense of abolition for the slaves, "We will be slaves no more, since Christ has made us free, as nailed our tyrants to the cross and brought our liberty". Liturgically the words of this slave hymn delineate hymns ancient and modern and at no time depicted the inner chamber, spirit and psyche of the enslaved.

The slave owners were afraid of meeting their slaves in heaven because the slaves would be the saints in heaven, and would punish them, mercilessly for enslaving them. This was their thinking. The slaves became conscious of their ontological innate manumission. There is no reference or evidence that African slaves ever accepted slavery. Indeed Dr. Richard Hart elucidated for us in his book 'Slaves who Abolished Slavery Volume II'. "There were constant revolts, mutinies, insurrections and rebellions". To the slaves Christ was their ontological consciousness for freedom. It had to be because Christ represented in the synoptic Gospels that salvation, liberation and freedom were essentially his message and ministry in consolidation with God's kingdom on earth. Dr. George Pixley in his book 'God's Kingdom' is right for the first time. Inflexible conservative approach has missed the relevance of the thesis of the Black Experience. Dr. Lamin Sanneh in his book 'West African Christianity – The Religious Impact', commenting on African Christianity not European or British Christianity reminds us in his book "The infant church like the holy child before him felt the full impact of contemporary political and social events, and in the struggle to interpret the message of Christianity, numerous obstacles were encountered and not always overcome. But whatever success there was in those early beginnings, some of it could be accredited to African Christians, some of whom had met Jesus personally and were presented in Jerusalem, Antioch and other places where the Christian movement began. Similarly, some of the apostles appeared to have landed on African soil, encouraging the setting up of churches. There is little doubt that Africa as well as other lands came firmly within the horizon of the first disciples and that Christian teaching was intended to apply to all peoples without respect to status, colour, political belief or geography. It is a matter of historical record that Africans participated fully in the mission of the church, and this is a matter of some significance for us today.

Elucidation of the missionaries, especially the liberal philanthropists was conceived as a means of social control, to instil in the Africans a proper attitude of subservancy towards the white man in connection with tilling the lands and producing materials to feed western industries and economies. It was further conceived that European traders could operate the slave trade better if a number of Africans were illiterate. Part of the Christian programme was therefore to keep the Africans in the chamber of illiteracy. Therefore, European Christianity was deeply oppressive and without any manumission for the slaves and Africans.

It is this cultural religion which has damaged the lives of Africans and African descendants to this very day. The result is that there is no black economic empowerment. No intellectual empowerment. No sociological empowerment and no theological empowerment.

St. Augustine (354-430) with his confessions and knowledge of God and Tertullian 160AD both born in North Africa are significant examples that European missionaries could not have taken Christianity to Africa. Rather, Africans took Christianity to Europe. What the Europeans took to Africa was nothing more than a culture. Dr Sanneh's statement "It is a matter of historical record that Africans participated fully in the mission of the church and this is a matter of some significance for us today".

Hugh Thomas' The History of the Atlantic Slave Trade 1440-1870

Hugh Thomas reminds us of the tremendous vicissitudes after the abolition of the slave trade by Britain and the United States. In 1820 the Ashanti King asked a British official (Dupuis) "Why did Christians not want to buy slaves anymore?" "Was their God not the same as that of the Muslims?" We are looking at the impact of the European Slave Trade on Africa. I am convinced that religion or Christianity from Britain and Europe readily messed up the brains of Africans. Such Christianity without any moral or ethical contents were logically stripped or extricated from any foreign religious cult. Gus John in his book *'Taking a Stand'* writing on the role of Africans and African Caribbean churches states "The churches had many functions".

1. Colluding with the dominant social order and validating the exploitation of black people.
2. Actively subjugating traditional African religion and peddling prejudices and stereotypes which we in turn internalise and use to oppress ourselves and one another.
3. Encouraging the belief that if we take care of our souls and ignore what people are doing to our bodies and to our fundamental humanity and basic dignity, our suffering would be a form of cleansing and held to greater rewards in heaven.
4. Encouraging the belief that poverty and suffering is good for the soul only when you are the oppressed and dispossessed. Consequently, not preaching to the oppressors that they could reap the same benefits from poverty and suffering and should therefore divest themselves of all their wealth and privileges.
5. Encouraging a view of morality and of sin which places responsibilities on the poor and needy, particularly with respect to property and to sex, while identifying with the exploitation and sexual predation indulged in by the rich and powerful".

Gus John goes on to say "Throughout history there have been gradation and variations across the churches with respect to the above. In the islands of the Caribbean, for example, the Church of England typically represented the land owners, former slave owners and the educated elite. The Roman Catholic Church had a following principally among the peasants and workers, and then there was and is the indigenous in the Caribbean.

CHAPTER 16
CORRECTING THE CRIME

Abolition of Slavery and Emancipation
1807 (Britain) and 1808 (USA)

Britain never embraced enthusiastically the need for Abolition. Rather, the abolition movement was persistently met with political recalcitrance. Indeed, reluctance was met at levels of the Government and society. Several abolition bills were defeated. Like it or not, British participation in the enslavement of Africans was based on the concept of the philosophy of inferiority and economic profitability.

Dr. Eric Williams' words are of complete remembrance "Those who owned enslaved Africans found it necessary to debase them in every conceivable way. They misused the words of the bible, attributed false claims to science, fabricated alleged genetic differences, perverted morality and turned intelligence upside down, even falling on chronology to prove themselves, to ensure their consciences that they were dealing not even with half men and half women but with property which could only be motivated and moved by the whip, hounded like dogs, chains and guns".

The British government and people were deeply or profoundly influenced by David Hume's structures on Negro capacity which was consciously and deliberately based on the Negro in a state of slavery.

Thomas Clarkson sought to invalidate and repudiate Hume's postulation. Dr. Eric Williams in his book, 'British Historians and the West Indies' Wrote, "For if liberty is only an adventurous right, if men are by no means superior to brutes, if every social duty is a curse, if cruelty is highly to be esteemed, if murder is strictly honourable and Christianity is alive, then it is evident that the African slavery may be pursued, without either the remorse of conscience, or the imputation of a crime. The remorse of conscience, or the imputation of a crime. But is the contrary of this is true, which reason must immediately evince, it is evident that no custom established among men was evermore impious since it is contrary to reason, justice, nature, the principles of law and government, the whole doctrine in short, of natural religion, and the revealed voice of God...how evidently against reason, nature, and everything human and divine, must they act, who not only force men into slavery, against their own consent, but treat them altogether as brutes, and make the natural liberty of man an article of public health. And by what arguments can they possible defend that commerce which cannot be carried on in any single instance, without a flagrant violation of the laws of nature and of God". Apart from David Hume's personal racist cultural and intellectual propensity and congenical racism, Hume used the context of slavery as his cannon to measure the Africans. Here, Clarkson was right to challenge and to remind David Hume, "The Negro race, even in servitude, had produced in time Phyllis Wheatley and Ignatius Sancho. People called them prodigies but there were only such prodigies as would be produced everyday if they had equal opportunities". To these prodigies I add St. Augustine.

Britain and Europe used the enslavement to deny the Africans equal opportunities. As I have expatiated proto, Britain and Europe extracted from Africa, they never put into Africa any technology, science, engineering, education or other cultural influence of significance.

The Abolition Movement contiguous with the British claim of humanitarianism is profoundly ambiguous and perfidious. On the left hand, Britain presented humanitarianism as the basis for Abolition on a moral and dare I say religious grounds because of the religious impact at the time. Simultaneously on the right hand there was the incubation of the apartheid system theologically, biblically and ethnocentrically based in South Africa.

It is a cultural and sociological fact that Britain had not been able to act unambiguously in dealing with Africa and African descendants throughout history.

Unreserved laudation is due to Thomas Clarkson, Grenville Sharpe and Lord Smith. Their contributions, energy, verve and dedication made them in the phrase of Drs. Oesterley and Theodore H. Robinson's statements, almost unique.

The Abolition Movement met with tremendous resistance from parliament, MPs, the Royals, the philosophers, the scientists and the slave traders. In some quarters the church vis á vis the Anglicans who were in the words of Gus John, "In the islands of the Caribbean the Church of England typically represented the land owners, the farm slave owners and the educated elite. The Roman Catholic had a following principally among the peasants and workers". We must not overlook who the major engines of the slave trade were. Without any doubt or reservation the prime movers in the slave trade were the states and churches. This we must not ignore or ever overlook. The states and churches combined in a symbiotic way as the prime movers of the slave trade.

Hugh Thomas provided a list of states and royals who participated in the slave trade. These range from Henry the Navigator whose captains looked for gold, but found instead slaves. Pope Pius II who declared that the baptised Africans should not be enslaved, Charles II of England who backed the Royal African Company on a golden voyage to Guinea. Ferdinand the Catholic, who as Regent of Castle, first approved the dispatch of African slaves to the Americas. Louis XIV of France who started the practice of giving bounties to French slave traders. Williams IV who as Duke of Clarence opposed Abolition in the House of Lords. Maria Cristina, Queen Mother of Spain in 1830 whose slave interest in Cuba was vast indeed. Humphrey Maurice, Governor of the Bank of England and London's major slave trader. John Blount, the brain behind the South Sea Company, whose main business was to ship Africans to the Spanish empire. Thomas Golright Mayor of Liverpool, who traded slaves up until the last legal minute in 1807. Sir Robert Rich, among the earliest entrepreneurs to carry slaves to Virginia, Pierre-Paul Nairac, the most active slave trader of Bordeaux who was refused a peerage because he was a protestant. Julian Zulueta of Havana, the greatest merchant in the last days of the Cuban trade, carried his vaccinated slaves by steamer to his plantation. William Wilberforce's place in political history and the Abolition Movement is somewhat solid. However, Wilberforce's motions for Abolition were defeated many times in defiance of justice and humanity. If we are looking for giants, people with remarkable extraordinary, spiritual, emotional, psychological and intellectual convictions and commitment for justice and equality, then we need to decorate Thomas Clarkson and Grenville Sharpe as far more prodigious in many instances than William Wilberforce. I am not dealing with personalities only, I am dealing with the facts of history, especially in relation to the mythological abolition of slavery that had been ascribed to Britain and which Britain maintained for far too long.

The internationalisation and institutionalisation of slavery was a deeply complexed problem. The complexities made it more difficult for the Abolition itself to succeed. In part, because of the powerful influence a number of people who had enormous financial and political power, were the merchants, the traders and politicians themselves who had enormous investment in the slave trade. It was equally the same major problem throughout Europe and also in the United States of America.

Philip Baker in 1795 through parliament stated unreservedly that he had £500,000 invested in 18 slave ships. Thomas Jefferson, the President of the United States of America, he spoke about the abolition with ambiguous tongues eloquently and unequivocally because he himself was deeply involved in the slave trade; hence abolition for Jefferson was personally and politically problematic. Why? Because President Thomas Jefferson's words were said delphically. In December 1806 Jefferson castigated and condemned the violations of human rights which prolonged the continuation of poverty and suffering on the unoffending people of Africa. In 1807, in the abolition of the traffic of slaves it is said slavery became outlawed and illegal. Even when the trafficking of slaves was made illegal, there still persisted the major problem which was the lack of effectuation of the law. In other words slavery was abolished on paper but not in reality. This was deeply pronounced in the major states of America, France, Portugal and especially Britain.

Britain and America were at the apex of the slave trade, especially in the late 17th and early 18th centuries. Making the trade illegal and abolishing the slave trade were a separate major problem for Britain and the United States because they were not authentic about abolition of the immoral trade. In other words, America and Britain spoke eloquently but they never had a convinced intention to abolish slavery. Their words of opposition were strong. Words such as, Peter Hurley of Georgia asked the question "What honour will you derive from a law which will be broken everyday of your lives?". King George III looked at Wilberforce's philosophy and activities repugnantly, "How go on your black clients?". Wilberforce and Pitt were both humiliated and Wilberforce experienced many setbacks with the bills being defeated, but Wilberforce used the energy of perseverance although the Abolition Movement truncated both Wilberforce's health and his life.

Hugh Thomas's 'The Slave Trade', Dr. Herbert S. Klein's 'The Atlantic Slave Trade' and Dr. Richard Hart's 'The Abolition of Slavery' have provided for us remarkable information on the true nature of the abolition of slavery. Dr. Hart's contribution deserves laudation and scholastic appreciation for his chronological legalistic tabulations, non-pedantically, Dr. Hart has juxtaposed with other scholars the recondite intention of Britain towards the obliteration of slavery and the extirpation of the economical dependency on slavery. It is of noteworthy significance that slavery was sustained and defended by the state and churches through the culture of the people. They sought even theological and moral justifications for slavery. There can be no separation of slavery from the history of Britain; they are indeed inseparable, because of the economic, political and religious propinquity between slavery, sugar, African free labour, oppression, exploitation, suffering, poverty and the massive underdevelopment of African and the development economically of Britain, Europe and the USA. Both Eric Williams and Dr. Richard Hart agreed by symbiotically postulating the relevance, importance and historical fact that there is a profound one-sidedness between the slave trade production and distribution of sugar from the Caribbean which supported the financial development of the technological innovations of the industrial revolution. It is from this economic development that the British economy became so powerful.

The legal abolition of slavery 1807 and 1808 was not a complete termination of the economic, cultural, sociological, and political and educational cancer of the slave trade. The ineffectuation of the abolition created the avenues for the immoral and inimical continuation of this heinous crime of slavery of African and African descendants.

The great hesitation and reluctance to adhere fully to the abolition movement was rather the commission of slavery as imperative for the West, Europe and Britain. The slave trade was definitely sociologically, economically, politically, genealogically, morally and theologically repugnant.

They were contiguous companions involved in the Atlantic Slave Trade and its dependents; the companion of the churches and their theology, economic and underdevelopment.

Africans were perceived as beasts of burden and that God had created them for whites to impart salvation to them. We see pellucidly why religion and European Cultural Christianity has always been a religious culture used to justify the dehumanisation of Africans. European Cultural Christianity was transfused psychologically and spiritually through the capitalist injection and infusion by a cultural brainwashing of Africans that poverty and suffering was cosmologically ordained for Africans in order for them to achieve redemption and milk and honey in heaven. Heaven was presented as a future hope and promise for the oppressed while white slave masters, the British, Europe and the USA were building and enjoying the material heaven here on earth. The teleos of the brainwashing of Africans was that black people have become spiritually intoxicated but economically and politically redundant.

Heaven was presented as future hope and promise for the oppressed enslaved Africans whilst the British and the Americans and Europeans were building and enjoying the material heaven here on earth. The teleos of the brainwashing of Africans is that black people have become the consequence of the legacy of the brainwashing process, spiritually intoxicated to this day and socio-economically and politically redundant and impuissant sociologically and technologically. Hugh Thomas kindly listed for us that the Prime Minister Lord Grenville and Thomas Erskine there was enormous debate in the House of Parliament and the Lower House to abolish slavery. A motion in favour of abolition was carried in both houses by 114 to 15 in the Commons and 41 to 20 in the Lords. The Act was quickly passed for enactment after August 1807 that no new ships should be employed in the slave trade. Hugh Thomas says "Grenville as Prime Minister felt in January 1807 by a most curious chance the same month as the congress of the United States took a similar step, to introduce a bill for full abolition in the Lords. This stated that the trade was contrary to the principles of justice, humanity and sound policy. Grenville spoke of the trade as not only detestable but criminal. To understand the intention and the motive of Grenville and the US we have to analyse the words of Grenville where he argued that abolition was necessary to ensure the survival of the whole of the Caribbean colonies "Are they not now distressed by accumulation of produce on their hands, for which they cannot find a market?" To elucidate and to apply a hermeneutical approach it must be said that the words of Grenville and others though pious and priggish in appearance the undercurrent was not a spontaneous moral crusader drive for the abolition of slavery. Abolition of slavery came about by the historical facts that the accumulation of produce from the slave colonies were both in abundance and inundation and could create enormous dissipation, because the slave trade was in decline and produce from the slave colonies were also in poor and limited demand. These two causes were not the fundamental reasons as I had stated elsewhere backed by competent scholars that it was the revolution in Haiti that saw the castigation and pulverisation of the French, the Spaniards and the British and the fear that such revolution was about to become pandemic culminating with the volume of rebellions, conspiracies and insurrections of the slaves in the West Indies. It was these culminated factors that precipitated the abolition of slavery. It is to be acknowledged and to be reiterated again that Dr. Moses D. E. Nwulia in his impressive pedantic book 'Britain and Slavery in East Africa', he made the substantive point that Britain did not abolish slavery as perceived and promulgated for humanitarianism reasons.

Indeed after August 1807 Britain, France, Spain and others escalated slavery in the slave colonies. Slavery only came to an end through the effective measures of the slaves themselves in procuring emancipation. Chronology is of vital importance. A heinous crime of repugnancy and magnitude such as the Atlantic Slave Trade Middle Passage, Transatlantic Crossing, the enslavement of Africans for 400 years. The gravity of this injustice, oppression and exploitation unprovoked by the Africans and executed by the Dutch, French, Germans, Spaniards and British all in the name of religion. All in the name of Christianity. The question therefore is even more pertinent. How could the abolition of slavery have various dates? For some it was March 7th 1807. For some other scholars it was August 1807. Others 1835, 1862, 1865 the dates are not concrete. We need to remind ourselves of what Hugh Thomas has said in his book 'The Slave Trade', "All Christian denominations were involved in the slave trade. But usually the dominating religion of the Port concerned decided the religious complexion of the merchants". In Liverpool, London, and Bristol, for instance, most slave merchants were Anglicans. In Nantes, Bordeaux, Lisbon and Seville and of course in Bahia and Luanda most were Roman Catholics, not to mention the Calvinists. Adge to these denominations were the Quakers and their Friends. The Quakers were important in the slave trade in the 18th century, especially in Newport where the Wanton family was still trading slaves in the 1760s. The Quakers also had their own gun factory in Birmingham. It is therefore not all that praiseworthy that the Quakers were active in the abolition movement of slavery. Was it a moral conversion or was it a sense of moral regeneration?

The complexities, conscious cultural and political perfidiousness of Governments, individuals and the churches, with social prevarications are historical facts that the abolition of slavery was not immediately effective. After 1807 and 1808 the Abolition of the slave trade was not founded on well intentioned moral, racial, economical and religious grounds.

Philosophically, abolition was a composition of complex confusions. It was insincere in the first instance and ambiguous. In the language of liberation theology, after the legal dates, the struggles for emancipation began. It was this struggle for real emancipation that now veered the attention. The Genesis of emancipation started with the continuation of slavery after the abolition act. Britain was always the chief sinner or chief of sinners. Britain escalated the slave trade. They expanded the slave trade. They moved the slave trade into "top gear".

I began with the temerities and audacious assumption that it was the slaves who procured their manumission. Manumission was not manufactured and disseminated by the British, Europeans, Americans and others. After the legal prohibition of the slave trade by the British Government, over one million slaves were imported into the Island of Jamaica alone. The slave trade had continued unabatedly after 1808, as it had been throughout the Atlantic Trade. Approximately 2,000 to 3,000 slaves per year says Hugh Thomas. The number of slaves of African descendants in 1922 actually doubled. Adam Smith's contention was in the wealth of numerous works, the uneconomic source of the slave trade with others of incorrigible propensity did not agree with Smith.

The slave population of Brazil was still staggering in 1817. African slaves were about 4 million in 1817. Cuba was very high on the list of slave population explosion. When the slave trade was abolished the number of slaves in Jamaica alone was approximately 361,657, but this is not to overlook the contributions of David Hartley in 1776. The Quakers and Grenville Sharp's vision and struggle for abolition. In 1796 William Wilberforce was astonishingly successful in getting his bill through Parliament.

The abolition movement drove home the brutality, dehumanisation, sufferings and the ethical, moral and social repugnancy of the trade that after the abolition the condition of the slaves did not change one iota. Thomas Clarkson and Olaudah Equiano travelled and perambulated the country, gathering reports, testimonies and facts in relation to the brutality of the slave trade. The practice continued because they changed terminologies in relation to the abolition movement and slavery. The concrete sitz im leben remained untouched. It has been said that the slaves were comfortably better off under slavery than after Abolition and emancipation. We once again look at the works of Dr. Richard Hart volumes 1 and 2. First there is no evidence that African slaves accepted slavery. The Anglican Church debated the theological justification for slavery. The major denominations proclaimed and were used for economical and political reasons to extend the slave trade especially for the economy of Britain, the expansion of Britain and Britain's control of the colonies.

The final immortal testimony of the immortal prodigious slave Sam Sharpe before he met his death with a degree of audacity which paralleled Socrates' approach to death by the stake. "I would rather die upon yonder gallows than to live as a slave". On 23 May 1832 at the tender age of 31 years Sam Sharpe was hanged. Another slave Cudjoe, also uttered the immortal words "I would rather die than to be a slave because nature made me to be free". Nature here is a deep spiritual ontological concept of the African Supreme Being manifesting its divine power in the cosmos. Nature is a feeling of the God who is present in the deep within. This God is the source and substance of life. The inner cry for manumission is the cosmos mind. Ontostheos culminating in the logos anthropos. Jesus who became the Christ of the black struggles and experience.

In deciding a critique and black hermeneutical enlightenment to the abolition and the emancipation we should never over praise William Wilberforce with any hyperbolical dressing for his historical appearance. Wilberforce as a conservative who used the abolition movement to further his political status and career. It is an important argument that while Wilberforce was gesticulating and verbalising the evilness of the slave trade and the wicked conditions of African slaves, he did not articulate any objection to child slavery in Britain with children sweeping the chimneys. Equally important is that Wilberforce was a sexist in that he strongly opposed to women participating in the publicity and position to the continuation of the abolition of slavery. Was Wilberforce moved by the power of compassion, love, kindness or a quest for justice? "Suffer the little children to come unto me" says Jesus.

Here is a gigantic paradox of perfidiousness, ambiguity and political dishonesty. Wilberforce had no time politically for the suffering children and human inequality with women. Yes, it is good that Wilberforce was a champion for the abolition but it does not make a rational sense. It has no cultural or religious rectitude. Wilberforce was like many others, especially those attached to the churches and the cultural so-called Christianity in deeds and practice without any morality or religious conduct. Religious virtues, concepts, beliefs and customs of universal brotherhood embracing the African slaves. The slave traders, the abolition of slavery, the emancipation of the slaves, the conspiracies, the rebellions the insurrections are all inseparable of the slaves whose groans and cries touched the inner being of the cosmic mind - God.

The gravitations of the power of sugar and the plantation slave society and the perpetuation of the plantation acts on economic greed was an awesome philosophy.

The chronological dates of 1807 and 1808 are significant. Abolition did not guarantee freedom for the slaves. Abolition had no teeth. Abolition never meant the immediate termination of the malignant cancer of slavery. The continuation of slavery was rampant throughout the colonies of the West Indies, Brazil and Cuba. The termination of slavery came about because of:

(a) slave rebellions and insurrections;
(b) slavery became increasingly uneconomical as a result of the slave resistance;
(c) the financial power generated from sugar and the germination and development of the industrial revolution made the trade uneconomical.

Elizabeth Halcrow in her book 'Canes *and Chains: a Study of Sugar and Slavery* says "From the evidence available, one may argue that it was the decline of the plantation system which helped to create a situation in which it became possible at least to end both the slave trade and slavery. Halcrow's thesis is persuasive but not convincing. Rather it was the "ontological freedom" of the Supreme Being, God created in man who inspired the slaves as clearly stated by Gad Heuman, *'The Killing Time - The Morant Bay Rebellion in Jamaica'*. Manumission was delineated in the various rebellions of the slaves and the Maroons. In the context of the plantation sugar slavery which was the foundation cornerstone of the economic basis for Britain and Europe. It was the slaves who through resistance and rebellions forced the end of slavery and finally emancipation.

It is a basic myth of the highest historical deception and mendacity with ineptness that abolition gave the slaves manumission. Abolition made the trade illegal but not the final termination of slavery. It is well documented in journals, periodicals, logs, schedules etc. that the names of those distinguished and undistinguished names of people who participated in the abolition process. We note with interest that the majority of these nobles and ignobles are in the main whites.

As always, sociologically, nobility is tantamount to whiteness and degradation sociologically related to blacks. It is both germane and appropriate that appreciation should be delineated to the prodigious slaves named and unnamed who God raised up to sacrifice their lives for the manumission of their African brothers and sisters who had been enslaved by a system founded on a philosophy of economic prosperity and the concept of a white master race called the British and the Europeans.

The methodology used to generate economical wealth was rapacious exploitations, oppression and dehumanisation of Africans through the churches' active involvement and participation in the Atlantic slave trade.

Men of anthropological inspiration such as Paul Bogle, Sam Sharpe, and Cudjoe were the 'Moses' of the sugar plantation slave trade. The measure of human suffering cannot be measured or estimated by any chronological means, conferences, committees, delegations or political eloquence. Rather it is measured by the sacrifice of the lives of slave men, women and children. The choice of death rather than slavery. The choice of manumission to enslavement. Human dignity rather than dehumanisation.

Paradoxically there are two sides to any situation. Emancipation was physical and economical. Labour for proper pay. Emancipation was psychological. Enslavement of the mind is still crippling. It is still strangulation of the whole personality, individually and collectively. Psychological emancipation is still a good distance away. Malcolm X's words are still a constant reminder "Liberate our minds".

Africans and African descendants are bodily free but mentally, psychologically, spiritually, economically and politically enslaved.

With political independence, the African diaspora of people are still not free. The slave syndrome and amnesia are truncative. Forces which are responsible for handicapping of the African race of people. I shall expatiate further on these two forces towards the end of this thesis.

Slavery was made illegal in 1807 and 1808 it is said in Britain and America. It was made to the detriment of the enslaved in the major plantations such as Jamaica, Cuba, Barbados and Brazil There was for the slaves, a tremendous dichotomy and ambivalence. Should they remain slaves sempiternally or surrender to the forces of the most degraded act on the pages of man's history? Black slaves chose through their religious convictions anthropological gift of freedom decided to eradicate slavery and to symbiotically move towards their liberation through rebellions and collective resistance. My thesis here is founded on the record in evidence of the plantation rebellions articulated by Dr. Richard Hart. It was the slave rebellions, insurrections and conspiracies along with the successful rebellion of the Maroons which led the British government to recognise the Maroons as a community with their own rights. The slaves' quest for emancipation was a very costly one. The Morant Bay rebellion in 1865 saw the death of its dynamic leader Paul Bogle.

Chapter 17
Effective Or Ineffective

Abolition and Emancipation

Abolition made the practice of slavery in the colonies illegal. Not on moral grounds, compassionate or humanitarian grounds, although the pretence was on humanitarian grounds by the British this turned out under critical heuristic research not to be so. The British ostentated without reservations their political, social and economical recalcitrancy to the Abolition of Slavery. Indeed, the bills presented to Parliament by William Wilberforce were faced with tremendous oppositions from the lobby from powerful members of parliament, the Government, Royals and merchants who were involved in the slave trade.

I have illustrated already the hypocrisy, reconditeness and perfidiousness of the British attitude towards slavery. The British delineated on the one hand the hesitant willingness, but then on the other hand, they delineated the recondite with poison, viciousness, mental, social, political and religious arrogance and a cultural philosophy of ethnocentric superiority.

Eric Williams in Chapter 5 of his book 'British Historians and the West Indies' declared, "Looking at Stubbs, Freeman, Macauley, Acton and Corlyee, if the barons of the Magna Carta were laying the foundations of Parliamentary democracy and the world was everyday getting better and better obviously, the struggle for abolition of negro slavery was merely part of the same general movement towards democracy and the abolition of special privilege and evil in general". If history was only the true demarcation of religion, if God was everywhere in history then obviously, the abolition of negro slavery was God's work. Williams here is taking a strong cosmological, sotereological and ubiquitous approach to God but at the same time Williams had no place for a pantheistic approach to God, not even philosophical. Dr. Williams has not failed to utilise the slave trade and abolition with an important word "remembrance".

In the 18th century, Britain with the opulence and economic wealth was conspicuous, and it was achieved from what Dr. Williams called the "Trinity":

1. Slaving
2. Slavery
3. Sugar

Although abolition was in 1807 and 1808 for America the final chapter for African slaves' termination was emancipation in 1838, chronologically over 30 years after the slave trade was proclaimed illegal. Abolition was not euphonious to the slaves because contextually, their conditions deteriorated. The real euphonious news in 1838 at the sound of emancipation day, the arrival of emancipation came from the struggles of the slaves themselves and not from any conscience, socially, culturally, politically and economically good for the white slave masters and the white establishments. Nor was emancipation effectuated by a white willingness "No, it was the struggles and rebellions which made efficacious emancipation.

My hermeneutic of abolition and emancipation is that British, European American abolition was made consciously dysfunctional and ineffective for economic and political domination. Hermeneutically therefore taking the whole spectrum and arguments for and against abolition it is reasonable without any black apologetic to say categorically abolition was definitely dysfunctional. It was impavid. It was people like Sam Sharpe, Nat Turner, Cudjoe, Paul Bogle and Kunta Kinte, who were replicated in the dysteleology of abolition into a fresh dimension of emancipation by the sacrifice of their lives and the inspiration of the Supreme Being of the African cosmology and epistemology of the binding guidance and persons of the God who suffers within the experience of the enslaved African slaves across the Atlantic, Middle Passage to the plantations in the West Indies.

In 1807 it was the prohibition of slavery, it was not abolition but the significant thing to remember and to acknowledge is that abolition or the prohibition of slavery was never based on humanitarianism, justice, morality, religious conviction, respect for human life, compassion, economic and political extrication of the slaves. Manumission for the slaves was never the economic, political, human, theological, moral, social or divine plan on the agenda or intentions of Britain, Europe and America. Even after emancipation, they continued never to regard the slaves or black people as having any value apart from their oppressed free labour as slaves for the extension, development and power of the master race - the white man.

Lord Scott remarked when abolition was introduced to him "Slavery is an economic necessity for the economy of Britain and Europe". Queen Elizabeth I remarked when told of John Hawkins' inhumanity and brutality of the slaves, "God will punish him", yet she had no moral, spiritual or theological hesitation in investing her money in the Atlantic Slave Trade. She gave John Hawkins her personal ship and the name of her ship was "Jesus", to guarantee maximum exploitation of African goods and slaves.

The conditions and brutality of the Atlantic Slave Trade Middle Passage and the addendum condition of the plantations in the West Indies, Brazil, Cuba and elsewhere makes it pellucid that prohibition and abolition were not grounded on moral or religious grounds, but rather because of the harms and physical struggles of the slaves with the result that these insurrections, slave rebellions and the slaves' consciousness that they symbiotically had the power to change the course of history and to rewrite history with their lives.

The Haitian revolution had impacted tremendously on France, Spain and Britain. The slaves were in greater numbers than their enslavers.

The rebellions were powerful. It will suffice for now without extra expatiation until later in this book that the rebellions caused much deaths to the whites. It was the end result which motivated the slaves to mentally extricate themselves and to use the power God gave them to reach out for positive and liberating experiences of the true meaning of a belief in the cosmic Supreme Intelligence, namely God. Whites were being killed daily. In retaliation the multiplication were proportionately staggering. The whites were limited, especially with the choice they were allowed to use for special occasions.

In these rebellions the death of 50 white men was equivalent to the death of 1,000 black slaves in retaliation. I am making now this bold statement that it was the slaves who through their rebellions, conspiracies and insurrections, are the ones who made these concrete audacious sacrificial measures. It was the slaves who made the slave owners' power over them become limited and sometimes impossible to deal with. It was this reality that prompted the anti-slavery movement in Britain. The Maroon wars were a significant situation and experience. Powerful impavid slave leaders, the killing of the whites, the destructions of houses and plantations were the driving force that brought about abolition. It was not a moral crusade, it was not a moral metanoia, it was not a moral consciousness, it was not even humanitarianism, it was the sheer force and power of the slaves. They moved towards their own freedom from the bondage of slavery and oppression.

I reiterate, abolition was not due to love by Europe, Britain and America. Endemic and congenical racism cannot be extirpated in the flesh. One needs only to look and to see that continuation of oppression and racism after the abolition of slavery things became worse for the slaves. They still had no rights, no protection, there was no compensation made to the slaves for 400 years of slavery. Whilst the economies of Britain, Europe and America were in a state of opulence and the inundation with economic wealth and power. In the USA especially in the South, the condition of the blacks of African descendants was greater than during the slave trade itself. In other words, the conditions for blacks after the abolition of slavery were in many instances worse than during slavery itself. Books such as '100 years of Lynching' by Ralph Ginzburg 'Breaking the curse of Willy Lynch' and 'The Science of Slave Psychology' by Alvin Morrow, 'Return to Glory' by Joel A. Freeman and Don B Griffin. Richard Hart's books 'Slaves who Abolished Slavery Volumes I and II', 'Blacks in Rebellion', these books are informative tabulated books that shed tremendous light on the abolition movement and who in concrete reality brought about the abolition of slavery. It was not Britain, Europe or the Americas, it was the slaves themselves. This truth had been kept recondite by the majority of British, European and American historians.

Dr. Richard Hart has accounted and articulated in his books how the slaves made the painful journey from oppression, slavery, dehumanisation and lack of human rights, their dignity was taken from them. The journey was painful to manumission. Through rebellions, and making the plantation economy ineffective to the glorious day of emancipation. Emancipation in reality was and is comprehensively different from abolition. 'Caribbean Slave Society and Economy' - A Student Reader' by Hilary Buckles and Vereen Shepherd. I cannot accept that a people and their culture that has been endemically racist, oppressive, perfidious and mendacious could overnight think of black people with mercy, compassion and the attempt to justify the hostility and brutal treatment of the slaves. It is a big moral and social mendacity for any continuation that abolition was made spontaneously. Mendacities have always been the methodology used by the British first, then the Europeans and lastly the Americans, to cover their immoral deeds of African slavery, the enslavement of the black race. Malcolm X is abundantly clear and correct when he said emphatically, "To know the Christians and Christianity one should just look at the deeds of Christians and Christianity".

CHAPTER 18
EVALUATION OF SLAVERY

Evolution of Prohibition/Abolition/Emancipation
The history and impact of the slave trade on African and African descendants cannot be ignored by historians, anthropologists, theologians and sociologists. Some scholars especially historians, politicians and theologians may find the slave trade chronological records uncomfortable both from a cultural, racial and sociological perspective. As I have laudated proto that scholarship must delineate rectitude and veracity, if it is to educate, enlighten and liberate the psyche. It would be like the black young woman dramatised by Miss X who consistently denied her blackness, but rather preferred to see herself as white, she even denied her black mother to be her biological mother, but when confronted by the death of her black biological mother's death which was psychologically precipitated by her rejection of her biological mother, the biological and physical facts which convinced her to live a life of denial was now at an end because it allowed her that illusion, deception, and ignorance to strangulate her freedom to her natural existence. Abolition and emancipation are indeed inseparable twins in the chronology of man's history. As Professor Moses I. Finley succinctly said "The President of the United States, Bill Clinton was challenged to issue an apology for slavery to the people of Africa, noting the role of European and Americans who had profited from the fruits of the slave trade, the

call was for an apology for the historical fact of slavery. To further document the historical facts of slavery we need to remind ourselves of what Dr. Finley says. "Even the founding fathers themselves have been made the subject of close scrutiny and revision in their roles as slave holders". George Washington's name on public schools has been made the object of a modern day Damanatio Menoriae said by Dr. Finley. Thomas Jefferson's hypocrisies covering a slave mistress Sally Hemming have been judicially investigated. In 1820 Thomas Jefferson in contemplating the current debate wrote to his friend John Holmes these words, "This cessation of that kind of property for so it is mistaken, is bagatelle which would not cost me a second thought, if in that way a general emancipation and expatiation could be effected, and gradually with due sacrifice I think it might be. But as it is, we have a wolf by years and we can neither hold him, nor safely let him go. Justice is in one scale and self preservation in the other". In order to make the point clear, two things we must tabulate:

1. That the historical founding fathers of the USA were themselves slave owners and dealers;
2. The great Thomas Jefferson President of the USA, his mistress was a black slave. He himself had his own slaves. He himself invested in the slave trade. There were tremendous discussions concerning the circumvention of the slave trade in the West Indies and also in Africa. There were three suggested arguments or solutions and these were: (i) prohibition; (ii) abolition; (iii) emancipation. It is imperative for us to recognise that the plantation slave societies came basically from the Atlantic Slave Trade. There were no moral, religious or ethical paradosis to slavery. But rather, the underpinning force was the economic philosophy which made Britain, Europe and America prosperous. To extricate themselves from this economic prosperity at the expense of free black labour, without conscience, morality, ethical responsibility or with theological justification it made the challenge and final termination impossible or complexed. Another way of looking at it is that British and European slave trade reveal the sharpest path of what the ambiguity inherent in slavery, the reduction of human beings to the

category of property. It also reveals for us the dialectics of the majority.

I very often wonder how the British, European and Americans used European Cultural Christianity and the bible to indoctrinate Africans to accept poverty, suffering, cattle ships in exchange for milk and honey in the hereafter. Why then I ask, did they the oppressors and exploiters not accept poverty and suffering for milk and honey in the hereafter? Rather Africa and all black countries are economically poor and socio-politically impuissant, some without good education, medicine, infrastructure and general facilities for a healthy society and environment. This is because of the consequence and the legacy of the Atlantic Slave Trade.

The pandemicism of Aids and HIV in Africa is rampant. It is a global disease facing humanity, but with Africa's economic, political situation the West, Britain and Europe seem to don't care a damn about Africa from which Britain, Europe and America built their economic foundations. Abolition was the political subject of Britain, Europe and America from the 17th to 18th centuries. The stages are many but what is undeniable, is the tremendous contributions of Thomas Clarkson, Grenville Sharpe and the few other fateful ones, their places are inscribed on the front pages of history.

The problematic situation is the abolition movement which was ineffective. Abolition did not constitute immediate removal of the British, European and American cancer from the African people's experience of slavery. Indeed, in some quarters it was the reverse, the increased power and control of the slave trade. Economic and social conditions had not changed for the slaves' perpetual oppression, exploitation and injustice was the unabated existence for the slaves.

The slaves with impavid spirit and courage took upon themselves the human struggles for their own freedom through rebellions and insurrections. Abolition was only a precursor to emancipation. It was achieved by the sacrifice of black slaves, especially the plantation slaves. Slaves who exercised their ontological innate freedom created by the cosmic Supreme Being, namely Almighty God. It was the freedom that the Atlantic slave traders and European cultural missionary Christianity used to truncate the will and the spirit of Africans.

Slavery was the diabolical denial of African peoples' freedom. The freedom created by God. It was the denial of Africans' humanity, personality, soulfulness, somebodiness, the denial that Africans were created in the image of God with the potential to become in the likeness of God through Jesus Christ.

Philosophically, theologically or anthropologically African slaves were biblically and historically Adams' children with an immortal soul. According to Socrates the European, British and American Cultural Christianity through slavery pronounced condemnation to the slaves. Slaves were only expendable property. The solidarity of Jesus Christ with the black experience in the slave trade episode. It is that profound experience which was like a volcano which emerged from the deep within which thundered out in the immortal words of Cudjoe, the Maroon slave leader "I'd rather die on yonder gallows than to be a slave, because nature (God) made me to be free".

CHAPTER 19
SLAVES' STRUGGLES

Struggle for Emancipation

Dr. Moses I. Finley says, "The first wish of a slave was to be free". This freedom is innate in man's nature. Freedom is God's gift to all creatures. It is part of the immutable human nature to be free. The culture of domination and superiority is a deep psychological and cultural sickness which historically and contemporarily is evident or rather is endemic in the British, European and American cultures. In the book 'The Myth Of Christian Uniqueness', Professor John Hick and Paul F. Knitter, Raimundo Panikkar says "Christians must recognise that they cannot and should not conquer the world because they represent only one phylum in human history and thus should not claim the universality of being the only true religion or race". This is pertinent and applicable especially to Britain, Europe and America.

The Europeanisation of Christianity was purely for political, economical and racial reasons. It had nothing to do with African prosperity, development and freedom. It was the oppressed, enslaved, exploited and subjudication of African people for the economic philosophy of superiority, the master race and domination of the world by Britain, Europe and America. The philosophy rather than theology to Christianise the world; that is the black race, was not for moralisation or spiritualization of the slaves but its dynamic purpose was to achieve total mental and psychological control of the slaves' minds namely Africans and the African descendants - black people. It is an audacious presumption and postulation of historical facts that abolition was not manumission for the slaves or the extirpation of the slave system and European philosophy. Abolition was not even an authentic intention. Another approach or perspective is that abolition was not manumission. Emancipation was manumission for the slaves and it was achieved by the struggles of the slaves' themselves and never because of Britain, Europe and America. Emancipation was the outcome of black power. It was the black power movement of Haiti which inspired the slaves in other slave environments and conditions which acted as a physical, psychological and mental dynamo which charged philosophically the battery of freedom to all enslaved people. It was this emancipation, struggle, death and sufferings that I want to stipulate some valid attention and energy.

Before I do this, I must confess that it is not very often I get the time to read a book from beginning to end. I have done so with Dr. Moses I. Finley's book 'Ancient Slavery and Modern Idealism'. His book is both radical and provocative. Some observations from his book are pertinent to my thesis. For example, on slavery and historians, Dr. Finley says the popular defence among the Portuguese for their leading part in the African slave trade was that by enslaving Africans they saved their body and soul. They saved their bodies from being eaten by cannibals and they saved their souls by baptising them. This hermeneutically was the most barbaric culture of European Cultural Christianity. Dr. Finley is implicitly agreeing that religion was also most important as a factor in the slave system. Finley delineated his hermeneutical jejuness and cultural vacuousness in his own statement, "The greatest of the revolts, which has become legendary. Nat Turner's rebellion of 1831 was a purely local affair of slave insurrection involving only a few hundred men and a mere three days of actual fighting. In 1912 rebellion American slavery reduced its place both in number and in harshness". Finley added his scholastic insult to Panikkar in the midst of Christian uniqueness which he called "The True Martyrs" the slaves for it is also a fact that for most of history, the exploited have done little to change their condition. Neither slavery or serfdom for instance, was ever abolished through the action of slaves". The few great slave revolts and jacqueries were moving and dynamic.

On emancipation my thesis was impetuous in that it was the slave rebellions and insurrections which brought about their emancipation because Britain did not authentically intend for abolition to consummate manumission for the slaves.

Finley in denying the dynamic power and impavid sacrifice of black slaves for their lives for emancipation was only looking at the slave societies of colonial Greece, Italy and Sicily but not Brazil, the Caribbean colonies and the southern states of the United States of America.

It was not only Finley who practiced a racial cultural scholarship, a pedantic scholarship, but equally Dr. Martin Niesson, the most reputed student of ancient religion of our time, who managed to produce a bloodless 1,500 page synthesis of Greek religion in which the word slave is absent from the index. In addition to Finley, the universally acknowledged leading ancient historian of the 20th century Edward Meyer, he insists that the Greeks and Romans had a mild form of slavery. Henry Wallon was a pious Catholic and he had compassion and sympathy only with the abolitionists movement because for him slavery was unchristian but says Finley, slavery denigrated and corrupted the slaves and the masters alike.

Dr. Eric Williams took a radical and different opine, when he concluded in his book 'Capitalism and Slavery', that slavery was not borne of racism but rather racism was a consequence of slavery.

African slaves suffered the totality of subjection, powerless and loss of rightness. With this degree of powerlessness and the reduction of human beings to cattle this was an incredible behaviour of the British, Europeans and Americans. It does resurrect the recognition that American slaves, north and south and the plantation slaves in the West Indies were forcefully uprooted. What then were the demographic, economic, social and political effects of the Atlantic Slave Trade on Africa? On the effects of Africans who remained behind? Whilst there are several scholars namely historians who are consistent scholars who argued that the slave trade was the key to the underdevelopment of Africa. Dr. Walter Rodney in his famous book 'How Europe Underdeveloped Africa', for Dr. Walter Rodney it was a massive underdevelopment economically, and with the forced enslavement of Africans.

Chapter 20
The Quest For Freedom

Emancipation

As a student of Philosophy of Religion, I was taught by two British philosophers that St. Augustine was a European. Later when I became a lecturer for Birbeck College, University of London, I discovered for myself through doctorate research that St. Augustine 354 to 430 was indeed an African. An African scholar of unmatchable academic eminence by any European standard. At one of my lectures on Liberation theology, I mentioned that St. Augustine was an African. I was immediately challenged by one of my English white students who was at the time a principal of a college. He claimed that I was wrong. The following week he came to my lecture and apologised to me for his audacity and academic stupidity. The significant point is that some white or Caucasian scholars deliberately teach mendacities especially in relation to prodigious black people or black paradigms. Contributions of black people are not often recognised regardless of the academic discipline.

Dr. David Bryan Davis in the fantastic collection of essays in the scholarly book 'Slavery, Colonialism and Racism', articulated the reconditeness of prodigious black people much better than I. For Dr. Davis, Thomas Erskine's approach helped to confine slavery to a marginal place in a curriculum. For example, a course on the history of religion in America never touched on the slaves' religion or on the religious controversies over slavery. "We simply took note of the dates when the major protestant denominations had divided along sectional lines. At best, slavery could be perceived as a variant on the history of immigration and ethnic conflict. After preparing for my PhD, in 1954 I remained totally ignorant of the works of such black historians as W. E. B. Dubois, later Woodson Charles, H. Wesley, Benjamin Quarles, Eric Williams, CLR James and John Hope Franklin".

There has been in my opinion scholarly dishonesty, which deliberately sought to isolate, invalidate and to make recondite the slaves' contributions for their own emancipation. Dr. Finley eloquently stated that the slaves played no part in their emancipation process.

Thanks sempiternally and abundantly to Dr. Richard Hart for his books on 'Abolition and Emancipation', 'Slaves who abolished Slavery Volumes I and II', 'The Abolition of Slavery and from Occupation to Independent'. A synopsis and tabulation of slavery, abolition and emancipation is significant. Dr. Sydney Mintz in the book 'Slavery, Colonialism and Racism' under the Caribbean region has provided us with a good outline. Dr. Mintz says, "Fernando Isabel's, when mentioning a shipment of 17 African slaves to Santa Domingo in 1505 declared a need for 100 more in order that all of these begetting gold for me". It was not until 1886 more than 380 years later that slavery was finally abolished in Cuba. Thus ending it for all time in the Antilles. Denmark illegalised the trade in 1802, England in 1807, America in 1808, Sweden in 1813, France in 1814 and Spain in 1820, but the illegal trade continued at least until 1860s and are freed but contracted African labours were also imported during much of the 19th century. Emancipation was accepted as reluctantly as the end of the trade had been. In 1838 in the British colonies, 1848 in the French colonies, 1863 in the Dutch colonies, 1873 in Puerto Rico and 1886 in Cuba.

Though most abolitionists frequently argued on principle, the complaints of the planters always originated in the warrant of labour; the concept of inferiority of the slaves was an embellishment for more basic arguments at every stage. Slavery was defended because it was first of all profitable, and only thereafter because it was rationalised and benign. Dr. E. J. Alagoa on Colonial Experience says, "Europeans sought to maintain control over Africans not only through technology but also through moral and psychological defeatism. Their view of Africans grew out of the traders accounts and fables of the slave trader's era compounded by the missionary propaganda and the racial theories of the 19th century.

Richard Hart has provided us with a comprehensive chronological synthesis of the various contributions of individual slaves and groups of slaves who cooperated in solidarity with the struggles for emancipation. His works on the subject has illustriousness both in contents and scholarship with rectitude. To Dr. Hart's contribution I now turn my attention to the question and situation in hand. There can be no critique of his writings but rather laudations and appreciations for what he has generously provided for us.

Most historians writing on the Atlantic Slave trade paid very little attention to the abolition movement and the abolition of the slave trade. They acknowledge the contributions of William Wilberforce, Thomas Clarkson, the Quakers and occasionally Granville Sharpe and the anti-slavery movement which was prompted by the slaves' rebellions, revolts and insurrections by symbiotic relationships with the Maroon wars.

Almost all white historians have consciously or unconsciously, it seems, ignored the power of the collective solidarity of the power of the plantation slaves in bringing about their emancipation and nothing historically to do with the abolition of the slave trade by Britain, France, Germany, Holland, Sweden and the USA.

We are forced by the gravity of the evidence and historical importance to acknowledge the functions of these groups and individuals by black slaves in achieving their ontological inner cry for manumission. Dr. Hart says, "Although a majority of those enslaved may have felt that there was no alternative to them adopting themselves to their situation everywhere, always there were substantial minorities who were unwilling to do so". Resistance was offered in many ways:
1. The inducement of abortions by some women to ensure that they did not bear children enslaved from birth;
2. By eating dirt;
3. Some groups of slaves extricated temporarily;

4. Mass escape, rebellion or conspiracies to gorilla warfare.

By 1657 and 1660 in Barbados there was the engagement of slaves involved in rebellious and runaway business for the Negroes. A great conspiracy in 1675 resulted in the dynamic leader Kofi (Cuffeo) and 51 comrades being sentenced to death. The manner in which they were killed is important to us:
1. Six were buried alive;
2. Eleven were beheaded;
3. Five awaiting trial took their own lives.

After the Spaniards were repudiated from Jamaica in 1660, slaves who had escaped before and during the fighting, re-established their own re-enslavement settlement. One of the leaders was Lubola. Sambo in 1692 tried a revolt, but it was dissipated immediately. From this encounter 92 conspirators were executed, four were castrated and 14 died in prison. In 1739 the first Maroon war lasted 10 years and a peace treaty which gave to the Maroons freedom and lands. The Maroon town was also given. In 1760 two major slave rebellions in Jamaica were suppressed. These rebellion were motivated by Tacky who was later killed by a Maroon. 400 were executed and 600 were transported from slavery for log cutting in the Bay of Andorra. In 1763 a tremendous national liberation struggle began. It was profoundly a time of great struggles. Rather than struggle for nothing Kofi committed suicide. These dates are significant in the slave struggle for emancipation. In Montserrat in 1768, 1770, in St. Kitts and in Tobago slaves rebellions were aggressively supported in 1770, 1771 and also 1774.

The New River rebellion is equally of significant delineation of the slave rebellion in 1765. In 1768 a memorial from a London businessman recorded the following:

"Matters are coming to this miserable past, but 23 British negroes armed had gone off from the New River to the Spaniards, and many more were expected to follow them, so that business of every kind was at a dead stand". All the slaves' rebellions had their impacts. Some of them were modicum rebellions and others were great. One of the most formidable slave rebellion was at the Bay of Honduras settlement in 1773 on the Belize River.

The vicissitude of the slave struggles was impressive. It is also significantly worthy to record that many British escaping slaves when freed by the Spaniards, once they profess their conversion to the Roman Catholic Church were protected by the Spanish refusing to return them. In 1776 a remarkable uprising in Westmoreland in Jamaica was also dissipated. 30 of the rising leaders were executed. In 1785 the Maroons had established so many free settlements that they had become a serious threat to many, many of the plantation owners and the government in many areas.

Balla was one of the most formidable slave leaders. Maroons from the Balla camp plundered the plantations and thereby brought about their dissipation by the Maroons and the settlement of a 500 strong military force were also engaged. In January 1791 a major slave rebellion commenced at Grand Bay in Jamaica, the leader of this rebellion was a man called Louis Polinoire, a freed mulatto in Martinique.

Major Events and Rebellions

Polinoire in 1791 carried out a tremendous condemnation whilst the macabre sentence was being carried out. Namely that he be disembodied and cut into four quarters. In 1795 Mr Julian Febdon a mulatto plantation owner in Grenada freed his own slaves and organised an army consisting of poor French residents and freed the slaves to drive out the British out of Grenada. Many other slaves joined the rebellion. The defeat of Febdon came when the British reinforcement arrived. There had been social and political vicissitudes between the black Caribs of St. Vincent and the British. The hostilities were great and lasted 5 months and in 1773 a treaty was reached. The black Caribs were indeed descendants of the Amerindian Caribs and African slaves. In 1795 hostilities began again. The main leader was Catoyer who was killed and 5080 survivors were dramatically removed to the Bay of Honduras. In 1795 there was a great crisis in the Trelawney Town. It was one of five communities in Jamaica. These hostilities became known as the second Maroon war and the great paradox was the surrender of the undefeated Maroons. They immediately signed a peace treaty.

Dr. Hart had done justice for us which we must articulate, laudate and acknowledge for he says, "The first Maroon war was in Jamaica. The freedom fighters, guerrilla warfare, the political victories, achieving freedom wars, the numerous conspiracies and rebellions that took place throughout the Caribbean in the 17th and 18th centuries all ended in great defeat, but these struggles were nevertheless significant in that they kept the torch of liberty burning in the hearts of the oppressed men and women and demonstrated equally, their determination to be free". These words are significant and dynamic for this thesis. The immortal words that form the consummation and made it both unjust and teleos for the oppressed slaves are, "Had so many of the enslaved that fought for their freedom the voices of those who condemned the slave trade and slaving would have been heard to less effect".

The slave trade and slave owners who had propinquity from the discomfort of their fellow human beings would have been able to assert with some degree of plausibility that those who it was alleged were suffering the indignities and tribulations of enslavement were not dissatisfied with their situation. The hermeneutical rationalisation conclusion from Dr. Hart's incisive understanding, articulation and most importantly his intellectual academic and passion, and conviction based on the rectitude of scholarship is profoundly pellucid. Both effected abolition and emancipation are concomitant ontological quest of the enslaved for their freedom. Freedom which is innate in man. This freedom was denied the enslaved Africans. This freedom was suppressed by the slave traders and plantation owners. Their freedom was negated scientifically, theologically and biologically. Not an extraneous gift from the Supreme Power or Energy but it was the Spiritual Being of the Supreme Intelligence we call God. It is from this source that this degree of freedom came.

There were replica Moses in the Maroon leaders and slave leaders who were raised up by the Supreme Being God, to liberate the oppressed enslaved Africans. Paradoxically and philosophically one man cannot fight a war. It is the symbiotic inner movement propelled by the drive for freedom against the military power of the oppressors in the fiery furnace of slavery and all its degradations, there was a torch person with the appearance of the Son of Man, the appearance changed into the Jesus Christ of the black experience of slavery. The Jesus Christ who was in the Maroons, in the rebellious leaders, in the enslaved people. It was the slaves who freed themselves. It was the blood and horrible deaths of the slave leaders who achieved manumission for themselves. The British, European and Americans, never, never gave manumission to the slaves. It would be an historical myth of the greatest historical mendacity to think otherwise that freedom was given to the slaves by Britain, Europe and America.

Physical plantation slavery ended 35 years and 65 years after the abolition of the Slave Trade Act 200 years ago, but economic, political, sociological, psychological and technological slavery continues into the 21st century. The language has changed significantly. Even the vocabulary has changed but African and African descendants are still in the grip of the slave trade legacy. The legacy of amnesia and synundrum. The legacy of psychological strangulations. The legacy of the lack of economic and sociological empowerment for Africa and African descendants. The encapsulation of real manumission must be inner consciousness of one's history. That consciousness is what the black American theologian James Cone said, "Anyone who is not conscious of his historical origin is like a tree without roots". The encapsulation of real manumission must be inner consciousness of one's history. A black man or woman with this degree of root consciousness cannot see, feel, think or function in anyway different from knowing and expressing empirically that I am black, I am an African, I am an African descendant. Black, not only in an epidermical complexion, but conscious conviction with somebodiness, mental, intellectual psychological, spiritual and physical to the point of language, food, woman, child and man. I am black. Historically, genealogically, and ethnologically I am an African. Jesus was black. There can be no sociological compromise. Blackness is Africanism, African necessity. I am black. To acknowledge one's Africanness is to acknowledge that historically African and African descendants were enslaved for 400 years. That slavery has enormous consequences and legacies. These consequences and legacies must be confronted, must be acknowledged.

Dr. Richard Hart has consciously and scholarly pointed out that German Moravians and the English non-conformist missionaries were the only Europeans to have demonstrated a modicum of proselytising the African slaves was the Quakers. The Baptists and Methodists who seemed active in this exercise were not in homogeneity with the great establishment.

The black Baptist missionaries also from the USA, their expectation and instruction to the plantation owners to provide with adequate qualifications, preachers acceptable to preach and instruct the slaves in Christian principles. In November the Jamaican assembly unhesitatingly exalted all slave owners to endeavour in the instruction of their slaves in the principles of the Christian religion. There was a specific stipulation from Dr. Richard Hart 'Slaves who Abolished Slavery Volume I – Blacks in Bondage' "...provided nevertheless, that the instruction of such slaves shall be confined to the doctrines of the established church in this island, and that no Methodist missionary, or other vestry preacher, shall presume to instruct our slaves, or to receive them into their houses, chapels or conventicles, under penalty of £20 for every slave proved to have been there...". There is a great paradox for us to face. According to Dr. David M. Thompson, the theology of the European churches is that they did not see slavery as a problem. In other words, they did not see any need to mention it in any formal theological works. Mr. Alpers believed that the Christians were aware that to see their fellow human beings in slavery could not be morally justified, yet the Christian churches made many excuses for the slave trade. Several priests carried on slave trading especially in Angola and many parts of the USA. The Catholic Church's excuse was that they were seeking to save African souls by baptising the slaves. The Protestants claimed the Africans had no soul. Hence the African slaves were a piece of property like a domestic animal.

With an incisive summation of the deeds of the Christian churches, the European and British churches fully and actively supported the Atlantic Slave Trade. I find therefore this so-called instruction to the plantation owners to give instructions to their slaves, was an act of instruction in the principles of the Christian faith, ambiguous, reckless, without morality or rectitude based on common human decency and conscience. The European church's level and standard of morality did not include the slaves because for them, the slaves had no soul. Furthermore, the slaves were incorrigible pagans. The treatment of the slaves, be they plantation or otherwise, the whole system was based on one economical principle within the British West Indies that it was more profitable to work the slaves to a point of premature and precipitous death and to replace them with more from Africa. To prolong their lives was unrealistic.

This subhuman Negro concept was a product of the pseudo-scientific theory which permeated the age, the Spanish and Portuguese plantation owners were engaged in a similar principle. Basil Davidson in his book 'The African Slave Trade', gave an eloquent account of an Englishman called Walsh who took a passage from Brazil in a British frigate – The North Star, and on crossing the South Atlantic they chased and stopped a slaver. Walsh himself went on board and described what he saw. The familiar horrors of the Middle Passage. "The slaving ship's cargo was five hundred and five men and women; the crew had thrown 55 overboard during their 17 days at sea and these slaves were all enclosed under grated hatchways between decks. The space was so low that they sat between each others legs, and stowed so close together, that there was no possibility of lying down, or at all changing their position by night or day. As they belonged to, and were shipped on account of different individuals, they were all branded like sheep, with the owners marks of different forms. These were impressed under their breasts, or on their arms, and as the mate informed me with perfect indifference, burned with a red hot iron". The conditions as described by Walsh was beyond comprehension, imagination or reality. It was a despicable and repugnant situation. It is pretty pellucid from the heuristic hermeneutical study in hand that the Roman Catholic Church and Protestant Church were at the station of ambivalence on slavery. The Roman Catholic Church upheld the humanity of the slaves but on the other hand it regarded the institution of slavery as divinely sanctioned. It is further evidenced by the fact that the slaves were brainwashed to patiently endure their lot in slavery until God in his wisdom would act to exchange it. The magnitude of brainwashing was tremendous. It was consciously and deliberately done without any Christian morality or ethical rectitude.

It is adgeable that the European churches' active participation and economical involvement was a theological, sociological and spiritual involvement in the context of oppression and enslavement along with educational and ethnological involvement.

The composition of involvement makes the character delineation of the British and European even more conspicuous from historical and chronological records. The churches were also the arms of the political and economical system, with the age of aggression and massive exploitation of the African race within Africa and the Commonwealth.

The buildings of the great cathedrals throughout Europe, especially in Portugal, Britain, USA and Germany are symbols of the power, influence and economical strength of the churches' function in the Atlantic Slave Trade. It is deeply questionable what the Atlantic Slave Trade would be like without the churches' active participation? No philosophical, sociological or theological conjecture can begin to tantalise the eyes or minds in the sphere of the most aggressive and gruesome inimical evil deeds ever recorded by man. There is no historical parallel to the slave trade period of 400 years. Even the biblical periods of wars and deaths were made by the biblical redactors in hyperbolical language and figures to heighten monotheistic awareness among the people. To return to the paradox and ambivalence of the Roman Catholic Church.

The affirmation of the humanity of the slaves and the noble status of the institution of slavery as divinely agreed. The Catholic Church's position was hermeneutically and sociologically provocative. It is definitely the case when we turn to the biblical narratives relating to the Hebrew slaves in slavery in Egypt by the Pharaohs. Yahweh never created Egyptian slavery for the Hebrew race. Rather, we know from biblical history the economical and genealogical prosperity of Jacob's family which resulted in the Pharaoh's decision to enslave Jacob's descendants.

I would vie with temerity and biblical Old Testament scholarship who dare postulate that the Egyptian slavery of the Hebrew people was divinely sanctioned. Rather, we see a powerful anthromorphic picture of God who hears, sees, and understands the sufferings of his people and his stupendous act of liberation and involvement to extricate his oppressed people. This act of liberation became the paradigm for the liberated Hebrew religion and faith.

Dr. Hart has postulated and articulated for us the institutional and historical place of slavery as the global institution dated back to ancient times. The ancient times go back to the Greek and Roman period. For example, the Greek philosopher Dion Chrysostomos in Rome in AD 100 castigated the institution of slavery. The philosopher Dion Chrysostomos expatiated eloquently on the abolition of slavery with the Roman Republic for the conditions of slaves were given legitimate rights in terms of acceptance. Even Hadrian in AD 118 redintegrated the law of killing slaves or selling slaves for the purposes of the amphitheatre pleasures and the relationship between slaves and masters.

Diocletian the pre-Christian era 284 to 308 made it illegal for a man to sell himself into slavery. A significant elucidation of distinction must be made between the Christian leaders and the Emperors through the paradosis and research in a situation establishing the rights of slaves and the Roman Catholic Church's acceptance of the paradosis handed down without challenging the paradosis. The validity of the slaves remained unchallenged. The Spanish and Portuguese colonies in the New World had legal foundations before the Atlantic Slave Trade began. The body of laws and traditions related to the institution of slavery. With this situation the state and church were symbiotic in the human category of slaves which were defined and many slaves were allowed to effectuate their own manumission.

There is the great temptation to pen other areas of the slave system institutionally, but this temptation must be resisted both at academic and pedantic cost. Suffice to say before any departure that the system of slavery had deep legal status with the church and sociological commixture. Slaves were allowed to marry. Slaves were allowed to purchase their own manumission. In places such as Brazil and Cuba slaves were free to purchase their manumission by instalments. Some slaves were able to obtain extrication after embracing the Roman Catholic faith. Thomas Sotheby substantiated this practice. According to CR and others, racial discrimination existed endemically in the church and state. It was also evident in religious orders, as early as the 15th century. Dr. Hart exemplified as follows, "A Congolese was ordained in 1485 to 1521. In 1517 a Congolese was ordained Bishop of Attica. Although racial discrimination was ostensible through the appointment of a new Bishop in 1774 when the Indian Clergy Goa complained that Pombal made his position very clear in a statement. The best summary for the state and church simultaneously active participation and involvement at different levels is best described by the Scottish clergy James Ramsay". "When buying slaves from the British foreigners except perhaps the unfeeling Dutch and Americans may boast that they take these wretches out of the hands of severe task masters".

CHAPTER 21
FACING THE CRIME

The Atlantic Slave Trade Holocaust
The late Pope John Paul II in the 90's issued a remarkable statement of apology to the Jews for the Roman Catholic Church turning a blind eye at the Jewish Holocaust. The Pope also apologised to other races of people who experienced oppressions and sufferings. From his apology I wrote an article published in the Methodist Recorder castigating Pope John Paul II for his biasness. His biasness was based on the fact that in his apologises the Pope never mentioned the following:
1. The Atlantic Slave Trade;
2. Africa;
3. The Apartheid system in South Africa which was set up by Britain and America.

No sane person can deny the moral repugnancy of the holocaust - the death of 6 million Jews. Dr. Vincent Harding in his magnificent book 'There is a River, the Black Struggle for Freedom in American' claimed that approximately 100 million Africans died in the Atlantic crossing. This figure is different from the millions who died on the plantations in the West Indies. 6 million Jews are immortalised and the Jews continue to hold the world to moral ransom today. The Jews are comprehensively compensated. There is no reference that they ever obeyed the United Nations resolutions. Israel is openly supported by the United States Government. There is no reparation for African slavery. Britain, Europe and America raped Africa. The measure of rapine is beyond vocabulary. The slave masters were compensated to a tune of £20 million while the slaves received no financial compensation. Not even a sham or resemblance of the indignity of the slaves who were reduced to the level of animals and what made the African slave trade unique in human history was the dehumanisation of Africans. Slavery made the black race the rugs of the economic world according to Dr. Richard Hart.

Dr. N T Wright, Bishop of Durham in his most recent book 'Evil and the Justice of God', the title which is a plagiarism of John Hicks 'Evil and the God of Love'. Dr. Wright looked at the subject from the perspective of philosophical theology and theological traditions academically. He also added to his thesis ontological dualism and sociological dualism, but he delineated the mentality of most white British and European theologians in showing with my contempt their disregard of the Atlantic Slave Trade, Middle Passage history. In a laconic way no mention of African slavery as a great moral evil enshrined on British and American history pages. Dr. Wright under 'Evil and Crucified God' considering political, science, personal, moral and emotional evil forces took into account the first world war, at Auschwitz, Hiroshima and September 11, 2001 (New York) as forceful reiterations; but he made no mentioned to the African slave trade. Is this academic ignorance? Is this academic stupidity or conscious unawareness of the greatest *de facto* in man's history? Scholarship, be it historical, philosophical, theological, political or sociological cannot occupy the place and library unless the scholarship is inundated with academic and pedantic rectitude.

Hart's thesis has been valuable and informative. On the other hand Hugh Thomas 'The Slave Trade'. Thomas made a radical statement with informative sources and intellectual audacity, Thomas said, "All Christian denominations were involved in the Slave Trade". His statement instigated my proto expatiations to a higher level, conviction and postulation that the European and British churches were active participants and fundamental pistons of the Atlantic Slave Trade. According to Basil Davidson in his book 'The African Slave

Trade', Davidson says that Britain and Europe used Christianity to pacify the slaves.

We find that the dominating religion of the slave ports used their intra-vires to decide the religious dimension, involvement and control of the slave business in Liverpool and Bristol, the two most powerful ports in Britain. The majority of the slave merchants were Anglicans from Nantes Bordeaux, Lisbon and Seville. In Bahra and Luanda the Roman Catholics dominated the situation while in L.A. Rochelle the majority of slave merchants were Huguenots because they were in the main Calvinists in Middlesburg. The Nairacs believed they were ignoble and the Laffons de Ladebat were so. Thomas says because their religion through the farmer had sent 25 ships to Africa between 1740 and 1792.

The encapsulation of the various denominations including the Quakers who became a powerful palladium in the campaign for the abolition of the Transatlantic Slave Trade. The importance of the Quakers in the slave trade in the 18th century especially in New England, in the geographic context of Newport where the Wanton families involvement in trading slaves was in the 1760s. In America, Friends conspicuous and permanent in slave trading as far as Pennsylvania. They even transported slaves from the West Indies also.

The names of great importance are William Frampton - he carried the first slaves to Philadelphia in 1680s. Jonathan Dickinson had his own ship which was typical of slave trade ships with illustrious religious names. His was the Reformation. Dickinson transported Africans from Jamaica to Philadelphia, but Isaac Norris had reservations as expressed in his letter to Dickinson in 1706. "I don't like that kind of business". Other names of significance are William Plumstead, Reece Meredith, John Reynell and Francis Richardson. The indication, attestation and active participation of the Quakers is that the Quakers had a gun making firm of farmers at Carlton in Birmingham.

The ship 'Perseverance' also took part in the shipment of slaves. The Perseverance carried 527 African slaves to the West Indies.

In Brazil the slave merchant Brachia and his private religious brotherhood met and assembled on a regular procession at Easter time, commencing at the church of San Antonio Da Barra. The stupendous burst of St. Joseph, long developed the aptitude to venerate the presence of such persons as at Elmina as the patron of the slaves.

The Bishop of Algarve in 1446 as head of the church posted out to African a Caravel. There were several spiritual leaders who invested as shareholders in countless voyages. The prodigious Cardinal Infante Enrique's propinquity to King Philip III of Spain is that he was a tremendous trader in slaves to Buenos Aires during the 17th century. Even the Jesuits were deeply positively involved in the Transatlantic Trade. In Spain and Portugal just as in the biblical days, as already attested by the minor prophets, especially Amos, the slave trade was tabulated and dominated by Jewish converts. Between 1580 and 1640 people like Diego Caballero, Sanlucar de Barranda and the George family sent slaves packing to the Spanish empire. These men were formerly Christians. Some were secret Jews.

Jews of Portuguese origin played a modicum part in the slave trade but when the slave trade was at its apex in the 18th century there is no indication of any single Jewish merchants in the gigantic European slave trade centre at the time. In places such as Liverpool, Bristol, Nantes and Middlesburg, sagacious investigation and examination of 400 hundred traders who were known to have sold slaves in Charleston, South Carolina, North America's largest slave centre in the 1750s and 1760s.

In Britain, home of the highest and most developed slave trading system, many of the slave traders were indeed deportees or full members of Parliament. This was effective slave trading in the 18th century. The chronology and tabulation included Humphrey Morris, George Rene, John Sargent, Sir Alexander Grant, James Larchie, Henry Cruger of Bristol. Ellis Cunliffe, Charles Pole, John Harman of Liverpool as well as Sir Thomas Jackson, Mayor of Liverpool. He was definitely responsible for one of the first ships to leave for Africa. Hugh Thomas has confirmed that in England most of the Mayors of Liverpool in the middle of the 18th century were traders in slaves. The contiguity of the Christian denominations and individuals cannot be separated according to the slave trade evidence. Most of the slave traders were also philanthropists, people of achievement and pronouncement as Foster Cunliffe. His name appeared on a plague in St. Peters Church, Liverpool. He is delineated as a Christian devotee and paradigmatic in private and public duty.

Brian Blundell of Liverpool was the founder of the Blue Coat School. Robert Burridge was immortalised for his charity to the aged in the infirmary and the poor who generally received the Eucharist. Philip Livingston of New York founded a Professorship of Divinity at the University of Yale. He also helped in the establishment of the first Methodist society in America.

What is veracious and remarkable is that the so-called religious thinkers and so-called philanthropists had no moral, ethical or deep religious convictions. It was not a matter of moral conscience or conviction. It was a psychological, economical and emotional legacy provided for the perpetuation of a racist inhuman and barbaric category and culture. I persist with reluctance to refer to the Europeans and British as Christians because of their diabolical, immoral and deeply irreligious participation and active involvement in the various manumissions in the Atlantic Slave Trade and especially for the plantation slavery. I precipitate to argue my thesis that the denominations were deeply enmeshed in the political philosophy of the slave trade. They had no theological conviction and they even sought theological justification for the enslavement of Africans. The attestation is confirmed by the Anglican Archbishop of Canterbury in 2005 when he made a public confession and acknowledgement of the Anglicans' conduct. The Anglican Church made a positive and public admission of their intractable involvement in the Transatlantic Middle Passage Slave Trade business and also their involvement in the plantation slavery by virtue of owning their own slaves.

CHAPTER 22
ACCEPTANCE AND REFUSAL

Slave Traders' Attitude to Slavery

It is an important reminder that definitions and categorisations of Africans were all made by the British, Europeans and Americans. Equally the French, Portuguese and the Spanish. No African was defined by himself or his people. Definitions were all made by foreigners to suit their ethnocentric and racist culture.

Jean Barbot who traded slaves in the 1680's claimed that despite the unpleasantness of being a slave in the Americas, "It was wonderfully better to be a slave or even to be a free man in Africa". We must remember that the description of slavery is hereby being defined and described by a European. He used the word unpleasantness. only the slaves themselves can define the experience of unpleasantness. His observation is one of the mendacities which was used time and time again to describe the conditions of the slaves. They claimed that conditions in Africa was more repugnant and diabolical. There is actually no historical evidence to substantiate such vacuous allegations, concepts or opinion. It was fabricated to placate, pacify and justify slavery. In order to highlight the conditions under which slaves were transported Walsh in 1829 described the conditions as follows:

"and these slaves were all enclosed under grated hatchways, between decks. The space was so low that they sat between each others' legs, and stowed so close together that there was no possibility of lying down, or at all changing their position by night or day. As they belonged to, and were shipped on account of different individuals, they were all branded like sheep, with their owners' marks of different forms. These were impressed under their breast, or on their arms and, as the mate informed me with perfect indifference, burned with a red hot iron...."

It is therefore unrealistic and unimaginable that Jean Barbot was able to describe the conditions of the slaves as merely unpleasantness. Sir Dalby Thomas the English commander of Cape Coast Castle in 1709 in an essay entitled "A True and Impartial Account of what we believe for the well carrying on of this Trade". Sir Dalby Thomas gave a bleak picture of mortality in Africa. The native here has neither religion or law binding them to humanity, good behaviour or honesty. They frequently for their grandeur sacrificed an innocent man. He thought that the blacks are naturally such rogues and bred with such roguish principles that what they can they get by force or deceit. This hermeneutically must be said is the kind of culture and semantical Christianity that was being promulgated by way of conscious and deliberate fabrications to stigmatise African culture. This he goes on to say, is mild in comparison to other euro-centric ethnocentric prejudices. A vicious and violent linguistic judgment is the bottom line, that blacks are naturally inclined to theft, robbery, idleness and treason. In general they are only suited to live in servitude and for the works and the agricultural of our colonies. This was said by Gerrard Miller in the late 18th century and Dr. William Chancellor Surgeon and Philip Livingston Wolfe wrote also in 1750 that the slave trade was a way of redeeming an unhappy people from inconceivable misery. Again by virtue of the most forceful reiteration all these prejudices and descriptions were consciously fabricated to justify the Atlantic Slave Trade's moral repugnancy.

The description of African people is motivated by inherent prejudices which related to the psychological preconceptions by Europeans and the British. For example, Dr. Cyril Eastwood in his book, "Life and Thought in the Ancient World" told this story of prejudice (removal of prejudice). Socrates wanted to substitute reason for prejudice. "There are prejudices for instance about the Jews and the Negroes. Some years ago an American research worker gave some school children the following silent reading test. "Aladdin was the son of a poor tailor. He lived in Peking, the capital city of China. He was always lazy and liked to play better than to work. What kind of boy was he? Indian, Negro, Chinese, French or Dutch? To his bewilderment, most of the children said the boy must have been a Negro." Socrates wanted to remove the unreasoned and unreasonable prejudice. Sir Dalby Thomas and Dr. William Chancellor were suffering from white ethnocentric prejudice. It would be a complete dissipation to expatiate further on their ignoble judgments. The only addendum is to say that they were desperately seeking to justify the diabolical slave trade practice by Britain and Europe. Just as the Anglican Church was seeking through an academic debate for a theological justification for the slave trade. The European Christians used Christianity to pacify the slaves.

There were some traders who professed that the slave trade was morally, ethically, socially and politically repugnant. The number was mainly in the modicum category. Such individuals as William Fisher, a merchant of Philadelphia, found the slave trade reprehensible. Laurens was the first person from the South of the United States to have expressed any measure of repugnancy about the Transatlantic Slave Trade. "I hate slavery" he confessed. His confession may well have been self placative. There were no serious considerations of the economic, social, political and demographical impact on Africa and the forced transported slaves culturally, emotionally, psychologically, spiritually and physically.

In 1773 Mr Moses Brown extricated himself from the Brown of Providence business and became an Abolitionist. Moses Brown sympathised and demonstrated his charity by giving slaves manumission immediately. The radical aid of the hermeneutical intellectual metaphorical knife delineates that these charitable deeds were expressed only lambently. They did not touch the background and foundation of commitment, justification and the circumvention of human thoughtfulness.

Some specific situations of slavery are worth mentioning in order to pinpoint the locations where black slaves were abundantly conspicuous. Nantes in 1780 had a large population of black slaves in France. In Liverpool in 1788 large populations of slaves, black and mulatto existed. The comparison of numbers of slaves cannot equate with Bristol and London. Nonetheless the slaves in Bristol and London were placed in a situation of oscillation between liberty and manumission.

In the 18th century Middlesburg in Zeeland was the largest slave port in Holland. So were Lisbon and Seville.

In addition to the Christian denominations active participation in the Atlantic Slave Trade, individuals such as Hugh Crow, who thought that the extraction of slaves to the colonies was a necessary evil. Hugh Crow veraciously believed that the Anglican slaves in the West Indies were better off than in their native colonies in Africa. Joseph Hawkins of Charleston, South Carolina in 1793 thought similarly to Hugh Crow that the Africans were better off in the colonies of the West Indies. On the other hand John Newton captain of the Duke of Argyle owned by the Monastery Brothers of Liverpool who was the future vicar of St. Mary's, thought deeply about his trade but paradoxically unlike Hugh Crow, John Newton never thought of justifying his trade.

John Newton became a Christian before he became a clergyman. In a letter to his wife on leaving Africa on the Duke of Argyle for the Caribbean with a cargo of slaves of innumerable dangers and difficulties which without a superior protection, "No man could escape or surmount and which by the goodness of God is happily over". John Newton had to face a slave rebellion for two days after which he wrote this sentence. After he overcame the great danger he remarked, "With the divine assistance". John Newton even prayed twice per day for his slaves and his slave crews. Here is the reinforcement of the power of this thesis and postulation that God, religion or Christianity had nothing in the eyes and minds of the slave traders or slave captains to do with the African slaves. After all the slaves were non-beings. They were cattle. They were not created in the image of God with the potential to become in the philosophical likeness of Christ.

Juxtaposed to this so-called cultural semantical Christianity were the medical surgeons. The surgeons were exceptionally important to the cargo and the slave ships. Medical surgeons such as Alexander Falconbridge, Thomas Trotter, William Chancellor and Reverend Stephen Hales, a leading physician and inventor in the mid 18th century invented the ventilator. The radical assumption which can be made without any reservation is that the medical surgeons and the clergymen never found themselves in the state of spiritual, psychological, theological, religious or social ambivalence. Morality or ethical conduct never came into play with them nor on the conscience of John Newton. He believed that the Transatlantic Slave Trade truncated the sensitivities of the crews. The real or supposed necessity of treating the Negroes with rigour gradually brings a numbness upon the crew and renders those who are enmeshed in the slave trade far too indifferent to the sufferings of their white fellow creatures.

The historical de facto of the Atlantic Slave Trade has nothing recondite in relation to the experiences of the slaves, the people who were deeply involved in the trafficking, exploitation and dehumanisation of the slaves racially, culturally, economically and politically.

The participation of the so-called European Christians and British Christians in the slave trade had no moral religious or ethical credence. The religious or African perspectives were used to further the enhancement of the trade and at times seeking a religious or theological justification. What therefore is the logical conclusion to this economical, cultural, social and religious propinquity between the Christian churches and their ministers from Europe and Britain? They were inseparable with their economic philosophy of the slave trade.

There are untold sufferings of the enslaved. They were brutally marched to the coast. They were kept in barracoons under diabolical, repugnant and appalling conditions. They were packed into slave ships like cattle. They were forced to face the horrors of the Atlantic crossing, euphemistically referred to as the Middle Passage. Most historians of the slave trade vividly presented the histories of the Atlantic Slave Trade's vicissitudes in moving languages. The languages are not semantical dramatisations but rather empirical, observational, experiences. It is sensitive and accountable to point out that the inventor of the ventilation system had two professions. He was a medical surgeon and also a Reverend of the Christian faith and he was involved in the slave trade, not to expostulate the slave traders but his function primarily was to secure the cargo medically for profit. In other words, his task was to secure the good condition of the slaves for the plantations in the colonies.

CHAPTER 23
SLAVE TRADERS AND SLAVERY

The Church, Slavery and Emancipation

The basic theme of my thesis is the diabolical function of the church, Christianity, religion, European and British culture, science and philosophy, in the Atlantic Slave Trade and especially the plantation slavery. All predications are made around the basic subject of this bold academic postulation and historical, theological, and sociological conclusion. Dr. Hart in volume I of 'Slaves who Abolished Slavery' and 'Blacks in Bondage' demonstrated and articulated the relationship between church, state and status. At no time whatsoever, is my thesis a critique of any singular scholar. This has never been my intention. This is not my aim or my purpose either but rather, Dr. Hart is to be thanked for his splendid contribution on a subject of such great importance and energy of the slave trade which had not been touched on before.

The originality is significant because of my academic and cultural propinquity to the history of the slave trade and Africa, culturally and genealogically.

Dr. Hart's laconic paragraphs at the genesis of Chapter 6 of 'Blacks in Bondage' must be quoted in order to locate and accommodate the scene and context of this part of this thesis. "Initially, in the English colonies, the slaves were represented as incorrigible pagans. This was part of the image, of a form of life incapable of receiving instruction in Christian beliefs, which the slaves own interest wished to create. When the Barbados assembly discovered that the Quakers were admitting slaves to their meetings they enacted in 1676 that "If any Negro or Negroes be found with the Quakers as hearers of their preaching he/she shall be forfeited (if belonging to any Quakers) half the money to go to the informer, the other half to the public use of the island... If the Negro should not belong to any person present at the meeting then the informer may bring an action... against any of the persons present... and so recover £10 for every Negro...". They declared that the conversion of the slaves will not only destroy their property but endanger the safety of the island and that as there is a great disproportion of blacks to whites. They have none greater Security than the diversity of their languages... and that in order to their being made Christians. "It will be necessary to teach them all English which gives them an opportunity and facility of combining together against their master and of destroying them". Dr. Hart has elucidated with academic pellucidness as an historian of remarkable eminence the political, economical, sociological, theological and anthropological conceptualisation of Africans by the church throughout history. The legal demarcations and legal stipulations about the church and slavery. The missionaries and most importantly the so-called Christian plantation owners, the farmers and traders.

The slave traders and plantation owners were all alleged Christians. Christians by the standard of European Cultural Christianity and the British. As Dr. Eric Williams said of those who opposed the abolition of the slave trade, "It is almost pathetic to have to deal today with the writers who opposed Smith and Clarkson, none of the defenders of slavery have any merit or international significance today".

Dr. Williams' wishing to adge more flesh continues, "If one had to mention Clarkson and Smith one could think only of Malachi Postlethwaite, who has ever heard of Postlethwaite?

I am forced by the gravity of the mentality, psychology, theology and commitment of the plantation slave owners to state categorically that European and British slave traders and in particular the plantation owners were semantical Christians in vocabulary only. They had no moral, ethical or theological fecundation or foundation. They had no moral rectitude or theological consciousness. Reiteration must be made forcefully with historical reliability. Britain and Europe expanded their European Cultural Christianity for the purpose of control and domination. British and European Christianity in the slave trade era was enmeshed with economic rapacity and a programme and philosophy in name based on exploitation and underdevelopment of Africa. The legacy of the slave trade is conspicuous economically and technologically today in all the major black countries of Africa, Latin America and the West Indies.

Plantation Owners' Christian Dilemma and Polemics

In 1710, Colonel Codrington by virtue of his will had established a fund to provide religious instructions for the negro slaves in the island of Barbados. His scheme was for the provision of missionaries to convert the slaves to Christianity and the establishment of a college. Codrington gave two plantations in Barbados over 300 slaves to the society for the propagation of the Gospel. There were difficulties with the council of traders and the plantation owners, "We must keep our awareness aye in spatation". It was the intention of the plantation slave masters to keep the Africans consistently ignorant. No enlightenment or the raising of their consciousness should be attempted. Even Christianity was used to keep the African slaves ignorant. It was a premeditated, deliberate and conscious plot. It was a programmatic strategy to extract from the slaves the maximum energy and even to the point of physical death. The slaves were only spare parts in a system which made them replaceable. They were immediately replaced because the supply was in abundance.

The polemics for the plantation traders were the common law of England which forbade the enslavement of Christians. Was this law applicable only to the slaves in England? Was the law also applicable to African slaves in the West Indian plantations? My conjecture is that the law was not ubiquitous nonetheless, there was tremendous bitterness and acrimony in the 17th century for the planters' ambition to offer religious instruction to the slaves. The African strangeness to Christianity, to European Christianity and British Christianity was a great polemic. This is seen in the castigation of Mr. Rishworth in 1635. It was in regard to Rishworth's sermon against slavery and especially his empathy with the Africans who had escaped to the woods. Rishworth received full condemnation for his insensibility which was due to the concept that Christians may not lawfully be imprisoned in slavery or servitude during their strangeness from Christianity.

The major polemic was the assumption that if the Africans were to overcome the strangeness from Christianity they would be entitled to manumission. The plantation traders and owners had a profound misunderstanding of the law. This is explicitly expressed in the diary of John Evelyn who was an official of the Council of Foreign Plantations in 1685. "That the negroes in the plantations should be baptised exceedingly, declaring against that impiety of their masters prohibiting it, out of a mistaken opinion that they would be *ispo facto* free.

Baptised slaves or converted slaves never meant freedom for the slaves. The symbolism of baptism was the completion of the brainwashing process, thereby allowing the inculcation process to be much easier psychologically and politically. European Christianity was only a cultural instrument used on the slaves. It had nothing to do with the removal of enslavement, the granting of freedom, the acknowledgement of biological and technological equality namely "death". There was no recorded situation where the common law was ever challenged. Even in the kings' hermeneutic it is pretty clear. In 1696, a Jamaican assembly accordingly to Sotheby enacted that "No slave shall be free by becoming a Christian". So what was the purpose of becoming a Christian? My contention is that to become a Christian was therefore dysteleological for the slaves only. In other words, Christian or incorrigible pagan according to Dr. Hart made no difference whatsoever. Although the common law gave or promised no freedom for the slaves, Thomas Sotheby defined the common law as "..the only efficient religious slave law which can be found". So this was specifically a slave law.

Education, technology, science, sociology, anthropology, economics, philosophy, theology or politics were at no time introduced to the plantation slaves. These disciplines were specifically for the British, European and American whites only. The only weapon that was used by the British and European to mentally, psychologically and spiritually command comprehensive control of the slaves' mind, soul, body and spirit was the said British and European Cultural Christianity. I reiterate with verve and conviction that at all times the vehicle or weapon used against the slaves was European Cultural and Semantical Christianity, not a religion because Britain and Europe had none. They were generally pagans and barbarians and this part of British and European history had been deliberately kept recondite by historians and scholars.

The progressive changes came not from a symbiotic religious consciousness of Britain and Europe but only singularly. That was with the case of Colonel Codrington who in 1710 financially established a fund to provide religious education for the negroes in the Caribbean islands. The basic aim of the project was to provide provision for the missionaries to convert the slaves to Christianity. In other words, to convert the slaves to British and European culture. It is very important to state here that the scheme was to convert the slaves to Christianity. This was their programme, this was their project, this was their cultural incubating chamber to convert the slaves only to Christianity in order to control and to subjugate them. It was not the other way round to expostulate the plantation traders. Their scheme, their missionary movement and their cultural incubation had nothing to do with the plantation traders. European Cultural Christianity was a Christianity of oppression, exploitation, enslavement, injustice, evilness and subjugation of the slaves, not enlightenment or manumission of the slaves.

Again, I cannot reiterate too frequently, throughout this heuristic thesis that the entire programme and purpose of European semantical Christianity or Cultural Christianity was to enslave, oppress, exploit and to subjugate Africans because of their genealogy, for the profitability of the economies of Europe, Britain and America, hence the centrality of the denominations in relation to the slave trade. Codrington gave two plantations and 300 slaves to Barbados for the propagation of the Gospel. When the college came into being many years later it was only for white children. No blacks were ever admitted to this Christian college. We must not be fooled by the appearance of generosity. The Codrington College never fulfilled the mission for which it was set up. It took 120 years for the college to begin the mission of educating the slaves to Christianity. This is extremely remarkable. In 1727 the Bishop of London emulated Colonel Codrington with an epistle to the English colonies, urging them to educate the slaves in the Christian faith. Again, Christianity was the central vehicle for the total psychological and spiritual brainwashing of the slaves. Nothing to do with science, technology, education, theology, philosophy, commerce, economic, even their freedom was denied from them by Christianity.

Dr. Richard Hart says "With the authority of the Bishop in London over the established churches in the West Indies the Church of England was now on record as recognising both the possibility and desirability of the slaves becoming Christians. In retrospect it was the said Church of England who had called into being a debate for the theological justification of slavery". It was a radicalisation and hermeneutical fact that of the Bishop of London was seeking education of the slaves in the Christian faith. The instructions for the availability of Christian education for the slaves was to use British, European Cultural and semantical Christianity to the slaves. Christian education in this context was not for the liberation of the slaves, rather it was to oppress the slaves into their submission to subservient, inferiority and for them spiritually and psychologically to accept slavery as God given and ordained by God in this life that in the afterlife they would find their tickets to heaven. This was purely a brainwashing process. A religion, a Christian faith that is inherently and theologically based on superiority via liberation from sin and all that pertains to sin was now used in a reversal way to dehumanise God's people.

This is another form of the brainwashing process by Britain and Europe. Christian education was to be interpreted by the whites only. First they were written by the whites, defined by the whites, and taught by the whites. Always from the whites' oppressive, dehumanised context, but never from the context of the oppressed or the enslaved. For the black slaves Christian education had nothing to do with ethics, morality, theology, justice, liberation and freedom. Christian education meant submission to the rules of whites only. Furthermore, it had nothing to do with the social, economic and political improvements of the conditions of the slaves. It is worthy of remembrance and reiteration that the entire Christian education, the missionary movement and European theology was to inculcate into the slaves by force that their sufferings and enslavement in this life was ordained by God and that they should accept the conditions without any rebellion, without any resistance and without any conspiracy, while for the British, Europeans and the Americans it was ordained by God according to their interpretation for them to enslave Africans and to build on the economic philosophy of prosperity and the master race culture and superiority.

In addition, the Church of England was also slave owners and plantation owners. Let this point be registered again. The Church of England was active participants, totally involved by owning slaves and they owned also large plantations. Therefore the church was actively involved in the practice of enslavement of Africans for economical reasons and nothing to do with religion or Christianity.

The Bishop of Exeter for example, retained his 655 slaves for whom he received over £12,700 in compensation in 1833. The Church of England had their theological debates for the theological justification of slavery. I hasten to add that the church had again no theology, no morality, no ethics, no sociology and no theological doctrine. In a nutshell, the church had no theology which embraced the slaves as human beings. The church claimed that the Africans were incorrigible pagans, therefore the question is pertinent, why the hell did they use Christianity to brainwash the slaves to become Christians except to enslave them? There is no record or reference that the slaves were perceived to be corrigible and not incorrigible. It was the plantation owners who in any language, in any society, in any understanding were incorrigible, not the slaves. They had no love, no justice, no peace, no shalom according to the socio-theological, socio-economical, socio-political and socio-anthropological meaning of shalom in all its dynamic functions for the wholeness and the intactness of man.

The long period of 120 years before the Codrington College began, it started educating and converting the slaves. The purpose of the college was to focus on educating and converting the slaves to be obedient slaves to their white slave masters. A critical hermeneutic will not find any difficulty in extricating the polemic for what it was, the programme for the college was the spiritual and psychological enslavement of the slaves. I note the concentration was on the conversion of the slaves. The plantation traders were economically powerful people. The church needed the plantation traders on their side. In other words the plantation traders held the economic power balance while the church was impuissant, so the church sided and became enmeshed with the plantation traders for economical and numerical reasons.

To convert the slaves to the Christian faith, what Christian faith may I ask? There were none. All that existed was a British and European Cultural Christianity, Semantical Christianity.

1. Not a Christianity embracing Christology, the resurrection of Jesus and the Pentecostal faith. The doctrine of the trinity and God's kingdom. To love your neighbour as yourself; to honour the two great commandments, thou shall love the Lord thy God with all thy heart, they soul and they minds; and
2. To love your neighbour as you love yourself.

Such Christianity could not have been real empirical experience.

The Dean of Middleham in a letter addressed to the Abolition Society, at its inception in 1787 wrote, "How invincibly unwilling are the white people to the admission of slaves to the privileges of Christianity?" What privileges of Christianity? Blacks throughout history of the British churches have experienced racism at all levels in the church. It was a vacuous scheme for the slaves. Its aim was for individual aggrandisement and individual esteem. Logically speaking, it had no value or significance to the slaves themselves.

Scholarship should at all times seek, practice and perform with rectitude consistently, in order to retain its scholarship integrity. There is no reason or grounds for frivolous placations and false, groundless decorations of the historical face of the church in the plantation system of black slavery in the Caribbean and elsewhere.

The Dean of Middleham in 1787 wrote about the privileges of Christianity for the slaves to enter into, after conversion, baptism and full Christian instruction in the Christian faith. There was no hesitation in the practice of segregated seating arrangements into the churches. In 1813, the Common Council of Kingston Jamaica was actively enforcing segregated seating in churches. Braithwaite stated that a resolution required that some pews should be "exclusively appropriated to the white members".

The church has never been genuine to its apostolic and patristic foundations of Christianity. They have used persistently European and British racist cultures, religion, politics and philosophy of the master race to permeate everything foreign and in particular African.

CHAPTER 24
SLAVE VICISSITUDES

Slave and Slave Traders' Conflict and Struggles
    Throughout this thesis, I have sought to delineate that European Christianity was a cultural Christianity. Furthermore I added that European Christianity was purely a semantical Christianity. In other words it was European and British Biblicism. Furthermore it was a cultural Christianity vacuous of any germ or resemblance of any meaningful religious rectitude. The slave traders were the chief protagonists in the full spectrum of the Atlantic Slave Trade. These slave traders were generally classified as European and British Christians. They were not theologians, sociologists, philosophers or social-anthropologists, yet they labelled themselves Christians. Most of the slave ships also carried Christian names. They used this purely to further justify the slave trade.
    I assume that they were Christians without any moral virtues, any theological convictions, any social convictions and any human convictions. They came not from a Christian perspective or environment, but rather from a pagan environment. During the 17th to 18th centuries, Europe and Britain were pagan countries. The question therefore arises immediately, What was the function of the traders as missionaries? To validate this question it would help us to obtain a good picture of the process, programme and economic motives of the slave traders.

It is indeed understandable historically before the slaves' emancipation in the Caribbean in 1865, European and American slave traders transported over 50 million slaves across the Atlantic. This estimate is not reliable because according to Basil Davidson in his book 'The African Slave Trade', his estimate is that, it was in the region of 50 million slaves across the Atlantic. For others, it was over 3 million slaves that died during the Middle Passage alone and the equivalent amount died on the actual plantations.

The Atlantic Slave Trade transformed the face of the Americas, economically it enhanced the economical and material well-being of the West and simultaneously wrought massive damage to Africa ecologically and demographically, socio-logically, culturally, genealogically and politically. The history of the slave trade and the consequences of the barbaric enforced transportation of the Atlantic Slave Trade attracted great scholastic interest over the past 25 years, in Britain, Europe and the US. Their interest have been geared primarily to careful historical tabulations and extractions from journals, minutes and records. No attempt has been made so far to scholastically, actually interpret the slave trade. In relation to the inherent involvement of the various denominations, this is the task that I audaciously seek to face in this book.

In the 17th and 18th centuries the slave traders were bitterly opposed to the conversion of the slaves to the so-called Christianity but as I have elucidated, it was purely cultural Christianity, semantical Christianity. Basic and fundamental reluctance, the fear of the traders was the possibility perceived by them that religious inculcation would automatically motivate the slaves to accept Christianity and furthermore that automatically it would lead to manumission for the slaves. This concept of the slave traders were inherently contradictory and not self-evident, because conversion to Christianity was never meant for the slaves' freedom, liberation or manumission, it meant further enslavement.

In the Caribbean regions of the slave communities missionary activities began to germinate around 1850. According to Humphrey Lamur 'Caribbean Slave Society and Economy Slave Religion on the Vossenburg Plantation', it is scholarly attested that slavery in the slave plantation in Virginian (USA) can be placed in the following groups or categories. 1750-1790, 1790-1830 and 1830-1860. The deciding factor was that the period distinguished the attitudes of missionary thinking to slavery.

The churches postulated that the slaves were their brothers in Jesus Christ. A slave converting boom period, along with a rapid and radical anti-slavery attitude to the slave society. The slave traders placed the slave owners under tremendous pressure. I find the concept that was proclaimed that the slaves were brothers in Jesus Christ, exceedingly vacuous and convenient. At no time during the slave trade were the slaves regarded as human beings, rather they were dehumanised. They were looked upon as incorrigible pagans. To mention Jesus Christ in relation to the slaves was not only an inherent insult but it was a lambent pretence to further brainwash the slaves.

The radical liberating mind of the slave traders also feared people like Nat Turner in 1822. Nat Turner in his insurrection in 1822 was a radiating time on the history of black Christianity. It was not the white missionaries, Baptists or Methodists who were at the forefront of the liberation struggle for emancipation and manumission, it was the black slaves of which Nat Turner was the most potent, dynamic and charismatic leader. Attempts had always been made by British, European and American scholars and historians to place European, British and American Caucasian into mythological paradigms. By so doing, they further raped and robbed the African slaves from their noble achievements and their noble sacrifice for themselves and the freedom of all slaves.

The slave traders and slave planters began gradually to accept European Cultural Christianity. They did so because they viewed Christianity as a social means of controlling the slaves. It was not to liberate the slaves. It was not to implant in the minds of the slaves their ontological consciousness or rather their ontological gift for freedom. It was used as a means of control. To control the slaves physically, mentally, psychologically, culturally and spiritually. Christianity was used further to puncture the minds of the slaves to amputate their intellectual capacity and to make them dysfunctional in mind, soul and spirit. For the slaves to think of their potential power for manumission through a growing consciousness by using Christianity and the missionaries was like the correct music to the slave traders and planters, not the slaves themselves. The slave owners were in constant conflict with the missionaries. Desideration to expostulate the slaves from their African past or African religious beliefs. There was the great Nat Turner conflict between the slave traders and the new black Christianity. Nat Turner was a proto liberation theologian and a pioneer in black religion and black Christianity. Across the Caribbean Sea in Jamaica there was Samuel Sharpe and Paul Bogle. Equally they were liberation theologians, pioneers in black theology, black religion and black Christianity, whilst Nat Turner was a dynamic engine in the USA.

A veracious admission must be made about the missionaries. The missionaries' purpose was to deculturise the African slaves. To inculcate a British and European Cultural Christianity, a semantical Christianity, thereby creating docile domesticated robots for the slave traders had the church's associates. The missionaries failed in their ambition to extirpate the African religious beliefs and customs. The missionaries had an agenda. They were the active embodiment of the denominations. Their sole purpose was to inflict psychologically and spiritually on the slaves a sense of inferiority, a sense of preordination and predestination, that they were born through the will of God to be slaves and mythologically in the hereafter they would have special privileges to enjoy milk and honey. Needless to say, it was not only an illusion and deception but it was and is total nonsense.

According to Genovese he postulated that the conditions of the new social life forced the slaves to symbiotically combine the African inheritance with a dominant fiat. They were confronted with a new culture and to shape a religion of their own. Reliable sources substantiate these facts as Jones, a Presbyterian missionary who preached the Gospel to the slaves in Georgia in 1840. According Genovese, Jones claimed that the slaves continued to believe in second sight apparitions, charms, witchcraft and also a kind of irresistible satanic influence. Hundley, a slave owner appropriately claimed that the slaves still believed in witchcraft, sorcery, conjuring many types of paganism. Eliza Andrews described forcefully the slaves' attitudes to Christianity. The slaves looked upon Christianity as oppressive and the source of their exploitation, not a source of liberation. The slaves no longer allowed by the slave owners to use Christianity to subjugate them into accepting slavery as their lot in this life. They saw Christianity as their major enemy, not their liberator. We observe also, that nothing pertaining to the slaves were laudative to the missionaries. Everything pertaining to the slaves were denigrating, were insignificant, were also stigmatic, witchcraft, magic, Satanism, all these were consciously fabricated by the missionaries to denigrate African religions and religious beliefs, traditions and practices. The missionaries, slave traders and enslavers were all profoundly inimical to the African slaves.

A significant laconic summation is that the missionaries failed to extirpate completely the African beliefs of the slave population in Virginia. In addendum, Jernigan, reached the same conclusion that the systematic efforts of the missionaries to dislocate the slaves' beliefs and to convert the slaves to Christianity was partly a massive dissipation of time, energy and purpose.

The ultimate purpose of the missionaries was to obliterate and to completely extirpate all aspects of slaves' lives, customs and traditions. That was the purpose of the missionaries to destroy everything that is African. To destroy the fabric of African culture, history and beliefs and to transplant into the Africans British, European and American cultures and so-called values. Another view to look at is that they failed to accept anything pertaining to African psychological development, spiritual, social and emotional development but at the same time all the natural resources from Africa and its people were accepted for the economies of Britain Europe and America and nothing else.

To replace the Africans historical beliefs with a British and European Cultural Christianity delineating oppressions, exploitations, sufferings, dehumanisation of the slaves and to make it theologically valid and divinely preordained by God and with God's approbation. It was a psychological and spiritual brainwashing, deeply inimical to the slaves.

Eradication and a black hermeneutical application is exigently required because of the depth of the legacy and consequences of the slave trade Christianity embedded in the psyche of black people, even to this day.

The slave trade missionary movement and European, British and American Cultural Christianity has left lasting roots, deep roots in the psyche and soul of black people. These roots must encounter not only hermeneutical elucidations but they are in need of de-rooting, de-culturising, de-theologising and de-missionising to cut the impact and influence that holds blacks today.

The majority of black people, especially the poor are deeply entombed mentally, intellectually, sociologically, theologically and educationally in the British and European cultural slave trade Christianity. Heaven is in the skies. God is with a long white beard. Milk and honey paradise is waiting. Dancing all over heavens floor. Putting on new shoes and walking over heaven. What diabolical rubbish! What codswallop! What about equality? Economic power? Political and economic independence? Appropriate education for black children? Appropriate medical care? Good housing conditions? Appropriate practical opportunities for blacks? Re and de-educating of our young black people to avoid drugs, prostitution, violence, self-centredness, complacency, selfishness, non-love, hatred, the list is endless. Theologically, what of God's kingdom being realised existentially in black individuals and communities today. I reiterate with every verve and energy that a new and exigent re-intellectualisation, hermeneutical, pregnant and fecund with blackness is now an imperative to correct the host of negative vibes, legacy and consequences of the Atlantic Slave Trade on the black race namely Africa and African descendants. It is a must – now – God and Jesus Christ must be seen as applied and experienced within with existential context of the African descendants and Africa today. As understood through the lens of the legacy of the Atlantic Slave Trade which has truncated culturally and demographically, socially and economically on black people ubiquitously.

The systematic conduct of the missionaries' attempts to obliterate and extirpate the slaves beliefs was basically in the first place for economical reasons, second for political, third psychological, fourth cultural, fifth theological, sixth, sociological.

At Vossenburg the following four categories were found among the plantation slaves.

1. A Supreme Being and lower than God.

2. Priest and mediums of lower God's.
3. Religious objects.
4. Rituals.

Many Old Testament scholars are still far away from theological and historical agreement on the various names ascribed to God in the Old Testament. This problem has been an ancient one. The slaves named and believed in a God called Adangra. The Old Testament conceptualisation of God took various forms, theologically, the monotheistic faith of the Old Testament is a very late development in the history of Israel. Even the anthropomorphic and the pantheistic beliefs in Yahweh was a prevailing historical nomadic belief. The name Adangar as a Supreme Being and lower than God. In Jeremiah and Christian theologies, the sociological language of the slaves understanding and relationship with Yahweh and belief in the Supreme understanding of Yahweh, the belief in one Supreme Being is not only a Jewish and Christian belief. A monotheistic faith is to be found also in other religious traditions.

The practice of Obeah or the Obeah Man or Myalism, these were practices of the slaves, so was human sacrifice in the Old Testament even to the time of the major biblical prophets. The witch of Endor is equally significant. All these forms of religious beliefs and practices permeated the bible in the Old and New Testament. I have claimed elsewhere in this heuristic thesis that the definitions and elucidations of God by British, European and American Cultural Semantical Christianity does call into question the existence of a moral God, a righteous God, a God of justice, love, liberation and equality. These characteristics of the cosmic mind or intelligence or Supreme Intelligence or Supreme Energy was not present in the Atlantic Slave Trade or even beyond the Atlantic Slave Trade.

In 1847, the Moravian Mission challenged the slave population at Vossenburg. Thus, the motive of the Moravian Brotherhood Mission was to convert the slaves to Christianity. We note the slaves, not the slave traders and the enslavers. Juxtaposed to the mission movement to convert the slaves, there was also the attempt to eliminate the religion of the slave population. It was considered inconsistent with Christianity. In other words, European, British and American Christianity through the missionary movement programme was to replace African religion and religious beliefs with a foreign unrelated culture. Paradoxically, did the Moravian missionaries succeed in brainwashing the slaves or did they succeed in eradicating and extirpating the slaves' beliefs?

Between 1847 and 1877 there were tremendous conflicts and religious vicissitudes at Vossenburg, between the slaves and the missionaries. Were they competitors? Were they struggling for survival or domination? The missionaries made their presence pronounced during the week and on Sundays too. The so-called religious services normally took place in the engineers or carpenters' shed. The missionaries gave so-called religious instructions. Catechism baptised both children and adults pastorally. They also visited the sick, the needy. There was a great ocean of ambivalence for the slaves themselves because conversion meant different things to different missionaries and slaves. There was no pandemic or universal agreement. Between 1847 and 1877, this period was the apex of religious and cultural ambivalence between the missionaries and the slaves. What is significant is that the missionaries used different approaches and tactics to convert the slaves to become more obedient, submissive and docile.

For example, in 1861 a tremendous epidemic attacked the slaves and a large portion of the slave population died as a result of this epidemic. The missionaries saw this as a divine punishment by God. The missionaries believed that the slaves shared this stupid belief. One report recorded was that for the first time, the slaves i.e. the negroes, were quiet and attentive. The Lord had addressed them seriously. Philosophically and otherwise, what of natural disasters? What of moral evil? What of natural evil?

In the Old Testament, time and time again, there is evidence of disasters that were beyond human influence.

The next significant event was the excommunication of a slave. According to the missionary on his death bed, "..he was buried as a pagan". This had a tremendous impact and impression on the minds of the slaves. Reiteration is necessary, the slaves were perceived to be incorrigible pagans. The missionary drive therefore was not on moral, ethical or religious grounds. It was basically to control the minds of the slaves. Once they achieved control of the minds of the slaves, then the body would also fall into place. Their customs and traditions would also fall into place. The missionaries worked primarily and psychologically on the minds of the slaves. The slaves showed metanoia and asked for re-admission to the church. The missionaries claimed that God's spirit had touched the slaves' hearts. A further tactic used by the missionaries was the statement that the slave who had been buried as a pagan was now standing before God's judgment to be punished for his idolatry. What a nonsense. The tactic had nothing to do with the slave's physical liberation from slavery. It had nothing to do with the oppressors of the slaves, namely the slave traders and the enslavers. The arrow was always pointing to the conversion and to the control of the slaves only. Nothing introspective on the part of the missionaries. And who were the missionaries? They were Christian oppressors of the slaves. They were British, European and American cultural Christians, who used Christianity as a religion to pacify the slaves.

Natural disasters or calamities, as can been seen from the Exodus, Deuteronomy, Numbers, Amos, parts of the major prophets, Jeremiah, Ezekiel and Second Isaiah, were not seen as natural calamities but rather as divine punishment, because of Israel's sin. In this brainwashing process, on chronos I note that the slave traders and planters were not included. Heaven they will go to immediately after appropriation, but not the slaves. The slave traders and the slave owners had no part in this process of the prodigal slaves. They were the oppressors. They were the opponents of the slaves. They oppressed the slaves. They denied that the slaves were human. For them the slaves were just properties. There is historical importance in a degree of such great and significant importance that the slaves had a cosmological belief in a Supreme Being, much superior and developed than that of Britain, Europe and America at that time.

Professor Paul Tillich in his tomb of 'Systematic Theology in the late 60's and 70's defined God as the ground of our being. Paul Tillich's postulations were not based on any solid or philosophical postulations, but rather on a Process Theology, of Systematic Theology. His Systematic Theology at no time embraced in its compass the Atlantic Slave Trade and the ground of Being. The slaves had for over 400 years before Paul Tillich perceived the concept of a Supreme Being. Both the missionary and Paul Tillich were very late in their theological and philosophical developments. Africans had preceded them. It was the plantation slaves who had the concept of a Supreme Being such as Breukelerwaard, Fortuin, and Schoonoor which were plantations where the Moravian mission started their activities to brainwash the slaves.

The missionary groups' sole purpose was to psychologically, spiritually and theologically control the lives of the slaves by brainwashing them religiously. The manumission of the slaves was not significant to the Moravian missionary people, it was only a matter of lambent pretence. Even baptised slaves had no guarantee of freedom. Baptism or conversion to Christianity never guaranteed the slaves their freedom. It further cemented their enslavement. In 1863 slavery was abolished in Suriname. Free slaves remained at Vossenburg. Here the Moravian mission flourished tremendously and continued to preach the so-called white Gospel. What kind of Gospel? This is not a conjecture or vapid statement, rather it is based on intellectual rapacity and emotional temerity of the writer of this book. The Gospel preached by the Moravians was not based on biblical theology, moral ethics or a programme of processed theology. The Moravians believed that the kerygma was for the slave traders only and that the slaves had no participation in this process of salvation. We must remember that with the power of reiteration the slave traders and the slaves' awareness were not indeed of the Gospel. The Gospel was aimed at the oppressed who at all times were the dehumanised slaves. The Gospel for the slaves was not the good news. The Gospel was the perpetuation of their suffering in slavery.

There is no evidence that the slaves accepted European Cultural Christianity or slavery. The slaves questioned Christianity. They questioned the missionary theology. In other words, the slaves, namely the African religious beliefs were endemic in their nature and culture. In addition, they had no hesitation in challenging and defending their religion against culturally orientated criticisms by the missionaries against their African religion. It is said that in 1864 the slaves were still practising the "bench dance" ritual.

The missionary movement was not smooth sailing. It had tremendous vicissitudes such as that which happened in April 1869. The missionaries told the Africans that they did not believe most of the themes which were still lifting up high their spiritual God. In 1879 the missionaries had a set back.

I have maintained throughout this thesis that European Christianity was a cultural semantical Christianity imposed dramatically and inculcatively on the slaves in order to obliterate their African culture and religious beliefs, whereupon the slaves would automatically accept European and British white orientated Christianity of moral, sociological, ethical and theological vacuousness. Indeed, European and British Cultural Christianity programmatically was used singularly for the enslavement of Africans. Baptism and conversion of the slaves had nothing to do with the abandonment of slavery. Rather, baptism and conversion of the slaves was a further implementation psychologically and culturally to guarantee the truncation and pulverisation of the slaves spiritually and the separation of the slaves geographically and culturally from their African roots and from their ancestral roots, culture, religion and God.

Dr. Beckles and Dr. Shepherd scholarly remind us that even baptised slaves had not fully accepted Christianity. In 1859 the slave Hiob Hermanus expressed the belief that his sickness was due to the actions of Abraham Hermanus. The missionary believed that his inculcation had extirpated the slaves' belief and practice of witchcraft even when the slaves had been baptised. The missionary therefore believed that the slaves had dissipated themselves back into the practice of paganism. All these were European definitions and elucidations and at no time had Europeans and the British shown any understanding, appreciation or value for that which was indeed historically and otherwise African. They discarded comprehensively all that pertains to Africanism.

A major psychological, spiritual and theological blow was in 1860 when the Moravian mission discovered by a missionary that a significant number of slaves, approximately 22 had returned to their former religious traditions, having meetings at their traditional altars in place of worship in the fields. It also came to his knowledge that the slaves had created a wooden image of their God. Was this monotheism or was this henotheism? Or was it Christianity?

The missionary with a racist European Cultural Christianity was profoundly surprised at the psychological and cultural behaviour of the slaves to their African tradition and at the same time to the missionary culture. This illusion became real for the missionaries because of the failure of European Christianity to suppress the African God. The significant surprise to the missionaries was the slaves' objection to remove their African icon. The missionaries refused to baptise any new candidates but continued with the belief that Jesus would be successful and that Jesus Christ would be all powerful to the Israelites. The message of disappointment remained for a very long time. What is of significance to note is that paradoxically there is no evidence that the slaves accepted European Christianity and also the slaves had not accepted slavery as previously indoctrinated in them that slavery was ordained by God for Africans. These two objections puzzled the slave masters. The slaves were responding and reacting to this type of inimicalism, morally, religiously and spiritually repugnant inculcation by virtue of their innate God consciousness and ontological consciousness to be free.

Equally, the Moravian missionary movement was relatively unsuccessful. It was unsuccessful because the missionary movement did not succeed in the elimination of African-based religion of the slave population. What logically happened was the development of dualism appropriate to both sides, or rather what developed was a form of henotheism by the African slaves. Opposition to the Moravian slave movement with more resistance continued for a long time. It was in part played by priests. It was also deeply significant especially because they acted recalcicrantly against the Moravian missionary movement. It was Jansa who introduced Christianity to Vossenburg in 1847. It was a black slave driver who with courage, temerity and a burning fire for freedom in his heart like the biblical Jeremiah, who opposed the Moravian missionary movement. Philosophically, spiritually and psychologically, the movement innate in man to be free is both indestructible and irresistible.

Slave driver priests were very effective instruments at the time, because time and time again these slave priests castigated and opposed the missionaries relentlessly and consistently. It is important to remember the depth of vicissitudes, tensions, and conflicts between the slaves and the missionaries. The slaves did not spontaneously or immediately accept the missionary Christianity. The missionary Christianity was a cultural and a semantical Christianity, designed to obliterate and to fully extirpate the slave religion.

Religion, Traditions and Beliefs

The Moravian mission was involved in the brainwashing process not in any dissimilar way to other denominations such as the Methodists, the Baptists, the Anglicans, the Catholics and the Presbyterians. They were all involved in the slave trade brainwashing process. They were all in the missionary business or movement for the same reasons; extirpation of anything religious and cultural relating to Africa and Africans. Along with the sociological and cultural programme to dislocate all forms of Africanism by inculcation of a foreign cultural and religious belief on the slave to secure the control, oppression and exploitation of the African slaves.

Both Beckles and Shepherd's postulation has weight and power for me. According to authentic records, the majority of conflicts between the missionaries and the slaves were the slave driver priests who used their deliberations with the Moravian missionaries as religious functionaries, priests or Obeah men. In all these situations, the missionaries were aware of the tremendous influence the slave priests had on the slave community. It was therefore a confrontation and a conflict between the slave priests and the missionaries.

It must be admitted that it was the slave driver priests who consciously and forcefully opposed the Moravian missionaries' attempts to replace the African religion with European Cultural and Semantical Christianity. It was the response of the slave priests' objection to oppression and exploitation of the slaves who actually motivated the emergence psychologically to form that all important palladium of oppressed people and to safeguard them from exploitation by the planters and also their slave owners.

The Moravian mission like other missionary movements considered the relation of the slaves as pagans. They used every conceivable method to destroy any slave religion.

Pantheism and henotheism was inappropriate for the African slaves, but paradoxically, the attempt made by the Moravian mission to extirpate the slave religion also threatened the basic fabric and foundation of the slave religion. The emotional support, their feeling of symbioticism culturally and spiritually. It is therefore pretty obvious that the conflict between the slaves and the Moravian mission was so strong and powerful, that the missionaries' task was to obliterate the slave religion and replace it with the European Cultural Christianity being imposed upon the slaves forcefully. The missionaries looked upon the slave driver priests functionally for the maintenance of the slave religion. If the Moravian missionaries were looking for dysfunctionalism from the slave driver priests they were in for a very rude awakening. Conflict and tensions were constant companions between the Moravian missionaries and the slaves. They called upon the slaves to dissipate their religion. They frequently called upon the slaves to act obediently to all the genealogical members of the politically and religiously dominant white groups. Who were these people? They were the directors, overseers, the bookkeepers and the artisans. There was also racial tension between the blacks and the whites. The whites believed that they were descendants of a superior white master race. This was an endemic European and British philosophy and culture. It was not a matter of assimilations or inter-racial connection, rather it was the inculcation of a European Cultural Christianity with contiguity of a white master race philosophy of economic oppression and exploitations of the African slaves. The Moravian mission even went much further in their psychological and spiritual programme. They tried to inculcate into the slaves such virtues as patience, submission and obedience for the creation and maintenance of a white social order over and against the slaves. Repudiation must be made radically and fully of the interconnectedness of the slaves through their identical existential experience of suffering caused by the said European Cultural and Semantical Christianity.

 I go further and proclaim that the slaves symbiotically shared one singular theme. That was the shared experience of slavery which was what made them want freedom all the more.

European Christianity and the Atlantic Slave Trade:
A Black Hermeneutical Study

The cultural Christianity while promulgating and inculcating the eradication of African pagan religion, the slaves' imperatives to embrace patience, submission and obedience. There was no mention of freedom or complete manumission from the diabolical and repugnant heinous crime of enslavement of Africans by force and subjugation.

The philosophy, conduct and policy of the Moravian missionaries in the despicable way described with full tabulation caused the slaves to see the Moravian mission and missionary preachers as integral instruments in promoting and preserving the philosophy of economic planters' culture of superiority.

In order to fully elucidate and hermeneutically postulate this sitz im leben of the slaves and the Moravian missionaries, we must look at the political and economical agreement reached in 1734 between the Moravian missionaries and the society of Suriname. Sociologically and economically the Suriname group represented comprehensively the planters' class. The pellucid agreement was made without any ambiguity that the society gave their approbation to the Moravian mission to preach the Gospel to the slaves in Suriname. A quotation from a letter with the chronology of December 1734 will illuminate the relationship and function of the society and the Moravian mission.

"On 4th December I met again the Directors in the West Indian home, to have talks… they only asked me how I felt about the slaves. I replied that one should try to convert, but at the same time, to admonish them to be loyal and industrious and therefore not to long for freedom… however to accept it with thanks when it is granted to them. They were satisfied with my answer".

It would be theologically and sociologically dissipatory to expend intellectual energy to elucidate the profound involvement and programme of the missionaries to keep the slaves subjugated. The quotation above delineates clearly the philosophy and programme of the missionary movement. To the missionaries the African religion and religious beliefs were paganistic. Paganism was illogical to European Cultural Christianity. The European and British had forgotten that Europe and Britain had always been paganistic and never Christian countries. It is noteworthy that European Cultural

Christianity did not promote manumission for the slaves. This is clear evidence that they were not Christians. The slaves were to be "loyal and industrious" and should have no desire for freedom in this life. This is not a simple brainwashing of the mind and spirit of the slaves, it was a deliberate, calculated and conscious premeditated inimical plot of a culture and cultural semantical Christianity, which denied the slaves their ontological gift from the Supreme Intelligence namely God, the gift of inherent and innate freedom.

If as purported and postulated that European Christianity was virtuous – why the hell did they not keep it to themselves? Why did they themselves not change places with the Africans? Rather they inculcated the Africans by force to abandon African religion for European Cultural Christianity. A radical deduction can be made from the vacuous and inimical statement just mentioned above. Nonetheless, account and responsibility must be fully delineated that there is no historical record of historical attestation and appellation of the missionaries and planters class in collaboration with the slave traders that the slaves accepted without resistance their bondage of slavery. In a nutshell the slaves had at no time succumbed to slavery. If they had done, that would have been a denial of their ontological innate freedom. At every opportunity, waking and walking for the slaves, they were looking and planning always to escape. Always to put in operation insurrections and conspiracies to organise equally rebellions. In this tremendous inner chamber of quest thousands of slaves sacrificed their lives rather than to surrender to the evils of slavery. Slavery was confronted and met with tremendous resistance from the slaves. It goes without saying that Britain, Europe and America never had any intention or they never gave freedom to the abolition of slavery. It was the slaves who abolished slavery. It was the slaves who procured their emancipation.

Second in line to the opposition of slavery in the form of resistance, be it confrontational or orthodox, is European Cultural Christianity and British ethnocentric Christianity. The slaves did not embrace spontaneously European Cultural Christianity and British ethnocentric Christianity. In reality the slaves did not understand the foreign religion and culture. Both the religion and culture of oppression and enslavement and the dehumanisation of the slaves.

The slaves were correct to object to these forms of repugnancy and heinousness.

The slaves were forced to abandon their culture, history, religion and historical traditions in all shapes and forms. Cosmology, witchcraft and Myalism were for the slaves part and parcel of their history and culture. In the Old Testament necromancy and various forms of magic grew up side by side with Israelite religion. There are instances when the slaves pretended to accept European Cultural Christianity in order to alleviate their conditions. Whatever was the source there can be no circumvention of the fundamental fact that the promotion and introduction of slavery was designed to extirpate that which had been all important to the slaves for their very existence and cosmological relationship with nature, namely Almighty God.

The gravitation of the separation between the African religion and foreign cultural Christianity demonstrated the importance to look at the Atlantic Slave Trade and European Christianity with a black hermeneutical incisiveness for what it was by nature and composition.

The Atlantic Slave Trade was a systematic, economic philosophy and system. The system began with the search for gold, palm oil, timber, ivory etc. The system then progressed to human cargo, namely slavery. The major countries of Europe were far from systematically equipped for the great slave trade. It was indeed the British who perfected or made the trade more systematic for the tremendous Transatlantic slave trade. Indeed Britain made the slave trade professional and sophisticated, even technological. Britain became the leading trade country in the Atlantic slave trade and colonies. Britain fought many wars to grab colonies from Spain, Portugal and France. We should never forget the 7 year war, and at the end of the war Britain had captured the majority of the colonies of Portugal, Spain and France. Another way of describing British trading system is that Britain became the master and prime mover of the slave trade.

Whilst Britain became the leading country dealing with slavery and expanding its colonies, the British churches were actually actively involved in the slave trade in order to keep Britain in power with the economic growth from African slavery.

Indeed, the churches were at the centre of the slave trade. Despite prevarications and countless mendacities, the logical summation is that in any language, theology, philosophy, morality, ethics, sociology, anthropology, even situational ethics, the Atlantic slave trade was morally and theologically indefensible and morally repugnant. In addition, British historians consciously made the history of the Atlantic slave trade recondite in order to prevaricate the truth. Eric Williams is most forceful in exposing this myth and mendacity in his book 'British Historians and the West Indies'.

The slaves remained contiguous to their religious traditions in the context of slavery as a radical, cultural and sociological response to the oppressive slavery conditions and psychologically it offered them the protection against exploitation by the planters, the enslavers and the aggressive ill treatment in the midst of their dehumanisation.

In a laconic sentence the European Christian churches displayed cooperation between themselves and the western organisations in colonies which was normal especially in the 18th and 19th centuries. The planters' class was kept in sublime esteem by people such as J.W. Kals in 1731 and 1756.

The Moravian and the Dutch Reformed Churches admitted that the slavery conditions were harsh, dehumanising and revolting. Paradoxically they considered slavery as a system that was imposed by God and that it should only be abolished by him. Again, such concept, such culture is absolutely revolting. It was the concept of the churches, the planters and enslavers. It was indeed a blatant audacity for the European churches to place God in the midst of the oppressions and exploitations. Nonetheless, it is also to be admitted that the European denominations and British concepts of God in the midst of slavery, oppression, exploitation and the repugnancy of the slave trade does pose not only a polemical situation or even problematic situation but rather a simple fact, and that is it calls into question the existence of a moral God, a God of justice, a God of love, a God of righteousness, a God of omnipotence and a God of mercy.

The concept was a general concept held by the so-called Christian slave traders and of various denominations, alongside the political leaders. The philosophers, sociologists and scientists also held the same identical concept that slavery was ordained by God. This God was the European and British God. The question is apt – whose God? Which God? The white man's God? The European and British God? Even karmically this is diabolical and repugnant. On the other hand, if slavery was imposed by God, why was it only for the Africans and not for the British and Europeans? Who said it was imposed and ordained by God? It was not the Africans and the slaves, but the oppressors and exploiters. It was therefore a calculated, deliberate and conscious postulation designed to inculcate, transfigure, amputate and to the full pulverisation of all that pertains to Africa and African descendants.

The view expressed by the Moravian missionaries created ambiguities, inconsistency, contradictions, reconditeness and unpellucidness concerning the behaviour of the missionaries who presented to the slaves in oppression and dehumanised enslavement and not to the oppressors and the exploiters. In other words, the missionaries promoted the dual concept of two Gods. One for the slaves confirming the conditions the slaves' were in that it was ordained by this God which was imposed culturally on the slaves. The God of the European Cultural Christianity and semantical Christianity. There was the slave traders' God who allowed the traders all the rights to keep the slaves in subjugation sempiternally for a heavenly brainwashed purpose. There was the exception and extraordinary not according to Beckles and Shepherd. The missionaries were used to keep the negroes in complete subordination and under psychological control. The exploitation was a joint and symbiotic policy and practice between the slave traders and planter class. The missionaries were not forced, they unconditionally participated in the slave system because the churches were enmeshed and instrumental in the furtherance of the economic philosophy for Europe and Britain.

The missionaries were not always successful. Failure was never alienated from the missionaries. Indeed the missionaries failed to obliterate the African based religion of the slave population. Even with subjugation alignment with the planters class. Psychological attempts to eliminate the African religion from the slaves, the missionaries did not make inroads deep enough to strangulate the African slaves' beliefs and paradosis of their religion. Obeah, myalism and witchcraft are entombed in the African psyche, culture and religion. African religion is psychological, spiritual, physical and particularly sociological.

According to Alpers, European Christians were aware that to sell their fellow human beings could not be morally justified, yet the Christian church came forward with excuses for the slave traders. Many priests carried on slave trading, especially in Angola, and many others owned slaves in the Americas.

Dr. Eric Williams in his book 'Capitalism and Slavery', claimed "The church also supported the slave trade". Hugh Thomas claimed that the denominations were enmeshed in the slave trade. Sherlock, Bishop of London assured the planters that Christianity and the embracing of the Gospel does not make the least difference in civil property. The church bells of the Bristol churches rang merrily on the news of the rejection by Parliament of Wilberforce's bill for the abolition of slavery. The slave trader John Newton gave thanks frequently to the Liverpool churches for the success, especially of his last venture before his so-called conversion and implored God's blessing on his cargo. Newton established public worship twice every day. He kept a day of fasting and praying not for the slaves for his crew. "I never knew the sweeter or more frequent powers of divine communion than in the last two voyages to Guinea". George Whitefield argued in advocating the repeal of the article of the Georgia Charter which forbade slavery. "It is plain to demonstrate that our countries cannot be cultivated without negroes". In 1766 according to record, there were 84 Quakers listed as members of the company trading to Africa, among them the Barclay and Baring families. Slavery was the most lucrative investments for English as well as American Quakers. The name of the slaver, the Winning Quaker reported from Boston and Sierra Leone in 1793 symbolises the approval with which the slave trade was regarded in Quaker circles. Europe was inundated with black slaves. Slaves were conspicuous among London bearers and were known as St. Giles blackbirds. So numerous were they that a parliamentary committee was set up in 1786 for relieving the black poor. Slave ships had Christian names and when ships loaded with human cargo sailed from Christian countries to the western hemisphere so-called Christian priests used to bless the ships in the name of Almighty God and also at the same time admonished the slaves to be obedient.

It never entered into their minds to admonish the masters to be kind to the slaves. This laconic final summary is both pertinent, conducive and significant and the cry therefore now is for radical rethinking biblically and theologically, ethnologically, culturally and sociologically for the acknowledgement that all human species are descendants of the singular anthropos – Adam and that we all belong to the one human race and the need is for universal brotherhood.

CHAPTER 25
ERADICATION OF SLAVERY

**The Abolition of European Slave Trade
- 1807 British and 1808 American**

The British Magna Carta is legally pellucid on two fundamental backbones of the Carta. They are:
1. That piracy was legally enshrined in the Magna Carta. John Hawkins earned his knighthood from Queen Elizabeth I for his piracy of Sierra Leone. The Queen even invested tremendous financial sums of money into the piracy business of John Hawkins. The Queen strengthened her commitment to John Hawkins piracy by offering Hawkins her ship with the name "Jesus". Needless to say, that the title or name Jesus had no moral, ethical or theological significance to the Queen in terms of justice, rectitude, freedom and equality.
2. Slavery was also enshrined into the Magna Carta as legal. The enslaved had no human rights to manumission. They were stripped of all attributes and characteristics of being human. Slaves were the properties of the slave owners, indeed the master enslavers.

It is historically acknowledged among different schools of history, geographical hearing and scholarship, that slavery formed an integral social function of man's life and society. Thus, sociologically and anthropologically, slavery is in the blood of human kind. Whilst this is historically carried, there are fundamental differences socially, culturally and politically about the different periods of slavery and slave societies. The biblical slave period of the Egyptians were due to the biological and economical conditions of the Joseph family with their genealogy and ethnic anthropology.

Hugh Thomas has instigated our attention to the different categories of slavery around European and others. Geographical and demographic contiguity of nations.

Among the dissatisfactions of slavery none can appropriately be compared with the Atlantic Middle Passage, Slave Trade. The comparison is unreachable and impossible, geographically, demographically, racially, economically, sociologically and politically enshrined. It is important to add that the religious, the theological, the African religion and African religious paradosis were henotheistic. We cannot separate these areas from the Atlantic Slave Trade movement. It was gigantic, morally repugnant by any standard of decency, humanity and religious connection to a moral and holy God. A Supreme Being, monotheistically conceived as creator and prime mover of the Universe. Sovereign God. The physical, psychological, cultural and religious ambulation of slavery and the African consciousness of cosmology and henotheism. The purpose was truncated by the European cultural movement. The cultural movement was Christianity, the co-mixture of the bible and acculturation.

A number of scholars of academic importance have written on the history of the abolition of slavery, the anti-slavery movement and the anti-abolitionists movement. Dr. Sydney W. Mintz has provided a chronological tabulation for the ending of slavery. His chronology is as follows:

1. It was not until 1886 that Fernando and Isabel when mentioning a shipment of 17 African slaves to Santo Domingo in 1505, declared, "A need for 100 more in order that all of these be getting gold for me." Slavery was abolished in Cuba thus ending it for all time. In the Antilles, Denmark illegalised the slave trade in 1802. England in 1807, America in 1808, Sweden in 1813, France in 1814 and Spain in 1820, but the illegal trade continued with modicum abatement at least until

1860. However, freed contracted African labourers were also imported during much of the 19th century. The chronologies of Dr. Mintz correspond to those of Hugh Thomas and others. What was the prime mover or driving force for the abolition movement? There are different claims made by historians, ranging from the British supposedly humanitarian to a Christian movement or conscience. I shall radiate these analytically, systematically, critically and particularly hermeneutically from a black conscious theological and moral perspective later in this paper.
2. Emancipation was accepted reluctantly as the programme to end the slave trade. In 1838 the British colonies, in the French colonies 1863, in the Dutch colonies 1873, in Puerto Rico and Cuba 1886.

Can we find a cannon with rationale to deal with the complexities of these unpellucid chronological factors? The best possible hermeneutic is that the dynamic force of the slave trade and its economic necessity to the various economies within Europe, Britain and the USA was so powerful that there was no leverage albeit political or legal that could stop the dynamism of the trade. In addition it is pretty clear that these countries had no homogenous agreement on the slave trade. There was no pandemic ubiquitous or international agreement. The agreements were politically and economically contextualised. Another point we need to highlight is that for Britain there are two separate dates 7th March 1807 and 7th August 1807. It is not logical to have two dates in the same year pertaining to the same problem or complexity namely the British abolition of the slave trade act on paper. These dates also delineate for us that the gravitation of individualistic economy and political power were of the greatest importance.

There were two major problems facing the end of slavery:
1. Did the abolitionists forcefully argued on the grounds of principal?
2. Did the planters equally forcefully argued for more labourers?

Dr. Mintz says "It was the congenical inferiority of the slaves which formed the basis for the arguments". Slavery was defended with the spirit of a prime lion spirit, because it was basically profitable. Indeed in the words of Lord Scott, "Slavery was an economical necessity for Europe".

I have elucidated in this thesis that my purpose is not to write a history of the Atlantic Slave Trade or rather the morally repugnant Atlantic Slave Trade or Middle Passage. My primary heuristic ambition is to provide a balanced hermeneutic by taking the volume of synthesis and like a biblical theologian apply redaction criticism as a theological tool to get behind the text or mind of the writer to bring out the theological message.

Far too many books have been written on the Atlantic Slave Trade. They have been written by white historians. This unequilibrium of academic historical writing on a subject of such historical magnitude without volumes of black contributions on the subject. Before my expatiation on the abolition movement and the prodigious achievements of the legal abolition of slavery there are some important and outstanding factors worth recording.

The contributions of the two best known anti-slavery opponents are:
1. Thomas Clarkson, deserves first prize with distinction.
2. William Wilberforce with measured reservations for his part in the abolitionist movement.

To these prodigious names I add the following:
1. Lord Palmerston
2. Fox
3. Pitt
4. Sir Philip Francis
5. Cannon
6. Sheridan
7. James Steven
8. Benjamin Hubb-House
9. Ignatius Sancho
10. Granville Sharpe
11. Olaudah Equiano

On the US side whilst the list is expendable, one name worth mentioning is President Thomas Jefferson. A careful analysis of his politics delineates that Jefferson acted with passion always as a perfidious, ambiguous president with an ambivalent mind.

Jefferson himself as president employed slaves; sometimes, Jefferson himself sold slaves. On the 27th January 1807 a bill supporting the Abolition of slaves was passed by the Senate and on 2nd March 1808 President Jefferson signed the Abolition bill which states categorically that unequivocally 2nd January 1808 it would be illegal for anyone in the USA to deduce any Negro, Mulatto or any person of colour as a slave. The Atlantic slavery has been seen as an historical problem. This cannot be right because Africa and her descendants globally reflect the legacy of the Atlantic Slave Trade. Juxtaposed with the negative dehumanising and psychological conundrum and amnesia of black people caused by European Cultural Christianity. Dr. Na'im Akbar in his book 'Papers in African Psychology. defined the slave trade as an insidious slave system. This slavery system was notorious as the most humanly degrading method of exploitation and abuse in the history of civilised man. A theological and hermeneutical deduction from Dr. Akbar's statement is that the legacies of the 18th and 19th centuries is still with black people today. Whether it is in Britain, Europe, America, Africa or the West Indies.

Zerdanoo Gifford in her book 'Thomas Clarkson and the Campaign against Slavery', said "Many of the world's most admired achievements have been built upon slavery. A logical and informative adding to Mrs Gifford's statement is the fact that Europe's economy and the US economy were built from the Atlantic Slave Trade. The American dream of tremendous opportunity and the global expansive capitalist system were all created by the sacrificing of the free lives of the slave trade people and also of the 18th and 19th centuries in which millions of African people were forcefully transported to the West Indies and the Americas.

The Slave Trade histories have been written by, again I reiterate white scholars. Entombed in their white culture which blinded most of them to the historical facts that they are wrong with their biased accounts which has been strongly influenced by their cultural perspectives.

Books on the Atlantic Slave Trade written by white scholars are classified as historical books, but accounts authentically written by blacks are classified as negative and part of literature. It is noteworthy that accounts written by whites are classified in libraries as under history but books written by slaves and black people generally are classified as literature or fiction. An outstanding example is that of Olaudah Equiano. The 'Interesting Narratives and other writings' and 'Ignatius Sancho's letters of the late Ignatius Sancho an African'. Hats had been taken off in their appreciative salutation of the illustrious Thomas Clarkson. But it has too often forgotten that black slaves were instrumental in the effectuation of destroying the pernicious slave trade system which denied slaves homes, family and identity. A system which denied the African slaves:

1. Human Rights
2. Human Freedom.

Clarkson was actively involved in opposing slavery on moral and economic grounds.

Clarkson managed through his physical intellectual and psychological astutely to turn the slave issue to the uttermost political topic. Through Clarkson's vision and physical, emotional and intellectual perseverance the topic was kept alive until the Slave Trade's abolition in 1807.

Finally, emancipation of British Slaves in 1834. The Wedgewood image of a slave in chains drew much attention to the fundamental question "Am I not a man and a brother?" This statement is ontologically significant. It is anthropologically significant. It is theologically significant. It is ethnologically significant. It is sociologically pregnant with meaning.

Thomas Clarkson was a gigantic force behind the abolition of slavery. Of all those in Britain who were involved, none can emulate the statue and the immortalised place of Thomas Clarkson. Clarkson worked with people who shared his vision and passion. The moral strength of Clarkson's argument was dynamic. He worked for the abolition at a time when religious intolerance and prejudice were endemically enshrined in British law, culture and religion. Clarkson even worked with the Quakers and the Quakers themselves though it had been claimed by several white historians that they were a paladium and a force behind the abolition movement it must also be acknowledged without reservations that the Quakers too had their gun factory in Birmingham where they supplied slave ships. In other words, there was tremendous moral, ethical and religious ambivalence on all sides. It is imperative to reiterate Hugh Thomas' statement that "all the denominations were involved in the slave trade".

Clarkson was contiguous to the moral arguments that each and every human being should be free. Historians of the Slave Trade have written laconically on the stupendous contribution of Thomas Clarkson. Clarkson was functionally instrumental in the movement for abolition of the slave trade. There are limited synthesis of Clarkson's work. Granville Sharpe's contribution is full of laudation and his illustrious gifts and strengths. It is not germane to compare Clarkson and Sharpe, but it is important to point out that although Clarkson had academic associations with Cambridge University where he was a graduate, the University's Latin competition essay was set by Dr. Pickard who was at the time Vice-Chancellor of the University. Anne Liceat invites "invitos scrvitutem dare". Is it right to enslave men against their will? Not only was Dr. Pickard a dynamic opponent of the Slave Trade but the Cambridge University Colleges received a tremendous amount of financial donations from slave owners and also from investment in the slave trade.

Another notable and ambiguous legal personality was Lord Mansfield, Chief Justice. Lord Mansfield as top judge was himself a slave owner and one of his slaves in London Elizabeth Dido was propinquitous to him being the daughter of his nephew.

Granville Sharpe had many conflicts with Lord Mansfield. His cases were all test cases. Even though Mansfield sought not to rule that the practice of slave trading was illegal in Britain, in the British Court it was said plainly "Slaves were merely a property not people. Therefore, slaves were perceived to be a mere possession with no individual rights or freedom". Granville Sharpe laid down the irrefutable moral foundations for Thomas Clarkson to build on. Granville Sharpe and Thomas Clarkson are conterminously illustrious in status and determination for the abolition of slavery. The same cannot be said for Wilberforce. Wilberforce was enmeshed in his own personal, political, ambitions and political involvement in the slave trade.

Zerbanoo Gifford summarised for us the realities of slavery in Britain.
1. Britain was deeply involved in the slave trade and this involvement was both horrific and morally disturbing. Britain sent ships to the coast of Africa to buy slaves against their will. Britain then transported them across the Atlantic to work without pay or compensation in the colonies of America and the West Indies. It was from this cycle which was extremely profitable to Britain that the philosophy of the triangular trade developed.
2. One ship surgeon described the condition on deck as follows: "The deck that is the floor of their room was so covered with blood and mucus which had preceded from them in consequence of the flux that it resembled a slaughterhouse. It is not in the power of human imagination to picture itself in a situation more dreadful or disgusting".

In 1807 when it is said that the slave trade was abolished but the slaves working in the colonies had not been set free. The white plantations in the West Indies were markedly outnumbered by their slaves. In order to keep the pressure of authority on the slaves the masters' ruled by fear and denied all rights to the slaves. The slaves faced a relentless variety of punishments, from whippings in the fields for laziness to mutilation, torture and death for anything from theft, running away to retaliation or even plotting against their masters. Any owner who accidentally killed a slave "shall not be liable to any penalty or forfeiture whatsoever". This was stated by the law. In other words, by virtue of reiteration, the slaves at no time whatsoever had any rights nor were they treated beyond that of an animal. We must remember that the subjugation, exploitation and the punishment of the slaves were conducted and done by men, European and British who claimed and professed that they were Christians.

Slaves could not give evidence against their owners in court, or even a white person because of this fact that the slaves were left without any protection against murder, except that they were there only as economic value as workers. They had no other purpose.

One law even stated the rights of a master to be everything and those of the slave, nothing. The master enslavers had all rights and legal powers, the slaves had nothing. They were not safeguarded. When slaves were executed, their bodies would normally be left to rot in the sight of their companions so as to give the punishment greater attention by the other slaves. The sum of this systematic subjugation and degradation of African slaves was the denial of the slaves' rights to be human. The slaves on the plantations were robbed, denied, psychologically, spiritually and physically raped, they were regarded as property to their master slavers. What is the paradoxical and ambiguous fascination is that although the slaves were treated with such brutality the missionaries were there to enforce their obedience to their condition. The missionaries were there to perpetuate the inculcation that the conditions of the slaves were divinely appointed. In other words, their conditions were appointed by European and British philosophy of superiority and the philosophy of economic prosperity at the expense of the slaves.

The power of Equiano's faith in his cosmological God was the basis for his voluminous appeal to end slavery. We see here that Equiano's courage, conviction and forcefulness had great significance. His immortal words are "O ye nominal Christians, might not an African ask you learned you this (slavery) from your God who says unto you, do unto all men as you would men do unto you". Although the words of Equiano are psychologically and spiritually and even theologically pregnant with meaning and purpose they were hopeless words because they fell on deaf ears of men without conscience. Men without morality, men without empirical knowledge or faith in the power of alpha and omega. They were men who carried the label Christians. Christians only by virtue of culture and philosophy.

The contributors to the Abolition of Slavery were people of imminence. Among the classical protagonists Equiano must be held high always because he had a tremendous influence on the mind of Dr. Pickard from Cambridge University. He also influenced Granville Sharpe tremendously. To take up the struggle for the abolition of slavery by taking up the slave ship's song in court. I believe Equiano's approach, philosophy, Christian convictions and his dynamic and persuasive letter to Lord Hawkesbury in 1789 which was put as evidence before a Parliamentary Enquiry in the Slave Trade was outstanding.

Equiano's argument was factual and realistic. He argued for "A fair trade with Africa. A commercial intercourse with Africa opens an inexhaustible source of wealth to the manufacturing interests of Britain and all with the slave trade is but a physical obstruction. His argument had moral and economical force. The abolition of the diabolical slave trade would give most rapid and permanent extension to manufacturers which is totally and diametrically opposed to what some interested people assessed".

Equiano worked till his death at age 52 in 1797. He toured and perambulated the entire country promoting the abolitionists campaign. Equiano was sempiternally dedicated to his African people and the basic historical legacy he has left us is the important evidence of his active contributions which African people passionately made to the abolition of slavery. It is hereby noted that white historians eloquently, expatiated with enthusiasm always by advocating the various places in history of Wilberforce and others of a similar vein. In the abolition of slavery the name Equiano is always and sometimes like a footnote. It is therefore of historical importance that people like Equiano must be enmeshed in history as immortal giants of moral conviction, experience, character and rectitude.

British plantation owners used their wealth to buy and build great country houses and to buy political favours.

Scholarship must have rectitude. Scholarship must have courage and audacity, to face critical, provocative, controversial and polemical issues be they history, sociology, anthropology or theology, scholarship must bear the hallmark of scholastic rectitude. Castigations therefore of historians especially British and European who have sought to suppress the African or slaves' positive contribution to the Abolition of Slavery, should be best judged by such black hermeneutical study in progress. Indeed, not only this vexed and exigent subject for honest research and postulations but also in the fields of theology and philosophy. No theologian or philosopher of religion can deny the sublime academic scholarship of the immortal St. Augustine, an African of unparallel academic ability at Rome University. Dr. Richard Hart has bridged for us the gap in his volumes 1 and 2. Volume 1 "Slaves who Abolished Slavery - Blacks in Bondage", Volume 2 "Blacks in Rebellion". For the first time, Dr. Hart as an historian has provided for us historical and authentic evidence that it was the slaves themselves who created the atmosphere and the effectuation of the abolition of slavery. Not British nor European or American politicians but it was the slaves themselves.

I make this bold statement that was conceived by me in my New York University Doctorate research on Education and Liberation. In that Doctorate, I used education to mean the ontological consciousness for manumission created in man by God. This ontological consciousness can not be suppressed sempiternally by man or the oppressors or the master enslavers. With this preamble I do state that there is no historical evidence that African slaves during the Atlantic Slave Trade period Middle Passage, plantation and cotton fields had at any time accepted enslavement. The struggle for manumission is congenical in man's nature. The words of the dynamic slave leader Cudjoe, "I rather die on yonder gallows than to die a slave because nature made to be free". Man was made in the image of God with the gift implanted in his nature to be free. Other men through their culture and economic philosophy stripped, denied, robbed, subjugated and exploited their fellow man especially because of their genealogical, ethnological and geographical context, namely Africa.

The slave traders and owners inculcated fear, inferiority, white superiority, white supremacy, dehumanisation, the lack of freedom, denial of human rights and human dignity to the slaves. In this inimical oppressive, brainwashing and enslavement of Africans, European Cultural Christianits did their best to destroy all African sense of being human. The church condemned and pulverised Africans with the biggest brainwashing scam. The slave suffering was alright. When they died, they will go to heaven. This was total bullshit.

No wonder John Newton was able without any conscience as a minister of religion like Clarkson in the Church of England, Newton had no qualms about torturing slaves and beating the daylight out of them and then thanking Almighty God for delivering his crew safely from perils. John Newton became William Wilberforce's spiritual tonic and advisor and chaplain. Three things cannot be denied. Reiteration, alliteration and appellation that the slaves were perceived biologically, scientifically and theologically to be non beings. To be animals. It was a concept they used on the African mind to destroy all senses, feelings, descriptions and purposes that they were human beings. The philosophy, campaign and the missionary movement was to force the Africans to accept their station of animalisation.

Dr. Richard Hart says, "Most historians have paid little or no attention to the frequent and formidable rebellions and conspiracies of the slaves or the extent to which these events influenced the British decision for the abolition of slavery. In other words, in simple unequivocal language, white historians have played the cultural game of not placing any significance or importance to slaves' contributions and in their hermeneutical context the contributions of the slaves themselves through their indestructible spirit, through their indestructible ontological consciousness gave their lives through suffering for their freedom. The way the slaves suffered and died for their manumission and emancipation runs parallel at times dominically and theologically to that of Jesus Christ. And this is why, the Jesus of the black experience, cannot be the Jesus of the historical quest in any New Testament school or approach, because the historical quest is a cultural quest to find a white Jesus, while the Jesus of the black experience is a black brother. Geographically, genealogically and historically. This is a fact that white New Testament scholars find impossible to accept.

Zerbanoo Gifford's conclusion is also pertinent for us here. She said "We shall not be taken in by a whitewash view of history which tells us that the abolitionists alone put an end to slavery, as it was the Africans who also brought about their own freedom and the collapse of the slave system, too often at the cost of their own lives".

Dr. Richard Hart says, "The denial of black contributions to the abolition of slavery through rebellions and non violence resistance, is like denying the contributions of the immortal Steve Beko or Nelson Mandela's contribution to the extirpation of the apartheid system in South Africa, which symbolically, chronologically, historically and biblically lasted for 400 years".

Contiguous to Dr. Richard Hart are Dr. Moses de Nwulia in his book 'Britain and Slavery in East African'. Dr. Nwulia says "It is one thing to profess and proclaim humanitarianism but it is another thing to feel it and manifest it. The concept and persistent humanitarianism, emerging and sustaining Britain's interest and activities in East Africa is a gross exaggeration. There is sufficient evidence to show that Britain's humanitarianism has exemplified in it's official attitudes and policies towards slavery and the slave trade in East Africa was more than humanitarianism of self-interest than of anything else". I add to the words of Dr. Nwulia that Britain at no time by virtue of conscience, moral or otherwise had any inner intention to abolish slavery. It never came by virtue of spontaneity or human conscience. It was done through the impact of the slaves themselves. Dr. Nwulia carefully reminds us that any academic critique of the abolition of slavery must be juxtaposed with the events of slavery. Let me ostentate my appreciation of Dr. Nwulia's contribution by tabulating some of his views further on slavery. "The principle agents for the trans-continental distribution of African slaves were white and Caucasian people. The trans-oceanic demographic rape of Africa has given rise to interesting academic debates. Nonetheless it was the Europeans who initiated the African slave trade across the Atlantic but the institution of slavery itself was already an established custom in Africa. This was the domestication of African slaves, while for Europe and Britain it was the dehumanisation and animalisation of Africans.

Dr. Walter Rodney further claimed that it has often been claimed that it was easy for African chiefs to begin by selling their own slaves. It appears that the sale of human beings was a new feature on most African societies which came about as a direct reaction to the presence and activities and perpetuation by Europeans.

The primary aspect of the slave trade that seriously engaged the attentions of Britain was the one lie told by Christians from the European world. Beginning with a modest share in the 16th century Britain graduated to the top of the list.

Mr. Granville as Prime Minister in January 1807, described the slave trade as "contrary to the principles of justice, humanity and sound policy". In his second speech on the bill for abolition, Grenville said "The trade is not only detestable but criminal". Granville's words are poignant. They are powerful words but one must remember that the Africans had no rights. No dignity, no humanity for 400 years of enslavement. They were legally defined as "no-beings" "none-beings", "cattle". Even philosophers and theologians defined blacks as inferior to the white race. At this juncture of hermeneutical elucidation, one can easily say the slave trade was both a cultural domination and at the same time, a cultural economic philosophy. In brief the slave trade was a system of antinomianism.

The Atlantic Middle Passage's figure of slaves to the Americas and the West Indies are only rough estimates. What scholars have overlooked is that there is no record, in other words no safe record of the number of slaves who have died during the 400 years of the most pernicious and diabolical racial slavery of Africans. It is not a conjecture, it is not philosophical, it is not theological, it is not sociological it is rather ethnological that racism is congenical in the European and British culture. This is showed by the evidence of history and the racial subjugation of Africans, the categorisations of Africans sociologically and scientifically as ignorant and inferior to the white race.

Words are cultural platitudes and this is coterminous among European whites especially dealing with racism, enslavement, exploitation and oppression. Was the abolition of slavery for the enslaved or for the expediency of European economy and moral image worldwide? The enslaved were robbed of their names, dignity and humanity; they were denied freedom and human rights. Take away a persons name and impose a foreign name on them, the names of the slave trade owners, and you will take away their dignity and humanity.

Kunta Kinte refused to accept his slave masters name. Kunte Kinte in *Roots* was whipped mercilessly for his recalcitrancy but he persevered.

The Christian Europeans and British churches were instrumental in the slave trade in imposing the slave master's name on the enslaved, thereby affirming the African slaves only as property. This was an inhuman strategy. A practice throughout the slave trade. Charles Ignatius Sancho was born in or around 1729, on a slave ship sailing in the Middle Passage from African to the West Indies via America. He was baptised by the bishop and named Ignatius by the bishop. Sancho's life as a slave boy was inimical and dramatic. He was kept in a state of ignorance in order to keep him submissive. Sancho's intellectual development and contribution as a literary writer became prodigious through his book, 'Letters of the Late Ignatius Sancho – An African'.

European Cultural Christianity and the major denominations had sought consistently to dress up their images and history but the reality is that no other institution has committed more evil deeds than the churches throughout history. Malcolm X was right when he said "Look at the deeds of Christianity, look at the deeds of Christians".

We need not look too far into the slave trade to see the culture and mindset of the British churches. The wickedness of the treatment and rejection of African West Indians from the 1950s to the 1970s. This is a period of testimony of British racism in the major churches. Even today, the major denominations see black people as economic props and dysfunctional numbers. I have been racially attacked by church officers whose mindset fits pretty well into the 17th, 18th, 19th and 20th centuries slave trade culture of disrespect, lack of appreciation that I am a human being and equally an ordained minister of religion. In my book, 'Suspension a Testimony of Faith, Suffering and Perseverance 2002', I expressed chronologically with tabulations my lived experiences. The church tried to ban my book which is my lived experience. It was 18th and 19th centuries mentality, attitude and racism at work. Obliterate from history black experience. Obliterate from libraries, the experiences and contributions of black people. That has always been the mindset and culture of the British and Europeans. A white person is not only laudated, but is being immortalised for his or her contributions. Blacks must not be immortalised.

It would be foolhardy and a serious sign of unconsciousness to ignore the evilness, spiritual, psychological and cultural historical deeds of the churches on black people worldwide. I reiterate, what the hell were the major churches doing at Elmina Castle with the holy communion table on top of the dungeons where the slaves were kept? Africans and African descendants, need to examine carefully their history, the slave trade history, theology, economics, science, technology, anthropology and philosophy of religion. They need to examine these always contextually from the black perspective.

A critical investigative approach is imperative. How psychologically and intellectually damaging it was to be told by one's Church History Professor, when I asked "Why is there no mention of the black church or black people in your Church History curriculum?" He answered, "it is not important. Professor James Cone had a similar experience with a white academic colleague, who when he asked, "How can you teach American history without the black contribution?" replied, "Black history is not important".

Black Slaves' Symbioticism

It would be unveracious to continue the historical myth that Britain abolished slavery spontaneously and for moral or theological reasons. The abolition of slavery was not motivated by moral compunction, or for purely humanitarian reasons. This has never been a characteristic of the British. It was the British who raised the level of the slave trade to its highest economic philosophy for Europe and Britain. Britain used the Atlantic Slave Trade and slavery for its personal economical prosperity, expansion, development and domination. Britain became the dominant force in the Atlantic Slave Trade in the Americas and the West Indies, Cuba, Haiti and Brazil. It was Parliament in the name of Christianity which passed laws, laws of subjugation for the slaves. It was Parliament who legally according to them, condemned slaves to hell here on earth in the name of the church and Christianity. The slaves were condemned to conditions of endless sufferings, indignity and dehumanisation by Britain. It was done to Africans, in the Caribbean islands where most members of Parliament had no geographical knowledge where the islands were in the universe. Their only knowledge was the economic profitability of the slave trade, because they invested in the heinous Atlantic Slave Trade Middle Passage act of slavery.

We should always remember that in the year 1618, King James I gave a charter of monopoly to 30 London merchants to deal in enslaved people and in 1562 England entered the trade through the person of Sir John Hawkins. Many merchants in London supported

Hawkins with the supply of three ships; they were Solomon, The Swallow and the Jonas.

Dr. Richard Hart has elucidated the slave uprising in Saint Dominique in 1791. The plantation slaves seized their freedom. This was their ontological freedom and consciousness. The victory of the blacks at Saint Dominique over the British and Spaniards with the aid of their mulatto allies established the independence of Haiti. Haiti became the first freed slave state from the British and this was done at the sacrificial dedication and commitment of the slaves to the pursuit and achievement of their human freedom. That human freedom was the beginning of their restoration as human beings with a soul, dignity, humanity and a God.

This piece of significant history of the contributions of the black slaves has not been universally acknowledged by white historians. White historians continue their cultural pedantic biasness towards recognition of the contributions of the black slaves.

The genesis of the abolitionist movement was limited to a small number of voices in Europe and Britain. These people were deeply moved by the brutalities committed to the slaves. The evilness of the Atlantic Slave Trade, transportation and exploitation of the slaves. Even this is questionable whether these people were actually emotionally, psychologically, spiritually and culturally moved. We need to remind ourselves of Queen Elizabeth I reaction to John Hawkins, when she was told of his brutality to the slaves from Sierra Leone to London, she remarked, "God will punish him". But when she was told later in the day of Hawkins' enormous profits she engaged John Hawkins in the slave trade expedition and trade, by giving John Hawkins her own personal ship with the name 'Jesus' on it. In addition to her financial investment in the trade she also knighted John Hawkins. In a nutshell, the economic profitability of the slave trade surpassed and replaced all fabrics of decency, humanity, morality, ethics and religion.

In 1776, David Hartley condemned the slave trade as a contradiction and affront to the laws of God on the rights of men. In 1783, a modicum group of Quakers prayed for the prohibition of the slave trade. The Quaker's humanitarianism fell on deaf ears and dead consciences. The Prime Minister Lord North had no time to dissipate on their appeals. For him, the slave trade was a fundamental necessity, economically to the European nations. The Quakers were active it is said in the liberation of the negro slaves in the West Indies. They planned systematically their publicity. In 1787, Granville Sharpe, Thomas Clarkson and a small team of convinced people formed a society. Their programme was to persuade Parliament to legally prohibit the slave trade. They were encouraged by William Wilberforce. Was it for their own ends or was it for the political expediency of William Wilberforce?

Among these prodigious people, are Olaudah Equiano, Bishop Samuel Ajayi, Crowther, Cudjoe, the Maroon leader in the West Indies, geographically in Jamaica, through whom the British were forced to recognise the Jamaican Maroons as fully manumitted people.

Nat Turner the charismatic preacher in the USA, was also part of the history of those who sacrificed their lives for the abolition, eradication and the extirpation of slavery.

I have said before, that during my doctorate research, that it is not possible to oppress a race of people sempiternally. Man's ontological inner will for manumission will eventually surface. The ontological will of freedom will always resurrect. It will always come alive. It will always be stimulated by the Supreme Intelligence we call God. This is typical of the refuted rebellions or insurrections throughout Jamaica alongside the Maroon community.

The Maroons beat the hell out of the British backside good and proper. They fought the British for 40 years and forced them not only to retreat, but to accept a treaty where the British once again deceived the Maroons perfidiously.

In Jamaica there was Paul Bogle the Baptist Deacon and Sam Sharpe. In 1831 Sharpe planned a tremendous campaign. It was a passive resistance similar to a non-violence movement to force the slave owners to pay the slaves good wages. Liberation theologians ought to be reminded that liberation theology had not started in the early 1960's as perceived by most Latin American liberation theologians and black theologians in the US and in certain quarters of the Caribbean. Liberation theologians were those of the slave trade period. Samuel Sharpe's campaign was promoting a tremendous concession for the slaves who were free and should be paid.

The Christmas riot and rebellion of 1831, rather the Baptist war must be acknowledged. In 1760 there was the Tatackys rebellion by the African rebel chief. The Akan slaves from the Gold Coast were at the centre of the rebellion. This rebellion was a major shock to the plantation slave owners because its aim was the comprehensive extirpation of the white community. The rebellion was laconic, it lasted for only 2 weeks. It caused tremendous damages to property. It is estimated that approximately 20,000 were involved. Property estimated at £1 million was destroyed.

Gad Henman in the 'Killing Time - The Morant Bay Rebellion' in Jamaica said, "The Christmas rebellion or the Baptist war as it came to be known was a crucial event in the abolition of slavery". At this point we must remember, that it had been promulgated throughout history that the British abolished slavery on humanitarian and moral grounds and sometimes religious grounds. It is a remarkable, fanciful mendacity. The Christmas war rebellion came at a time of economic and political vicissitudes for Britain and Europe. This was a crucial turning point in the history of the slave trade and those who were the palladium and vanguard and warriors and Moses for the liberation of the slaves.

From the synthesis of records of the volume of black slave rebellions, insurrections, non-violence and passive resistance it can be said with tremendous confidence it was the slaves who in the end secured their manumission from slavery. Britain and Europe found the rebellions too expensive and as a result slavery became uneconomical and unprofitable. That was the basic fundamental and historical reason for the termination of slavery. It was these forces which motivated and forced Britain and Europe to manufacture a moral high ground with so-called conscience, thrown in and dressed up as European Cultural Christians. No such thing happened. It was the African slaves who through God's divine implantation of spiritual manumission with contiguity in man that which is endemic and epistemological gnosis and awareness that the cosmological African God despite European Cultural Christianity attempted to eradicate African's concept of God. The same African God, who was on the side of the oppressed, exploited, dehumanised and degraded African slaves.

It was a symbiotic effort with particular acknowledgement of the African slaves' contributions to the abolition of slavery that many historians have ignored this historical and documented fact. As Dr. Richard Hart's books Volumes 1 and 2 clearly states 'Slaves who Abolished Slavery' "It is time for the whole footnotes participation of whites as essential figures to be removed from the foot pages of the history of the Abolition of Slavery". It is hoped and it is the ambition and heuristic desire of the author of this thesis that this thesis will help in the process of correcting misleading conscious or unconscious biasness in history.

Elizabeth M Halcrow in her book, 'A Study of Sugar and Slavery'said "Now it is realised that the main events and institutions of West African history were primarily the African minds dealing with slavery. Slaves were available on the scale required by the master enslavers and planters only because African chiefs and traders were prepared to supply and develop a high effective organisation for making them available". The fact of the matter albeit uncomfortable, albeit unsettling or not, the African chiefs and kings were actively involved and they were active participants in the Atlantic Slave Trade.

The Atlantic Slave Trade began not with poor men driven by need, not with law breakers, but with royalty, the rich and the law makers in Europe and Britain. This applied to Europeans as well as Africans. Some African states suffered and were ultimately destroyed by the slave trade demographically and economically. The best known kingdom which was destroyed was the kingdom of Congo 1526. In 1526 King Alfonso complained to Portugal that the extraction of slaves was harming his people.

Dr. Robin Walker in his recent book 'When We Ruled' published September 2006, reminds us not only in a pedantic way but with scholastic authority of imminence as follows. The relationship between Congo and Portugal eventually soured. In 1508 the first slaves from Congo were sent as presents to King Manuel to pay for the Christianisation programme. The Portuguese workers were sent to the Congo and in return they failed to deliver on the work that was agreed. In addition their shabby and arrogant conduct was a cause for concern. Nor was it long before the enslaving activities and abuses of Congo women got out of hand. Dr. Williams wrote "The Portuguese Christianisation of the Congo created something more than chaos. It was a revolting mess, no matter from what angle it was viewed, to begin with, priests were not only among the lead slave traders, but they also owned slave ships to carry the black cargoes to distant lands. Priests also had the harems of black girls, some having as many as 20 each. One of the main attractions that drew thousands of British and European men was their unlimited sexual freedom with the black girls and women who were enslaved and helpless in the power of their masters. These "wholesale raids" on black womanhood continued to swell the mulatto population, the majority of which as in the case of Egypt and the Sudan became the faithful servants and loyal representatives of the conquering races to which their fathers belonged". George Kay said Robin Walker, an English journalist, reports that Hawkins "had great pleasure to behold the Africans fleeing from them, crying out and leaping in the air, mystified when pellets from the pursuers ambushed them. Firearms caused almost invisible but crippling wounds". This was the same John Hawkins who commanded his crew "to serve God daily and love one another". We see here that religion for Hawkins and others had nothing to do with the Atlantic Slave Trade. The trade was seen by them as legitimate and ordained by God. To drive home the force of my argument I place on my intellectual and hermeneutical surgical table Boyd Hilton's book, 'The Age of Atonement – The Influence of Evangelicalism on Social and Economic Thought – 1785 – 1865'. Dr. Hilton failed disgracefully and academically to look at the impact and legacy of the Atlantic slave trade.

Black History in the Atlantic Age

Dr. Robin Walker in his book 'When We Ruled' provided for us information which is pertinent to this postulation and thesis.

Black history in the Atlantic age is therefore composed of the rebellions and the Maroon societies. Dr. W. E. B. Du Bois provided a list of important rebellions by enslaved Africans which showed that the docile nigger slaves in America is a myth.

1522	Revolt in San Domingo
1530	Revolt in Mexico
1550	Revolt in Peru
1550	Appearance of the Maroons
1560	Byano revolt in central America
1600	Revolt of Maroons
1655	Revolt of 1,500 Maroons in Jamaica
1663	Land given to Jamaica Maroons
1664-1738	Maroons fight British in Jamaica
1674	Revolt in Barbados
1679	Revolt in Haiti
1679-1782	Maroons in Haiti organise
1691	Revolt in Haiti
1692	Revolt in Barbados
1695	Palmers;, revolt in Brazil
1702	Revolt in Barbados
1711	Negroes fight French in Brazil
1715-1763	Revolt in Surinam
1718	Revolt in Haiti
1719	Revolt in Brazil
1738	Treaty with Maroons
1763	Black Caribs revolt
1779	Haitians help the United States revolution
1780	French treaty with Maroons
1791	Dominican revolt
1791-1803	Haitian revolution
1794	Cuban revolt

1794	Dominican revolt
1795	Maroons revolt
1796	St. Lucian revolt
1816	Barbados revolt
1828-1837	Revolt in Brazil
1840-1845	Haiti helps Bolivar
1844	Cuban revolt
1844-1893	Dominican revolt
1861	Revolt in Jamaica
1895	War in Cuba

There is irrepressible spirit among the Koromantyn including an Ashanti family deported to Jamaica. The family members were Cudjoe, (Ashanti) Accompong (Achaempong), Kuffee (Kofi), Quanco (Kwaku). To these irrepressible names and paradigms, we must add the name of Nanny who according to legend could have been either the wife or the sister of Cudjoe. 'A history of Negro Revolt' by CLR James is a useful contribution.

Once more Dr. Robin Walker in his book outlined for us the effectiveness of slave rebellions that precipitated the abolition of slavery. Dr. Walker said "The Haitian revolution demonstrated to the world that the European enslavement of Africans could not continue indefinitely the way it had. By the late 19th century it was over, with millions deported and many more killed. All serious scholarship estimated the loss as upward of 50 million. Dr. Basil Davidson puts it "So far as the Atlantic Trade is concerned it appears reasonable to suggest that in one way or another before and after embarkation it caused Africa at least 50 million souls". The Haitians destroyed two French invasions, a Spanish invasion and an English invasion. After the victories Jean-Jacques Dessalines tried and then executed thousands of Europeans for high crimes against the blacks of Haiti. On 22 February 1804 Dessalines gave the relevant orders to dispense justice on the criminals. A second effect of the revolution says modern authority was the decision by Britain to end the slave trade and the eventual dismantling of the cattle slave system entirely by the late 19th century. Actually, abolition was part of a larger plan designed to prevent the blacks from taking over the rest of the West Indies and portions of Central and South America. Britain, the United States and other European powers begun covertly, and supported by white Creole revolutionaries to offset the possibility of a repetition in Haiti. Indeed in less than 20 years after the black nation gained its independence all of South America and Mexico became independent under white Creole leadership. The willingness of the United States to recognise and support newly independent countries was not merely to prevent Europeans from coming back but also to guarantee that insipient black revolts were stamped out before they became torrent. Thus, it can never be overstated that it was the slaves who procured the abolition of slavery and finally their emancipation. Abolition was never a British or European intention, it was precipitously brought about by the rebellions and revolutions of the slaves themselves.

Robinson A. Milwood - March 2007.

BIBLIOGRAPHY

Author/Editor	Title	Published By	Year
Robin Walker	When We Ruled	Every Generation Media	2006
N.T. Wright	Evil and the Justice of God	SPCK Publications	2006
Bob Brown Pan African Roots	Slavery and the Slave Trade – Where and are Crimes against Humanity	African Diaspora Publishing Corporation, Columbus, Ohio	2005
Alvin Morrow	Breaking the Curse of Willy Lynch – The Science of Slave Psychology	Rising Sun Publications	2004
Mark Christian	Black Identity, Expressions of the US and African Diaspora	Hansib Publications	2002
Robert C. Solomon and Mark C. Murphy	What is Justice?	Oxford University Press	2000
Verene Shepherd and Hillary Beckles	Caribbean Slavery in the Atlantic World, A Student Reader	Ian Randle Publishers Kingston	2000
Herbert S. Klein	The Atlantic Slave Trade	Cambridge University Press	1999
James Walvin	The Slave Trade	Sutton Publishing Limited	1999
Vincent Caretta	Ignatius Sancho	Penguin Classics	1998

Author/Editor	Title	Published By	Year
Amos N. Wilson	Blueprint for Black Power A Moral, Political and Economic Imperative for the 21st Century	African World Infosystems	1998
Richard Hart	Occupation to Independence – A Short History of the People English Speaking in the Caribbean Region	Pluto Press	1998
Moses I. Finley	Ancient Slavery and Modern Ideology	Marcus Wiener Publishers	1998
Susanne Everett	The History of Slavery	Grange Books	1997
James Walvin	Questioning Slavery	Ian Randle Publishers, Kingston	1997
Hugh Thomas	The Slave Trade, The History of the Atlantic Slave Trade 1440-1870	Picador	1997
Bev Karey	The Maroon Story, The Authentic and Original History of the Maroons in the History of Jamaica 1940-1880	Agouti Press	1997
David Haslam	A Race for the Millennium	Churches Commission for Racial Justice	1996
Zerbanoo Gifford	Thomas Clarkson and the Campaign against Slavery	Ant Slavery International, London	1996

Author/Editor	Title	Published By	Year
Basil Davidson	The African Slave Trade	James Curry, Oxford	1996
Olaudah Equiano	The Interesting Narrative and Other Writings	Vincent Carretta, Penguin Books	1995
Dr. Eric Williams	British Historians and the West Indies	A and B Books Publishers	1994
Gad Heuman	The Killing Time – The Morant Bay Rebellion in Jamaica	Warwick University, Caribbean Studies Department	1994
Marimba Ani	An African Centre Critique of European Cultural Thought and Behaviour	African World Press	1994
James Walvin	Black Ivory – A History of British Slavery	Fontana Press	1992
Thomas C. Holt	The Problem of Freedom. Race, Labour and Politics in Jamaica and Britain 1832-1938	Ian Randle Publishers	1992
Edt. By Joseph E. Inikori and Stanley L. Evangerman	The Atlantic Slave Trade - Effects on Economies, Societies and Peoples in Africa, the Americas and Europe	Duke University Press	1992
Hillary Beckles and Verene Shepherd	Caribbean Slave Society and Economy A Student Reader	James Currey Publishers	1991

Author/Editor	Title	Published By	Year
Alex Haley	Roots	Vintage Books, London	1991
Paul C. Boyd	The African Origin of Christianity Volume I A Biblical and Historical Account	Karia Press	1991
Wosef AA Ben Jochannan	African Origins of the Major Western Religions	Black Classic Press	1991
A. P. Antippas	A Brief History of Voodo – Slavery and the Survival of the African Gods	Hemb Conex	1990
Richard Hart	The Abolition of Slavery	Community Education Trust	1989
John Hick and Paul F. Kniffer	The Myth of Christian Uniqueness	SCM Press Limited	1987
Fred Lee Hord	Black Culture Centres Politics of Survival and Identity	Third World Press	1967
Cheikh Anta Diop	The African Origin of Civilization Myth or Reality	Lawrence Hill Books	1974
James H. Cone	Martin and Malcolm and America a Dream or a Nightmare	Orbis Press Books	2005
Theo Witvliet	The Way of the Black Messiah	SCM Press Limited	

Author/Editor	Title	Published By	Year
Gayraud S. Wilmore	Black Religion and Black Radicalism an Interpretation of Religious History of Afro-America People	Orbis Books	1973
Richard Hart	Slaves Who Abolished Slavery Volume I – Blacks in Bondage	Institute of Social and Economic Research University of the West Indies, Jamaica	1980
Richard Hart	Slaves Who Abolished Slavery – Volume II Blacks in Rebellion	Institute of Social and Economic Research University of the West Indies, Jamaica	1985
Boyd Hilton	The Age of Atonement – The Influence of Evangelicalism on Social and Economic Thought 1785-1865	Clarendon Press, Oxford	1986
Lamin Sanneh	West African Christianity – The Religious Impact	C Hurst & Co, London	1983
David T. Shannon and Gayraud S. Wilmore	Black Witness to the Apostolic Faith	William B. Herdmans Publishing Company	1988

Author/Editor	Title	Published By	Year
Cornel West	Prophetic Fragments	William B. Herdmans Publishing Company	1988
Marcus Garvey	The Philosophy and Opinions of Marcus Garvey	Majority Press	1986
James Walvin	Slavery and the Slave Trade – A Short Illustrated History	The MacMillan Press Limited	1983
Vincent Harding	There is a River – The Black Struggle for Freedom in America	First Vintage Books Edition	1983
J.E. Inikori	Forced Migration – The Impact of the Export Slave Trade on African Societies	Hutchinson University Library	1982
Albert van Dantzig	Forts and Castles of Ghana	Sedco Publishing Limited	1980
Dr. Eric Williams	Inward Hungar – The Education of a Prime Minister	Andre Deutsch	1979
George Pixley	God's Kingdom – A Guide for Biblical Study	Orbis Books	1977
Sydney W. Mintz	Slavery, Colonialism and Racism	W.W. Norton & Co, New York	1974
Moses De Nwuilia	Britain and Slavery in East Africa	Howard University, Washington DC	1974

Author/Editor	Title	Published By	Year
Walter Rodney	How Europe Underdeveloped Africa	Bogle L'Ouverture Publications	1972
James Walvin	The Black Presence – A Documentary History of The Negro in England	Obach and Chambers Publishers	1971
Dr. Eric Williams	Documents of West Indian History	A and B Books Publishers	1994
Dr. Eric Williams	Capitalism and Slavery	Andre Deutsch	1972
Cornel West	Prophecy, Deliverance an Afro-American Revolutionary Christianity	Westminster Press	1982
Gus John	Taking a Stand	Gus John Partnership	2006